WATER RESOURCES MANAGEMENT SERIES : 1

WATER FOR SUSTAINABLE DEVELOPMENT
IN THE TWENTY-FIRST CENTURY

WATER RESOURCES MANAGEMENT SERIES : 1

Water for Sustainable Development in the Twenty-first Century

Edited by
ASIT K. BISWAS
MOHAMMED JELLALI
GLENN E. STOUT

DELHI
OXFORD UNIVERSITY PRESS
BOMBAY   CALCUTTA   MADRAS
1993

Oxford University Press, Walton Street, Oxford OX2 6DP

Oxford New York Toronto
Delhi Bombay Calcutta Madras Karachi
Kuala Lumpur Singapore Hong Kong Tokyo
Nairobi Dar es Salaam Cape Town
Melbourne Auckland Madrid

and associates in
Berlin Ibadan

First published 1993

© *Oxford University Press 1993*

ISBN 0 19 563302 4

Printed in India
Typeset by Vibrant, Rohini, Delhi 110085
Printed at Crescent Printing Works Pvt. Ltd., New Delhi 110001
Published by Neil O'Brien, Oxford University Press
YMCA Library Building, Jai Singh Road, New Delhi 110001

Contents

Contents / vii

Contributors

S. Abdel-Dayem
Water Research Center
22 El Galaa Street
Bulak
Cairo
Egypt

M. Abu-Zeid
Water Research Center
22 El Galaa Street
Bulak
Cairo
Egypt

Randolph A. Andersen
Chief
Operational Services
Technical Department
Africa Region
World Bank

Fatma Attia
Groundwater Research Institute
El Kanater
Egypt

Juan J. V. Bentancurt
Geography Department
Energy Research and Studies
  Center
University of Brasilia
Caixa Postal 04655
70919 Brasilia
Brazil

Asit K. Biswas
International Water Resources
  Association
76, Woodstock Close
Oxford
England

Michael Curley
Hall, Curley & Co. Inc.
50, East Forty-second Street
New York 10017
USA

A. Das Gupta
Asian Institute of Technology
G.P.O. Box 2754
Bangkok 10501
Thailand

K. R. Datye
Centre for Applied Systems
  Analysis in Development
68, Prarthana Samaj Road
Vile Parle (E)
Bombay 400 057
India

R. L. Dewan
Director
Oriental Bank of Commerce
77/40 Bailey Road
Patna 800001
Bihar
India

Marco Alfredo Di Lascio
Electrical Engineering
  Department
Energy Research and Studies
  Center
University of Brasilia
Caixa Postal 04655
70919 Brasilia
Brazil

Norman J. Dudley
Centre for Water Policy Research
University of New England
Armidale
NSW 2351
Australia

Mohamed T. El-Ashry
Director
Environment Department
World Bank
Washington D.C.
USA

Malin Falkenmark
Natural Science Research Council
Box 6711
S-113 85
Sweden

Genady N. Golubev
Professor
Department of Geography
Moscow State University
Moscow

K. Hefny
Groundwater Research Institute
El Kanater
Egypt

Hiroshi Hori
Hori-Hori and Associates
Tokyo
Japan

Maynard M. Hufschmidt
Senior Consultant
Environment and Policy Institute
East-West Center
Honolulu
Hawaii

C. B. F. Kuijpers
Department of Environmental
  Studies
State University of Utrecht
P.O. Box 80115
3508 TC Utrecht
The Netherlands

S. Y. Kulkarni
Director
Irrigation Research and
  Development
8, Moledina Road
Pune 411 001
India

J. Lundqvist
Department of Water and
  Environmental Studies
Linkoping University
S-581 83 Linkoping
Sweden

Warren F. Musgrave
Centre for Water Policy Research
University of New England
Armidale, NSW 2351
Australia

Babacar N'Diaye
President
African Development Bank
Abidjan
Ivory Coast

Mario D. Araujo Neto
Geography Department
Energy Research and Studies
  Center
University of Brasilia
Caixa Postal 04655
70919 Brasilia
Brazil

M. A. Rady
Water Distribution Research
  Institute
El Kanater
Egypt

Gert A. Schultz
Ruhr University Bochum
Institute of Hydrology
Water Resources and
  Environmental Techniques
P.O. Box 102148
4630 Bochum
Germany

M. R. Semaika
Water Distribution Research
  Institute
El Kanater
Egypt

W. Robert Rangeley
Consultant to the World Bank
Washington D.C.

Y. Takahasi
Shibaura Institute of Technology
3-9-14 Shibaura
Minato-Ku
Tokyo
Japan

Albert Tuinhof
IWACO
Rotterdam
The Netherlands

Jan A. Veltrop
Harza Engineering Company
150 S. Walker Drive
Chicago
Illinois 60606-4288
USA

Series Preface:
Water Resources Management

In recent years there has been increasing realization of the importance of water in the continuing well-being and development of mankind. In nearly all countries of the world, ranging from Algeria to Zimbabwe, more and more planners and decision-makers have started to realize the critical importance of efficient water resources management for their sustainable development. Even in an advanced industrialized country like the United States, water availability and its rational management has become a major socio-political issue, especially in the western and south-western parts of the country.

On the basis of extensive analyses carried out, it is now evident that compared to earlier generation of water development projects, new sources of water are becoming scarce, more expensive to develop, require more expertise and technological knowhow for planning, design, implementation and operation, and are contributing to more social and environmental disruptions. Accordingly, it is being increasingly realized that water can no longer be considered to be a cheap resource, which can be profligately used, abused or squandered without noticeable consequences for the future of mankind. Like oil some two decades ago, the day when water could be considered a cheap and plentiful resource is now over in most countries of the world.

If the current trends continue, the situation is likely to deteriorate even further in the future for two important reasons. First, the global population is increasing rapidly, and is likely to continue to do so till about the year 2050, or even beyond. This means more and more water would be required for domestic and industrial uses, agricultural production and hydropower generation for this expanding population. Second, as more and more people attain a higher standard of living, per captia water demand would continue to increase as well. Current analyses indicate that the total global water consumption during the period 1900–

2000 is likely to increase ten-fold, and this trend is likely to extend well into the twenty-first century.

In addition, as human population and activities increase, more and more waste products are contaminating available sources of surface water as well as groundwater. Among the major contaminants are untreated or partially treated sewage, agricultural chemicals and industrial effluents. These contaminants are seriously affecting the quality of available sources of water for various uses. Thus, water quality management is becoming increasingly an important concern all over the world.

Another major factor which could affect water management in the future is likely to be increasing delays in implementing new projects. Higher project costs and lack of investment funds would be two major reasons for this delay. Equally, social and environmental reasons would significantly delay project initiation time, certainly more than what has been witnessed in the recent decades.

Since on a long-term basis the amount of water available to any country is limited, the traditional response of the past to increase water availability to meet higher and higher water demands would no longer be a feasible solution in the future. This means that water professionals will come under increasing strain to make the management process more efficient than it has ever been at any time in human history. However, the transition period available to us to significantly improve the water planning and management processes is likely to be short, certainly no more than a decade or at most two. While technological problems, though complex, may prove comparatively easy to solve, economic, political, social and environmental constraints are likely to be more difficult to resolve. Thus proper approach to the solution of water problems is one of the most difficult challenges facing water management in the twenty-first century.

The Water Resources Management series of books, monographs and state-of-the-art reviews consist of authoritative texts written by some of the world's leading experts in their field. The series as a whole will consider all aspects of water—quantity and quality, surface water and groundwater—from the viewpoints of all the major associated disciplines, i.e. technical, economic, social, environmental, legal, health and political. It will also consider all types of water use: domestic, industrial, agricultural, hydropower generation, navigation, recreation and wildlife enhancement. Individual books may of course have more specific focus. The books of the series would not only be of direct interest to students and professors but also to all professionals associated with water resources planning and management.

ASIT K. BISWAS
International Development Centre
University of Oxford
76 Woodstock Close
Oxford, England

Preface

Water, said Pindar, the eminent Greek philosopher, is the best of all things. Though some may consider it to be an over-statement, events in recent years have clearly demonstrated the wisdom of the Greek sage more than two millennia after his death. Extensive and prolonged droughts in many parts of Africa, Asia and the United States have categorically demonstrated the unique position and importance of water for mankind's social and economic development. In fact, human and animal survival in some parts of Africa is seriously threatened due to the continued droughts and floods witnessed in recent years.

Human population and livestock are increasing at a significant rate nearly all over the developing world. This means that the demands for water for various uses are increasing as well. The best current estimates indicate that these trends will continue for at least the next half century.

On a long-term basis, the quantity of water that is available to a country is limited. Also, nearly all the economically exploitable sources of water have now already been developed, or are in the process of development. This means it would be increasingly difficult to find new sources of water which could be developed economically and in an environmentally-safe manner in the future. Many arid countries are already facing this serious situation. By the early part of the twenty-first century, nearly all developing countries would be facing this problem.

Accordingly, water professionals and users—which means the entire humanity—will have to learn very quickly how to do more with less water. This is likely to be the main challenge facing the water profession in the twenty-first century.

It has to be admitted that theoretically it is not a difficult problem to solve. Agricultural activities now account for 80 to 90 per cent of all water used in most developing countries. Since water use in the agricultural sector is inefficient, considerable improvement is possible through policy changes (e.g. water charges), technological solutions and other alternatives. However, what is likely to be a most difficult process would be to change the mind set of the users, who have always considered water to be a cheap resource, which is for them to use, abuse or squander—as they see fit. It would not be an easy process to wean the general population from the concept of cheap or even free water, which has been the general pattern throughout history. The situation would be further complicated by the fact that agriculture is a major economic sector in nearly all developing countries, as well as in many developed countries. The farming community forms an important lobby and the current indications are that it will not be an easy task to convince the farmers of the need for water pricing policies to improve agricultural water management.

Thus, water management and development will be an increasingly complex task and sensitive political issue in the twenty-first century. This was the main reason as to why the theme for the VII World Congress of the International Water Resources Association was 'Water for Sustainable Development in the Twenty-first Century'.

Some 700 participants from 55 countries attended the World Water Congress in Rabat, Morocco. Over 200 papers were presented during the Congress. These papers were peer-reviewed, and only about 1 in 7 papers were selected for publication in this volume. On the basis of the peer-review, several of the papers published herein were extensively modified.

Finally, I would like to express my personal appreciation to my co-editor, Mr Mohammed Jellali, whose leadership and hard work made the VII World Water Congress an outstanding success. As the President of the International Water Resources Association, it made my life much easier to have a person of Mr Jellali's calibre organize this important Congress.

ASIT K. BISWAS
Past President
International Water Resources Association
Oxford, England

I / Main Lectures

1 / Opening Statement of His Majesty the King Hassan II

Praise be to God! May peace and blessing be on the Prophet, his kin, and companions.

It is a great pleasure for us to open in Morocco the VII session of the World Congress on Water Resources. Our country is honoured to host this international scientific meeting. We pray God for success in your work and fulfilment of your objectives.

Humanity has always been led to adapt its own needs to its environment. This has enabled it to develop and intensify the available potentials in stride with historical evolution.

The successive phases of human life have been marked by several transformations translated by the use of a variety of resources ranging from stones to the atom, through iron and coal to gas. In parallel, human needs have forced man to transcend his narrow environment to link continents, conquer space and land on the moon, thanks to the extraordinary skills with which God has blessed him.

Water, always been in a privileged position, has played a vital role. *The Book of God* compares this element to life: 'We made of water all that lives.' Water which, by God's grace, gives life to earth and to all kind of plants, is an important factor for progress and development and represents the basis of the development of authentic civilizations through the ages.

God has provided humanity with a valuable gift—the changing seasons—for which we must thank Him. For if there were *only* nice weather, we would have to face droughts, diseases and epidemics; or if rain were uninterrupted, fields would have rotted and devastating floods submerged the land.

God has also endowed us with the ability to reason and the skill to understand and has led us onto the path of wisdom to help us harness our water resources, to make the best use of this vital element and thereby to face natural hazards.

The law of supply and demand is applicable in the different domains of production in relation with human activities. However, water supply depends on the will of God 'He generates water from the sky in determined quantity.' (Koran).

The available amounts of water have not changed with regard to geographical and seasonal distribution. Regions with water shortages continue to suffer from this necessary resource. Moreover, usable water quantities are decreasing owing to pollution.

On the other hand, water demand is continuously on the increase. It has doubled during the last thirty years as a consequence of galloping population growth, rising living standards, and increase in individual consumption. It is also the result of industrial, technological and agricultural progress characterized by adverse effects of pollution.

Today, all the countries in the world have to concede that water belongs to all and must be shared. As God has said in the Koran (Verse: 'the Moon'): 'tell them that water was bestowed on them to be shared'. So, it is common property wherever man may be. Thus, we have to assist one another, and exchange techniques and expertise to master the complex systems of nature.

God has located our country in a semi-arid region. We have promoted national solidarity and have instructed our government to seek possibilities of transferring water from rain-fed regions to parched regions, and to secure water supply on a sustainable basis not only to meet current demands but also to address those of future generations. We are always willing to share our know-how with neighbouring countries as part of the international solidarity pattern that must govern a vital field.

It is our duty to proclaim that we have been able, with the help of God, to achieve this ambitious target in thirty years: we have worked out plans; set up orientations; fixed positions and scheduled a programme and a philosophy to follow, being aware of the key role of water in social and economic development. In our water plans, we have developed a global vision which will, in the long run, allow us to organize this vital sector to pre-empt any crisis and any misuse of water and to preserve its quality.

To achieve these objectives, we have to persevere towards a sound understanding of our surface and groundwater resources and to provide the necessary equipment for meeting water demands. In this regard, we have built different size dams and sunk thousands of wells and boreholes in order to irrigate one million hectares of land and to supply different regions with drinking water. We have been engaged in developing sprinkle irrigation systems and other modern techniques of irrigation. Our goal is to cope with climatic changes and ensure cereal self-sufficiency.

We have also exerted effort to master water management methods and water saving to avoid any waste or loss of this resource. Moreover, we insisted that water policy must be based on the principle of dialogue and concertation. In this regard, we have incepted the Water High Council (le Conseil Supérieur de l'Eau) which we preside over. The objective of this institution is to discuss orientations and options of our country in water issues. Deputies, politicians, users and experts are represented in this institution and all participate in the decision-making process.

In the same context, we decided to carry a modern code which will allow us to better run our water resources, to control its use and quality and combat the pollution and squandering of water. We ordered our government to intensify research for a thorough knowledge and a better use of our climatic data. In this regard, important studies are underway in the field of dendrochronology to help us know better, by means of the age of trees, the history of our country's climate and particularly the cycle of droughts.

We have a particular interest in research and experiments on climate changes and their impact on water to prevent negative incidence, particularly in the dry zones. We set up an ambitious research programme on man-induced rain in order to increase our water reserves. We decided to create a specialized institute for social and economic research and promotion of the arid zones in connection with water management.

All these actions highlight the ultimate goal of our water policy, that is, national utilization and preservation of water, along with adequate management of this sector, for the benefit of both present and future generations.

Therefore, Morocco is ready to face, during the coming years, the challenge of water and is indeed willing to contribute to the effort made for this purpose by the international community.

While convinced of the urgent need to boost international cooperation in the field of water, Morocco has organized various international meetings in order to discuss issue of international concern such as drought, water management, construction of small dams, agricultural production, pollution, and ecology.

These initiatives elicit the concern of Morocco in contributing to the enrichment of civilization. Such readiness is a testimony to a determination to transcend borders and barriers, time and space.

This experience, conducted by Morocco, associating a prestigious past and promising present, has allowed the country to acquire a knowledge admired worldwide. The qualifications and performance of its engineers and technicians are highly appreciated by international bodies. While presenting to you such an experience, we intend to contribute to finding an appropriate solution to the international issues of water.

Your Congress is timely. We sound the alarm so that the world take heed of the importance of this vital element and of the looming dangers which may prove explosive in the next century. We are indeed convinced that other countries, regardless of their geographical and economic conditions, are concerned about water issues. This meeting is indeed a forum for the discussion of water issues, particularly in developing countries. Through this Congress we call on all states to hold, in the next few years, a priority meeting, with participation of the countries of what we call the South and those of the developed North, to discuss water issues which may be raised in the near and long term, and to work out a technical and financial assistance programme to developing countries threatened by water scarcity.

We also make a call for the creation of an international fund for a programme for the struggle against pollution of world water reserves, and for assistance to developing countries in the field of water operation, as well as for the transfer to these countries of the necessary scientific and technical know-how to prepare them fend for themselves in setting up appropriate and sound bases in the field. We suggest that a part of the debt of the developing countries be earmarked for this international fund.

The foregoing reasons are behind our interest in this Congress. We deem it necessary to implement the resolutions to be endorsed by the Congress for the well-being of mankind.

We wish, with God's help and with your initiatives, that water become a factor of concord and fraternity between peoples and a source of peace for all countries. We pay tribute to the organizers of the Congress and praise the efforts made to convene this gathering.

We wish you all success in your work.

2 / Water for Sustainable Development in the Twenty-first Century: A Global Perspective*

ASIT K. BISWAS

It gives me great pleasure to welcome you all to the Seventh World Congress of the International Water Resources Association. The former venues for this congress have been North America, Asia, and Latin america; this is the first time that this important event is being held in Africa. Morocco is a most suitable location for this World Congress because of the importance of water to the country's development as well as its long history of water resources development.

We are meeting here at an important crossroad in the history of mankind. Not only is it the beginning of the last decade of the twentieth century, but also during the past few years there has been increasing realization of the importance of water management in the continuing well-being and development of the developing countries, especially those located in the arid and semi-arid regions. More and more planners and decision makers have started to realize the critical importance of efficient water management for the sustainable development of their countries.

New sources of water are becoming scarce, more expensive to develop, and require more expertise and technological know how for planning, design and implementation. Accordingly, decision-makers are beginning to realize that water can no longer be considered to be a cheap resource, which can be used, abused, or squandered without much consequence for mankind's future. Like oil some 15 years ago, the day when water could be considered a cheap and plentiful resource is now virtually past. During the next two decades, water will be increasingly considered

*Presidential Address, VIIth World Congress On Water Resources, Rabat, Morocco, 13 May 1991

to be a critical resource for the future survival of the arid and semi-arid countries, so much so that the political tensions between certain neighbouring countries over the use of international rivers, lakes, and aquifers may escalate to the point of war during the early part of the twenty-first century.

WATER CRISIS

The water crisis, which some arid and semi-arid countries are already facing and which more and more other countries will start to face as the twenty-first century dawns, may be considered to be the direct result of four important but interrelated phenomena.

First, the amount of fresh water available to any country on a long-term basis is limited. Since nearly all the easily available sources of water have now been developed, or are in the process of development, the unit costs of future projects can only be higher. For example, a recent review of domestic water supply projects indicates that the cost per cubic metre of water for the next generation of projects is often two to three times higher than that for the present generation. This is an important consideration, since many developing countries are now saddled with very high levels of debt burdens, and the amount of new investments available, both internally and externally, is limited. In addition, the demands and competition for available funds are intense. These factors, both individually and collectively, are sure to affect the next and later generations of various types of water projects, probably somewhat adversely in most cases.

Second, world population is increasing steadily. Consequently, water requirements for domestic, agricultural, and industrial purposes and for hydroelectric generation will also increase. This, of course, is not a new trend. For example, current estimates indicate that the total global water consumption during the present century (1900–2000) is likely to increase ten-fold. The total agricultural water requirement is likely to increase 6.5 times during this century. There are, however, changes in the pattern of water requirements. In 1900, agriculture accounted for nearly 90 per cent of total water requirements, but by the year 2000, the corresponding figure is likely to be around 62 per cent. Industrial water use, which was about 6 per cent of the total water consumption at the beginning of the present century is likely to increase four-fold, to nearly 24 per cent by 2000 AD.

The general trend is likely to continue well into the twenty-first century because of the steady increase in world population. Present estimates indicate that the current world population is likely to double to 10.64 billion by the year 2050, out of which the less developed countries will contribute nearly 8 per cent or 9.29 billion. The population of China would still be higher than India's (1.637 billion against 1.525 billion). The current estimates of population in a few select countries by the year 2050 are (with 1990 estimates within parentheses): Bangladesh 253 million (113), Egypt 117.4 million (55), Morocco 57.44 million (25), and United States 280 million (249). Viewed differently, a country like Bangladesh, with a per capita GNP of $179 in 1988, and having an area of 144,000 km^2 (approximately similar to that of Wisconsin), will, by the year 2050 have a population level that would be rapidly approaching that of the United States as a whole, with a per capita GNP of only $179 in 1988. It would not be an easy task to provide a reliable water control system to all the citizens of Bangladesh in the future under such adverse conditions.

While it is not easy for most individuals to grasp the real meaning of billions of people, it should be seen in its proper perspective. If we resettled all 5.368 billion people of today's world (early May 1991 estimate), in an African country like Zambia, whose area is 753,000 km^2 a family of four will have an area of 561 km^2 which is a typical single-family one-storey house in North America, with a front and a backyard!

While there is no one-to-one relationship between population and water requirements, it is clear that substantial increase in the world population, the total water requirements will increase as well. Furthermore, past experiences indicate that as the standard of living improves so does per capita water requirements. Hence, if the present poverty alleviation programmes succeed, both water requirements will increase further and the water management process will become significantly more sophisticated-two facts that have often not been considered by our policy planners, both nationally and internationally.

Third, as human activities increase, more and more waste products are contaminating available sources of water. Among the major contaminants are untreated or partially treated sewage, agricultural chemicals, and industrial effluents. These contaminants are seriously affecting the quality of water especially for domestic use. Already, many sources of water near the urban centers of developing countries have been severely contaminated, thus impairing their potential use.

Since comprehensive water quality monitoring programmes in nearly all developing countries are either in their infancy or even non-existent, a clear picture of the status of water pollution and the extent to which water quality has been impaired for different potential uses is simply not a available at present. On the basis of anecdotal and very limited information available, it may be said that the problem is already very serious near urban centers, especially for groundwater and lakes and for some rivers as well. It should be noted that once groundwater is contaminated, it cannot be easily decontaminated. Furthermore, for developing countries cost-effective technologies simply do not exist for removing pollutants such as nitrates from water. Equally, alternatives such as forcing people through regulations to use bottled water for babies, because of high nitrate contents of local drinking water, as currently practised in 38 towns in Nebraska, are not feasible because of widespread poverty.

Even in advanced industrialized countries of North America or Europe, despite all the recent rhetoric, no clear picture is available for water contamination. The monitoring and detection process have focused mostly on selected chemicals that are toxic and mobile. Equally, it is only the parent compounds that are being monitored: monitoring of their metabolites is seldom carried out. Thus, at our present state of knowledge, we simply do not know the extent of contamination that has already occurred which may render some water sources unusable in the future without expensive treatment. On the basis of the present trend, it is unlikely that a clear picture of the global water quality situation will be available by the beginning of the twenty-fist century at the very earliest. Thus, it is possible that many sources of water may not be considered to be appropriate, especially for drinking purposes, in the future.

The fourth major factor is the likelihood of increasing delays in the implementation of new water projects in the coming decades. Higher project costs and lack of investment funds will be two major reasons for such delays. Equally, social and environmental reasons will significantly delay project initiation time, certainly much more than that witnessed in the earlier decades.

There is no doubt that the water requirements of developing countries will continue to increase significantly during the next several decades. However, the traditional response of increasing water availability to meet higher and higher water demands will no longer be adequate in the future for two important reasons:

(i) Many countries simply do not have any major additional sources of water to develop economically.

(ii) Even in those countries that may have additional sources of water, time periods required to implement those projects are likely to be much longer than expected at present.

This means that water professionals will come under increasing pressure to improve the efficiency of the management process. However, the transition period available to us to significantly improve the management process is likely to be short-certainly no more than a decade or, at the most, two decades. While technological problems may be comparatively easy to solve, political, institutional, and social constraints are likely to be very difficult to resolve. Here in may lie the most difficult challenge facing water management in the twenty-first century.

MAJOR ISSUES IN THE TWENTY-FIRST CENTURY

On the basis of an objective analysis of the current status of water development and management all over the world, and the present trends in other areas that may affect water management practices, the following major issues may be identified for the twenty-first century. These issues are not mutually exclusive; in fact, they are often interrelated. Also, some of these issues are already visible, but they are likely to become significantly more important and complex in the next century than they are at present. Furthermore, these issues cannot be listed in any order of priority on a global basis since their importance and relevance may well differ from one country to another, and over time.

Water Conservation and Efficient Use of Water

Until today, water conservation and efficient use of water have not received the attention they deserve. Water conservation has thus far received only lip service.

Since agriculture is by far the largest user of water, efficient irrigation management will undoubtedly be a major conservation option of the future. At present, it is fairly common to find that more than half the amount of water abstracted from a river does not even reach the fields being irrigated. In addition, there is considerable scope for improving the efficiency of application of water once it reaches the field. This means that not only is a critical resource being used inefficiently, and thus uneconomically, but also such poor practices are directly contributing to the development of unwanted environmental impacts such as waterlogging and salinity, which are actually contributing to the reduction of the production potential of the areas.

During the past decade, limited progress has been made improving the efficiency of irrigation management, but the overall system efficiency is still far to low for complacency. The reasons for such poor efficiency have now been well-documented and the solutions are also well-known. However, in spite of this knowledge base, it has not been possible to appreciably improve irrigation efficiency in most countries. On the basis of the current trend, it is unlikely that major progress can be made until well into the twenty-first century.

Considerable scope also exists for practising water conservation in the domestic and industrial sectors. In many urban centers of developing countries, more than half the treated water is lost due to leakages. Similarly, appropriate design change can significantly reduce water requirements for the industrial sector. For example, extensive use of recycling can reduce by 96 per cent the amount of water needed to produce one tonne of steel. In the early part of the twenty-first century, some countries may be forced to institute water audit to ensure an efficient water management system for the agricultural, industrial, and domestic sectors.

Water Pricing and Cost Recovery

During the 1980s, there have been periodic discussions on economic aspects of water allocation, including the issue of water pricing and cost recovery, in many arid and semi-arid countries. Conceptually at least, water pricing could affect:

— water allocation between competing uses;
— water conservation;
— generation of additional revenue which could be used to operate and maintain water systems, and even repay part or all of investments costs;
— cropping patterns;
— income distribution;
— efficiency of water management; and
— overall environmental impacts.

A noteworthy feature of the 1980s was the number of papers that were produced in the western academia on water pricing, especially for the agricultural sector. The overwhelming thrust of the hypothesis was that if right water prices could be charged to the farmers, they would become rational optimizers. If farmers have to pay an economic price for the water used, its distribution would become more reliable and equitable. Government departments would receive the revenues generated by water pricing, which would enable them to operate and properly maintain their irrigation systems. Thus, water pricing would contribute to a desirable win-win situation. These hopes, however, have remained unrealized thus far.

While water pricing and cost recovery will unquestionably be an important policy instrument in the twenty-first century, at least two fundamental issues have to be considered before it can be effectively implemented. First, water pricing has thus far been viewed primarily as an economic instrument for efficient water management. Its socio-political and cultural implications in developing countries have generally not been understood, and much less addressed to, by the Western academics. Second, water has been traditionally subsidized to achieve very specific socio-political objectives of food security, provision of clean drinking water, and increasing the income and health of the rural poor. If economic water pricing is to be introduced, other policy instruments have to be developed to achieve the same objectives. These alternative options may not necessarily make water use more efficient. For example, crop subsidies could encourage excessive water use. Thus, decision-makers have to carefully analyze the various policy options available holistically and in their totality. Compartmentalized policy making, which is often practised at present, will generally not be optimal.

Second, on what criteria should the water charges be based? Should the beneficiaries pay the operation and maintenance costs of the water systems? Or are they expected to pay total investment costs as well? Should such pricing include external costs such as environmental and social damages? If so, how should these costs be calculated? These difficult issues will have to be resolved during the present decade, if water pricing is to be an effective policy option in the twenty-first century.

Social and Environmental Considerations

Social and environmental considerations of water resources development and management will, in all probability, become even more rigorous in the twenty-first century than they are at present.

Water quality management will increasingly become as important as water quantity management, though the former is at present mostly considered as a poor cousin. Water quality monitoring will become essential for efficient water management. This transition, however, will not be easy. This is because water quality monitoring is significantly more difficult, time-consuming, and complex than water quantity monitoring, and expertise and equipment required are also correspondingly of a much higher order.

In order to achieve a functional water quality monitoring system, the following issues need to be considered: institutional arrangements within which such a system can be properly established; developing an effective network, selection of water quality parameters that need to be monitored at different locations; choice of these locations, frequency of monitoring different parameters in each location; development of indigenous expertise to carry out the necessary analyses; dissemination of information to potential users; and regular presentation of appropriate information to decision-makers in a timely fashion. It will take more than a decade before these issues can be effectively resolved. However, without such information, water management cannot be efficient in the twenty-first century.

Institutional Response to Better Management

Water management can be rational only if the institutions responsible for such management are efficient. As a general rule, it may be said that most water management institutions in developing countries need significant strengthening. While considerable progress has been made in some selected countries in the recent past, much needs to be done to successfully face the challenges of water management in the twenty-first century.

In addition to institutional strengthening, nearly all countries have to substantially improve their inter-institutional collaboration in order to practise efficient water management policies in the future. At present, water-related policies are developed in a fragmented fashion. For example, irrigation and large-scale water development generally come under Irrigation or Water Resources Ministry, domestic water supply under Ministry of Public Works, navigation under Ministry of Transport, hydropower under Ministry of Energy, environmental impacts under Ministry of Environment, and health issues under Ministry of Health. The co-ordination between these various ministries leaves much to be desired. Sometimes the ministries are even adversaries! Thus, in this generally unsatisfactory milieu, efficient water management policies are not easy to develop.

If the nations of the world are expected to manage their water resources properly in the twenty-first century, major institutional changes will be necessary.

Management of International Water Bodies

One of the critical issues of the twenty-first century would undoubtedly be the management of international water bodies. The global magnitude of this potential problem has not been generally recognized thus far. Nearly 47 per cent of the area of the world (excluding Antarctica) falls within shared water basins. Expressed differently, there are 41 countries (20 in Africa) where at least 80 per cent of the total area lies within international basins.

Estimates made in 1976 indicate that there are 214 river and lake basins which are shared by two or more countries, of which 57 are in Africa. Of these 214 basins, the vast majority, 156 (or nearly 75 per cent) are shared by two countries. There are nine basins which are shared by six or more countries, of which only two—Danube and Rhine—are in the developed world. Such estimates are clearly erroneous. The magnitude of the problem is much higher than the above estimate.

A very limited number of objective and in-depth analyses of international water bodies in developing countries are available for arriving at definitive conclusions. To a great extent, international organizations have deliberately stayed away from the development and management of international water bodies, mainly because such issues have been considered to be politically sensitive. The leadership shown by President Black of the World Bank in the 1950s, who was instrumental in expediting the Indus River treaty, has been generally missing. A lone exception is Mostafa Kamal Tolba, the present Executive Director of the UN Environment Programme, who engineered the Zambezi Action Plan.

As the demand for water increases in the Third World, and the exclusively national sources of water are developed, the only major sources of water that remain to be developed in the twenty-first century are likely to be international in nature. Herein will lie a major opportunity or a serious problem for the future.

Unless proper treaties are negotiated between the co-basin countries, international water bodies are likely to be a fertile area for emerging conflicts in the twenty-first century. Unilateral exploitation of shared water resources by one country, without the prior agreement of the other co-basin countries, could contribute to serious regional instabilities, or even wars, during the latter part of this decade and beyond. The number of such conflicts is likely to increase significantly during the next century, unless the seeds for their solutions are properly planted in the present decade.

Proper Analytical Frameworks

In order to successfully meet the challenges of the twenty-first century, water professionals have to critically review the reliability of some of the existing analytical frameworks. Some of the present frameworks, which have been used for at least two or more decades, and are thus now automatically accepted, need to be seriously questioned and, hopefully, significantly improved. Only two widely used methodologies will be briefly mentioned here.

First is the common technique of generating synthetic streamflow based on whatever short periods of data are available. Analyses of climatic fluctuations observed during the past five or more decades in many parts of the world clearly indicate that the concept of generating synthetic streamflow on the basis of short periods of data is seriously flawed, to the extent that its continued use to plan and manage large-scale and high-investment water projects should be seriously questioned. It is becoming increasingly evident that complex mathematical manipulations are no real substitute for getting better information, if the short period of data on which such manipulations fundamentally depend upon are unrepresentative of the long-term pattern. Since the probability that short period of data available is really representative of the long-term pattern cannot be very high, continued use of synthetic streamflow generation must be reconsidered.

Second is the current practice of environmental impact assessment (EIA). The methodologies used have serious shortcomings. At a macro level, the linkages of EIA to the planning of social and economic development are not clear. While considerable expertise has been developed on the application of EIA at the project level, commensurate progress at policy and programme levels simply has not been made.

Even at the project level, EIA considers almost exclusively negative impacts: positive impacts are completely ignored. If EIA has to be effective, this all-pervasive bias has to be eliminated. The overall thrust must be modified to maximize positive environmental impacts, a step that is completely ignored at present, and to minimize the negative ones. Such a balanced and holistic approach is urgently needed to maximize the benefits of water projects and thus enhance the future welfare of mankind.

CONCLUSION

On the basis of the present review, it is clear that the water management profession will face a problem in the twenty-first century, the magnitude and complexity of which no earlier generation has had to face. In the run-up to the twenty-first century, our profession really has two choices: to carry on as before with a 'business-as-usual' attitude and endow our future generations with a legacy of suboptimal water projects, or continue in earnest an accelerated effort to plan, manage, and use the world's water resources sustainably and fairly.

All the major issues facing the world are interrelated, and the dynamics of the future of mankind will be determined not by any one single individual issue but by the interactions of a multitude of issues. An increase in population means more food, energy, and other raw materials. Augmenting food and energy supplies necessitates sustainable water management. The common requirements in all practical responses to the solution of all these major problems must include greater investments, more technology and expertise, and intensified co-operation. The interrelationships are global in character, and hence they can be best understood and then resolved within a global framework. While the framework could be global, within this there must be a wide variety of integrated national and regional responses. Within this overall framework, water professionals must also play their own constructive part. Mankind has a common future: we survive or perish together, North and South, East and West! Should we ignore that salutary exhortation, we can only be reminded of the warning of William Shakespeare that: 'men at some time are masters of their fates. The fault dear friends is not in our stars but in ourselves that we are underlings.'

3 / Water and African Development*

BABACAR N'DIAYE

It is an honour for me to participate at this meeting of the VII World Congress on Water Resources. I should particularly wish to thank Professor Biswas for the very kind invitation. Allow me also to express my sincere gratitude to His Majesty, the Government and people of the Kingdom of Morocco for hosting this conference. I am particularly gratified because the sub-theme of sustainability is one that is of great concern to me and to the institution that I head. It is therefore my fervent hope that, over the next few days, you will succeed in addressing the major issues of management and conservation of our natural resource base (water) and the orientation of technological and institutional changes that should ensure the attainment and continued satisfaction of human needs for now and for future generations.

I am confident that your combined wisdom and knowledge will direct our efforts towards consolidating the strategies for better use and management of our water resources. I hope that the delineation of issues, and the analysis of perspectives relative to sustainable development, will guide your discussions and the content at this gathering.

The theme of the Congress, 'Water for Sustainable Development in the Twenty-first Century' is most opportune, since the need to focus on new and innovative strategies has become inevitable, resulting from the lessons we have learned from the immediate past. What is needed now is to take stock of the actions and strategies we applied in the past decades and to reorient our approaches if we are to safeguard the quality of life on this planet. The lessons learned from past decades ought to provide solutions that should enable acceleration of the development process and greatly enhance the management and utilization of natural resources such as water. The development process and rational use of resources should not be contradictory. To develop today at the expense

---

*Keynote address by Mr Babacar N'Diaye, President of the African Development Bank, Abidjan, Ivory Coast.

of the quality of life of future generations is not only shortsighted, it is suicidal. But neither can we halt development in order to safeguard the future. Such an approach would not be acceptable.

Of all natural resources, water is probably the most essential for life. In general, the availability of water varies from one locality to another and is dependent on climatic patterns worldwide. Natural conditions and human activities have, over the years, affected the quality and quantity of available water. Many of these activities consume the available water without any consideration to the welfare of future generations. Many of the great migrations of humans and animals are linked to be presence or absence of water. And yet, much of its scarcity has been man-made in so far as it has tended to be taken as a free good. However, it is its acute shortage that oftentimes reveals the true value of this critical resource.

I have referred to the complementarity of development and rational resources management. In the case of water, one of the by-products of development has been the pollution of the very water resources on which we depend. Industrial location theory suggested that a number of important industries be located near waterways or water bodies in order to facilitate transport as well as handling of the resultant effluents. Such an approach made good financial sense, but it was disastrous for the water and the associated life, resulting in pollution that rendered the water supply unfit for various human activities. We have witnessed how such pollution has affected natural biological systems leading to eutrophication of lakes and coastal seas, as well as causing the accumulation of unsafe levels of organic residues and metals in fish and other marine life. Rivers and lakes died. Water, far from being a source of life, became a carrier of death. Fortunately, water can be resurrected, but at what cost! These are issues that I believe should form part of the development agenda that should be pursued so that development is sustainable.

I shall now discuss briefly the situation in the African continent on issues of water resources affecting the region. The locality of the continent has given her a problematic climate. Rainfall as a source of water varies from region to region. In the humid forest zone, rainfall amounts to 1500 mm or more each year. To the north is the sub-humid zone of open woodlands and savannah, with rainfall between 600 and 1200 mm. Moving still farther north, the Sahel is dominated by grassland with sparser trees and shrubs. Precipitation here is below 600 mm. The largest expanse, accounting for almost half the continent is of arid and desert zones. The rains are too short. In southern and eastern Africa, rainfall varies with altitude. The mountainous areas enjoy the highest rainfall, the lowlands the least. This situation calls for properly coordinated management of the water resources if sustainable retention of water at acceptable levels is to be maintained.

Water bodies such as rivers, lakes, marshlands, coastal waters, and oceans support life for both humans and wildlife, but they are under increasing pressures. Factors causing pressures vary, ranging from the physical to socio-economic, and are interrelated in many cases. Rivers and lakes supply water for drinking, power, irrigation, transport, and recreation. They support substantial harvests of fish and crustaceans and serve as habitat for water birds and other aquatic organisms. Again, prudent management of these sources is necessary if we are to maintain balanced ecosystems.

Fresh water in the continent is unevenly distributed with chronic and seasonally acute water shortages occurring increasingly. Several of the rivers and lakes have been undergoing a marked reduction in flow rates, leading to increased conflicts over water resources use in rural, urban and agricultural areas. Other sources of water such as wells are under threat by desertification and are depleted, thus accelerating the migration of pastoralists into marginal lands.

Land clearing for agriculture, encroachment of poor people into the forest, and subsequent felling of trees pose a threat to the water-retaining capacity of forests, which leads to the reduction of available water. On the other hand, siltation by soil erosion continues to shorten the life span of reservoirs. The reduction of water volumes in reservoirs, due to siltation, triggers conflicts in the use of water among various users. International friction arising from water usage may become a feature of relations within the region.

The exploitation of aquifers has also become a problem in arid and coastal areas. Aquifers have been unsustainably utilized in arid and semi-arid areas. In certain coastal zones, excessive pumping has lowered the water table to such an extent that polluted water enters the aquifer. This is unacceptable as it pollutes groundwater.

The encroachment of poor people into the forests' surroundings and the cutting and clearing of these forests cause deforestation and subsequent soil erosion, resulting in the deterioration of water quality and shortening of the life span of reservoirs. To avoid this situation, it is essential to integrate rational settlement programmes in the development scheme of things. I believe that without integrating appropriate rural and community development programmes focusing on poverty elimination, water resources management will invariably continue to be of concern, and will be adversely affected.

In order to effectively address issues of water resources management, and those of easy availability of water for development and personal use, the focus should be widened from forests and soils to more comprehensive issues relating to the general supply of water for various uses as well. Africa is losing 3.6 million hectares of its tropical forests annually and rehabilitating only a few thousand hectares during the same period. The average annual loss rate is estimated at 5.2 per cent. It has been observed that the deforestation of forest resources leads to the decrease in evaporation of water retained in the forest and subsequent decrease in rainfall, thus making the climate more dry at a meso-scale level. Soils, particularly the fertile topsoil, are the direct victims of deforestation.

African soils are characterized by low proportions of clay and organic matter, which makes them particularly susceptible to erosion. Vegetation cover protects these vulnerable soils from erosion. Once vegetation is removed, the soil is exposed to the power of wind and rain, and its valuable topsoil is driven to rivers and lakes, causing eutrophication and siltation in the water bodies and leaving the lands unproductive. This is a serious loss of valuable water resources for the continent. We therefore need to emphasize the importance of incorporating forests and soil components into water resources management.

Water resources in Africa are under severe natural and social pressures. Although water is in abundance, shortages have become evident due to pollution and other factors. Poverty, on the other hand, has a tremendous impact on Africa's water resources. The problems related to water, water use, and pollution should therefore be addressed in the context of sustainable growth and development. In other words, we should opt for public policies and financing programmes that avoid rapid depletion of natural resources and the degradation of ecological systems. Our future strategies ought to emphasize and promote sound environmental management to ensure sustainable growth.

The majority of our population reside in rural areas where potable water supply is still a struggle. Women walk miles and waste valuable time in drawing water for use in their homesteads. Some of the water available is not potable and is subjected to pathogenic microoogranisms that affect humans. At the start of the International Drinking Water Supply and Sanitation Decade in 1981, 66 per cent of the urban population, and only 22 per cent of the rural population, in Africa were served by adequate supplies of potable water. And only about half, and hardly a fifth, of urban and rural dwellers respectively had access to adequate sanitation. Midway through the decade, water supply coverage had risen to 84 per cent in urban areas and 46 per cent in rural areas. Sanitation coverage had also improved, although less spectacularly. That this was done in the face of rapidly growing populations makes these achievements even more remarkable. It also throws a ray of hope in an otherwise bleak picture as to the results that concerted effort can produce.

The Bank Group, in this regard, has been financing various projects and programmes that relate to the provision of potable water supply to its member countries. The Bank Group has assisted, generally, in enhancing the capability of countries to manage best the available water resources from various sources. It has been strengthening the incorporation of forest and soil management components in the projects it finances, such as afforestation in upper stream areas or banks of reservoirs; appropriate zoning of land use around the reservoirs; soil conservation programmes; bench terrace techniques, etc.

The African Development Bank has contributed to the attainment of the Decade Objectives. During the same decade, the Bank committed over US$900 million for water and sanitation in support of investments of about US$3 billion. Its commitments supported water projects in rural and urban areas in all parts of Africa.

In addition to these investments, the Bank has, through its technical assistance window, supported a variety of activities to strengthen the institutional capacity of the water authorities. We believe that this is an essential input into the sustainability of the investments. We plan to expand this activity into the broader areas of master plan design that will fully integrate the various elements outlined in my discussion.

I will now make a brief reference to an ongoing effort to strengthen national planning mechanisms. One of the outputs during the preparations for the New Delhi Conference of 1990 was the creation of a Regional Orientation Committee, supported by Subregional Committees, to review sector progress and strategies and recommend adjustments. The Bank is providing the secretariat for the Regional Committee and we plan to launch the consultative mechanism later in the year. It is envisaged that this consultative mechanism will facilitate regional and sub-regional coordination and planning amongst donor agencies and member countries as well as foster information exchange and sharing of experiences.

As a follow up of the activities of the past decades, it seems that there are some issues that we need to continue to focus on in order to enhance success in the endeavours for sustainable development. The Bank will, in future, continue to include in its programme of activities the financing of various key activities that will promote effective and efficient running of sector services for member countries, such as:

— Strengthening public and parastatal institutions in the water sector that are responsible for the implementation of water and sanitation projects, as well as the operations and maintenance of systems already installed. Such strengthening will include training of management staff and provision of logistic support.
— Building the capacity to coordinate and take relevant decisions related to the rehabilitation, operations, and maintenance of existing systems. Oftentimes, handsome returns are obtained from rehabilitating existing capital facilities rather than creating new ones. For instance, the restoration of drilled wells and the capacities of treatment facilities and pumping stations for water supplies to their rated capacities produces improved lower per unit cost than the installation of new equipment.
— Building the capacity for institutions to put in place financially viable systems and policy structures that allow for flexibility in responding to changing economic situations.

The long-term success of managing water resources lies in comprehensively incorporating all issues of development in strategies that aim at sustainable development. The Bank is actively incorporating the essential components for the institutional building in water-related development projects. However, it should be stressed that the desperately needed basic institutional setting must be strengthened. These institutions should reflect positive activities such as appropriate education, human development, flow of appropriate technology, and programmes that ensure that technology is used positively to foster growth and development without much damage to our natural resources. I believe that forums such as this Congress will go a long way in strengthening the supply capacity of water as well as in water resources management in Africa, and spread the necessary messages for the development of the Continent. I have no doubt at all that the results of our deliberations in the next days will provide us with a concrete start for the twenty-first century, and will further contribute to the design of a development process that is human-centred and sustainable.

4 / Environment and Development: Urgent need for a water perspective

MALIN FALKENMARK

INTRODUCTION

Today's predicament is an extremely blurred picture of the field of environment and development. The international dialogue contains more words than genuine understanding, and a heavy load of climatic bias. Analysis of different documents on major environmental problems shows that water functions are at the core of the problem. This makes it fundamental to involve a cross-section of water scientists and professionals in the dialogue.

During the preparations for the Earth Summit 1992, held in Rio de Janeiro, attention was being concentrated on the linkages between environment and development. The aim of that conference (Preparatory Committee for the UN Conference Environment and Development, 1991) was to 'find a common basis for action to protect the future of the planet Earth and to secure for all its inhabitants a more sustainable and equitable future'.

Although the linkages between fresh water issues and other environmental issues were focused already at the first meeting of the Preparatory Committee (1990), difficulties have remained in assessing the contribution of water-related phenomena and functions to the environmental problems. The reason may be that the focus has been more on causes and end-effects rather than on the processes generating the end effects from those causes. The Preparatory Committee (1991), by the organization of its work, also decided to separate fresh water issues from the issues of atmosphere (including climate change), land and agriculture, forests, biodiversity, toxic chemicals, and hazardous wastes. The former was handled at a specialized pre-conference, the latter within the UNCED working groups.

The linkage problem is probably closely related to basic paradigms.

The necessity to bring in the functions of water in the broader environmental issues has not been evident for the temperate zone ecologists, which seem, even after three decades of environmental debate, to be retaining the problem-formulating privilege. Their temperate zone experience has allowed them to take water for granted, i.e. leave it outside the analyses. Their interest has therefore been concentrated on analysis of energy balances and biogeochemical flows. This approach has however *carried them to a situation where more attention is paid to emptiness areas than to inhabited areas and to the fundamental development problem of how to feed the extremely rapidly growing population outside the fences of the national parks and reserves.*

Water issues have, however, strong relevance as soon as focus is on the development of the arid tropics and subtropics, i.e. the region occupied by majority of the poverty-stricken countries. The conceptual problems are illustrated also by the framework reflected in UNEP's Environmental Perspective for the 1990s and beyond (1988). There, the basic focus was laid on sectoral issues and on instruments for environmental action respectively. The *sectoral issues* represent mainly driving forces: health and settlements needs; and international economic relations. The *instruments of environmental action* arrived at in the document refer mainly to mechanisms in problem solving: assessment; planning; legislation and environmental law; awareness building and training; and institutions.

What is lacking is a description of the *system on which the driving forces are acting,* which produces the critical environmental problems. The text on the sectoral issues indeed outlines a number of what we may call goals: to achieve a balance between population and environmental capacity; to reach food security without resource depletion; to get sufficient energy at reasonable cost; to achieve sustainable improvement in levels of living; to secure improved shelter and essential amenities; and to secure equitable economic systems. But there is no discussion of how these goals might be achieved. Thus, it may well be asked how it is possible to draw conclusions in respect of the mechanisms needed for problem solving without first asking *how the problems should be solved.*

What follows is an attempt to relive some of the constraints introduced by the past water illiteracy among environmental experts. The discussion on *environmental problems* focuses on regional differences and on water functions in the landscape as manipulated by man for livelihood purposes. *Development problems* are considered when the emphases on water-related vulnerabilities. Finally, an effort is made to link environment and development as seen from a water perspective. Attention is given to crucial measures needed to minimize the risks of environmental degradation. There is also emphasis on the need to balance the water consumption in biomass production for livelihood security against the water needs for various fundamental purposes of the human population, since these two water needs are competitive. The analyses basically carries a set of messages:

— the need to develop clear concepts, which are now predominantly aimed at the temperate zone problems;
— the need to develop a conceptual framework on the linkages between environment and development;
— that, due to hydro-climatic peculiarities of the low-income countries, hydrologists are, in fact, crucial in bridging environmental and development issues;
— that, fundamentally, the inhabitants on the Water Planet are in fact living at the mercy of the water cycle.

OFFICIAL PERCEPTION OF ENVIRONMENT AND DEVELOPMENT

The truncated character of the present perceptions are difficult to pinpoint a scientifically reference-supported fashion. This section will present the conclusions arrived at after analysis of a number of key documents from the Stockholm Conference in 1972 and onwards (Tolba, 1988).

Perceptions of Environmental Problems

The environmental issues of main concern according to the official view can be seen from the formulations in the General Assembly resolution on the Rio Conference (United Nations). Key words in paragraph 12 of this resolution are: protection; conservation; environmentally sound management of biotechnology and waste: improvement of living and working conditions; protection of human health. If characterized in short, the solutions to the environmental problems of the *humid tropics* are approached basically from a biodiversity protection perspective with the need of combating deforestation. The problems of the *arid tropics* are mainly characterized as land degradation with the need for measures aiming at combating desertification and drought. The earlier idea of tree barriers to protect the expanding desert, as stressed at the UN Desertification Conference in 1977, has however been erased-probably because it was later realized that trees will not grow on the desert border. The problems in the *temperate zone* are mainly, (besides output of greenhouse gases and ozone-depleting substances) exposition of the individuals to toxic substances in the surroundings, on the one hand, and losses in biological diversity, on the other.

Dominating Water Perceptions

The perceptions of water as related to development are apparent from the wording in para 12 of the General Assembly resolution: 'protection of water quality and supplies'. The formulation indicates that water is seen in either of two ways:

1. Water as the *victim* of pollution, which is the traditional perspective held by aquatic ecologists with their focus on water bodies as habitats for aquatic biota;
2. Water supply as a *technical issue*, which is the perspective dominating in the follow-up of the UN Water Conference in 1977 within the International Drinking Water Supply and Sanitation Decade.

Perception on Linkages Environment/Development

The formulations in the early preparatory work to the Earth Summit gave the general impression that technology and protection are two fundamental components of the solutions to the low-latitude country development problems. The technology was thought of as already existing in the high-latitude countries so that it can be more or less easily transferred to the poverty-stricken countries, speeding up their development.

WATER-CYCLE RELATED ENVIRONMENTAL PROBLEMS

The environmental problems in the temperate zone are pretty well known-pollution from a whole set of different sources: air exhausts, fertilizers, dry waste deposits, wastewater habits, etc. Are these the crucial environmental problems in developing countries as well? Or are their problems maybe completely different? Let us start by analysing the major environmental problems as they were reported to the World Bank

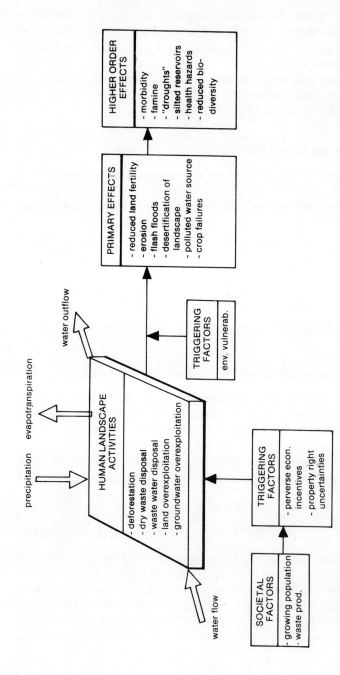

Fig. 1. Systems views on relation between main factors involved in environmental problems reported by World Bank's borrowing countries (ref. 6).

in their inventory to some 70 borrowing countries (World Bank, 1989).

The first observation is a general conceptual chaos. Further analysis by the author (Falkenmark, 1991) indicates that what we tend to speak of as environmental problems are basically caused by human activities in the landscape, belong to three different categories (Fig. 1):

— human activities in the landscape as such;
— primary effects of those activities;
— higher order effects of these primary effects.

Four causes are identified in the Bank study as giving rise to these environmental problems. They are however of two different types: societal factors (growing population, waste production) on the one hand, and triggering factors (perverse economic incentives, property right uncertainties) on the other. The particular environmental vulnerability that is related to the tropical climate tends to intensify the environmental side-effects produced by human activities.

At the core of the environmental problems dominating in the Third World countries is man's dependence on the resources in the landscape

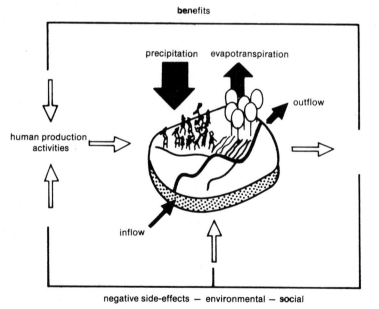

Fig. 2. Man's dependence on resources in the landscape. (Dark arrows = water flows; light arrows = linkages).

(Fig. 2). This leads to the following conceptual framework: basically, man depends on the resources produced by the natural environment: water, crops, fodder, fibre, fuelwood, timber, energy. In order to get access—'harvest' these resources, he *has to manipulate* (i.e. skilfully regulate) the environment: dig wells, drain, cut trees, fertilize, etc. The environmental system being a complex held together by natural laws, these disturbances of the system will—besides the benefits intended—produce negative side-effects.

A multiple set of driving forces compels man to manipulate his environment: population density and growth, food needs, energy needs, industrial activities, health needs, settlement needs, economic relations. In order to satisfy those needs, man manipulates the system by interfering with landscape functions and water flows, and by chemical outputs. The result is disturbed processes in the system: disturbed water cycling, water quality genesis, biomass production, etc. These disturbed phenomena will result in disturbed environmental components: air quality, groundwater recharge and quality, river flow and quality, sea quality, land productivity. The ultimate end result is not only higher-order biological effects on flora, fauna, and human health, but also persistence of famine and poverty.

In order to be able to address the multicause dilemma, we need a better idea of the system as a whole, on which all these parallel perturbations are acting. In the mesoscale, the landscape concept in Fig. 2 may be interesting to develop further. Also in the macroscale, we need a conceptual idea of the Total Earth system and of man's manipulations of that system. Figure 3 shows one way of visualizing the system so that it includes the propagating of disturbances related to the integrity of the water cycle. Conventional wisdom within the life sciences (upper half of Fig. 3) shows the Total Earth system as a broken mirror with a set of main subsystems (climate, terrestrial ecology, aquatic ecology, and marine ecology) mutually connected basically by regression formula, which will change when climate changes.

In the lower half of Fig. 3 the perceptional vacuum between the different subsystems in the upper figure has been filled by the water flows which link the atmosphere, the landscape, and the water bodies, carrying nutrients and waste products.

Man's influence on the Total Earth system is indicated by the four horizontal arrows to the left:

(a) waste gas output to the atmosphere

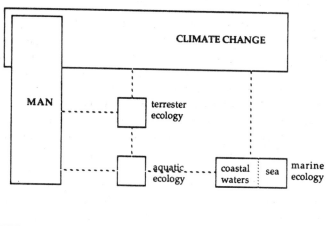

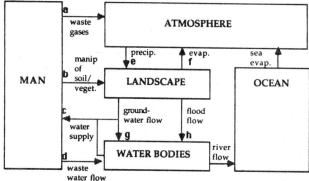

Fig. 3. The Total Earth System and Man

(b) manipulation of soil/vegetation
(c) waste withdrawals from aquifers and rivers
(d) waste water output to water bodies.

When population grows, these arrows will grown in size, whereas the water flow arrows in the Total Earth system change only when climate changes.

In this water-continuity related version of the Earth system, the earlier conceptual void between terrestrial and aquatic ecosystems has been filled with the main water-related functions. Man influences the environmental system in basically four different ways:

— He sends air exhausts to the atmosphere, such as CO_2 changing the energy balance of the atmosphere, heating the ocean, and speeding up the water cycle; acidifying gases which get dissolved in water droplets in the atmosphere, transform the precipitation into a dilute acid which plays havoc with the soil and vegetation (forest dieback), later acidifying also the shallow groundwater while the flood flows may, during the snowmelt season, convey acid shocks. This was the way the acid rain problem was originally detected in Scandinavia where 20,000 lakes are biologically severely damaged only in Sweden.

He manipulates the soil and vegetation in the landscape-physically (clearing, draining etc) and chemically (agricultural chemicals)-, which is necessary to harvest its biomass resources; other chemical manipulations include drywaste deposits, landfills, cesspools, consumer products, etc.

— He withdraws water from aquifers and water bodies to supply the society with water for households, industry, and irrigated agriculture-a society where the activities are often 'lubricated' by water.

— He finally returns the wastewater to the water bodies.

In a long-term perspective we may distinguish two main phases:

(1) the next three decades, when the population growth will dominate and multiply the arrows to the natural system; basically, two influences are controllable by technology, i.e. the air exhausts and the waste water return flow which may both be strongly reduced by technological means; the other two are, basically, population-driven and therefore involve heavy and unavoidable manipulations of the land and water systems;

(2) by the year 2025 or so can we expect that the ocean has warmed up to such a degree that the evaporation increases with all the consequential changes of the precipitation pattern, the evaporation, the groundwater recharge and water table, the river flow and seasonality, and the water quality genesis and therefore the natural water quality in groundwater, rivers, and lakes (Brouwer and Falkenmark, 1989).

WATER-CYCLE RELATED DEVELOPMENT PROBLEMS

Figure 4 shows a striking analogy in geographical location between the

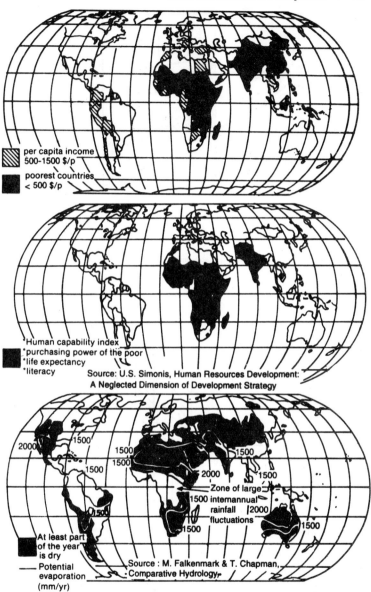

per capita income
500-1500 $/p

poorest countries
< 500 $/p

*Human capability index
*purchasing power of the poor
*life expectancy
*literacy

Source: U.S. Simonis, Human Resources Development:
A Neglected Dimension of Development Strategy

2000   1500
            1500   1500
1500   1500
            2000   1500
            Zone of large
1500   internannual
            rainfall   2000
            fluctuations
            1500   1500
1500

At least part
of the year
is dry

Potential
evaporation
(mm/yr)

Source : M. Falkenmark & T. Chapman,
Comparative Hydrology

Fig. 4. Three global maps: (a)low income countries; (b) countries in
category low human development index; (c) dry climate zone also
showing regions with high evaporative demand.

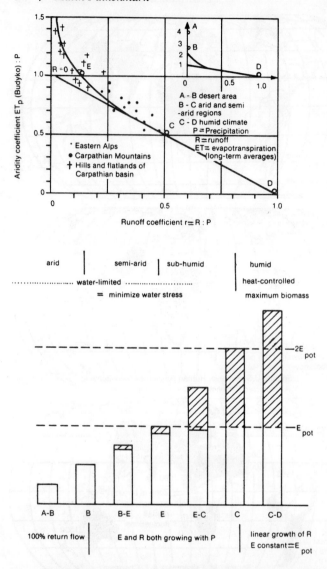

Fig. 5. Interrelation between aridity, return flow to the atmosphere, and the runoff-forming portion of precipitation. Upper diagram shows Budyko's curve together with river basin data from mid-Europe according to Szesztay (1979). Lower diagram shows how the water partitioning changes with changing hydroclimate. Codifying letters refer to upper figure.

most poverty-stricken countries; countries with low human capability index; and the dry climate regions in the world. The map invites the conclusion that the most poverty-stricken countries have a double challenge: on the one hand, part of the year is dry and/or there is a large risk for interannual droughts, and on the other the evaporative demand of the atmosphere is exceptionally large (three times as large as in Scandinavia, twice as large as in mid-Europe), greatly reducing the efficiency of the precipitation.

Why is it that the poorest countries tend to accumulate where the atmosphere is particularly thirsty? Figure 5 shows the characteristic curve of Budyko as validated by Szesztay (1979), relating the water partitioning at the ground surface, between what returns to the atmosphere and what goes to recharge the aquifers and rivers, to the aridity of the hydroclimate. The lower diagram visualizes how this partitioning alters as the precipitation increases and the climate changes from arid to semi-arid to subhumid to humid. The diagram illustrates the tremendous differences between the humid region where water is easily taken for granted, and the semi-arid and sub-humid region where most of the poverty-stricken countries still remain. In the latter countries, most of the rain returns to the atmosphere, making life a struggle for livelihood security on the hydrological margin. The predicament is further validated by the congruences discussed in an earlier paper (Falkenmark, 1986) between three African zones; the zone with severe famine during the 1984–85 drought, the zone with a short growing season, and the zone where there is less than 100 mm left of the precipitation to recharge local aquifers and rivers.

Earlier studies by Falkenmark have shown that the water scarcity dilemma in Africa involves four superimposed modes of water scarcity (Falkenmark, 1989; Falkenmark, Lundqvist and Widstrand, 1989):

— *two hydroclimatic modes:* (A) the short rainy season in combination with the high evaporative demand producing a short growing season; and (B) the large interannual fluctuations in rainfall, involving a persistent risk for crop failure due to intermittent droughts;
— *two man-generated modes:* (C) desiccation of the landscape due to degradation of soil permeability for various reasons (dryland degradation, highland degradation)-this type is often misleadingly spoken of as desertification; and (D) high population pressures on a finite and limited water availability, producing increasing levels of water stress in society. The first two have to be adapted to and mitigated as

they are part of the climate; the latter two can however be avoided by careful land conservation and population control. The four modes combine into a risk spiral, driven by population increase which intensifies both C and D, and is released during intermittent drought years (B).

The water scarcity D (Fig. 6) is worth a separate discussion as this consequence of population growth does not seem to be well understood. It seems that development experts sometimes tend to confuse the fact that water is a *renewable* resource with the fact that it is a *finite* resource. Some people contend that a renewable resource can never get scarce (Rogers, 1991), while the conventional wisdom suggests that water scarcity can easily be controlled by raising the price: let people pay. There seems, in other words, to be a conceptual confusion between the

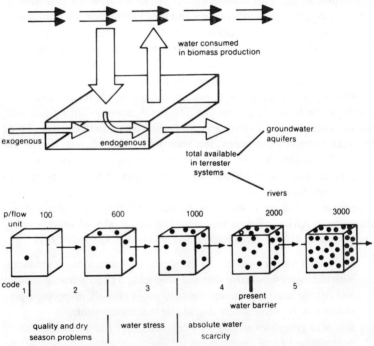

Fig. 6. (a) Freshwater availability—endogenous and exogenous.
  (b) Visualization of different levels of water competition. (Each cube indicates one flow unit of one million cubic metres of water per year available in aquifers and rivers; each dot represents 100 individuals jointly depending on each flow unit).

water delivered in technical systems and the water that is regionally available in the rural landscape, i.e. the life-support base for humans, cattle and rural food security.

Figure 7 illustrates the relation between water demand expressed as multiples of a household demand of 100 l/p day (denoted H), and the per capita water availability. The *horizontal axis* shows both per capita availability (cubic metres per person per year) and water competition level (persons per flow unit of one million cubic metres per year). Circled code numbers at the top of the diagrams refer to the population pressure intervals indicated in Fig 6b.

The *vertical axis* shows water demand expressed both as cubic metre per person per day. Crossing lines shows different mobilization levels of water availability, achieved through water storage, flow control, and other measures of water resources development. Roman numbers. Five positions can be distinguished: I, II, III, IV, and V.

The principal options as population grows in a *country type I* is demand reduction through rationalizing and restructuring of agriculture towards water-saving crops. It gets more and more important to avoid pollution as human activities per flow unit of water increases in intensity. A central water authority will be needed to secure maximum coordination between water-related sectors in society and an integration of land use and water resources.

The challenge meeting a typical *country type III* as population grows is tremendous. The task is to mobilize as large a part of its overall water availability as possible by storage above and (preferably) below the ground surface. Integrated land/water management will be important in order to secure the best possible use of the very limited amount of water available. Strong efforts are needed to abate and avoid water pollution to increase usability of the scarce water.

The typical *country type II* may have difficulties in keeping the current high demand level as population grows unless there are ample possibilities for resource development. The medium-term task will be to solve problems of regional imbalances.

The typical *country type IV*, finally, is the one with virtually the largest degrees of freedom to meet a demand increase even under population growth as seen in a medium-term perspective. Even under such fortunate conditions, the broad margin may however be consumed rapidly wherever there are problems in mobilizing a large fraction of the water availability due to lack of topography, already silted reservoirs, etc.

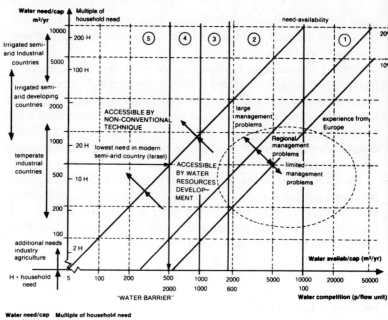

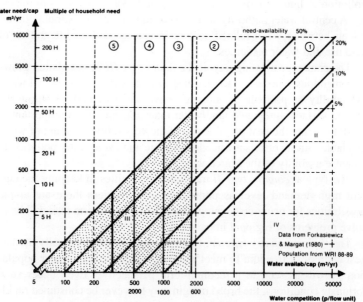

Fig. 7. Logarithmic diagram showing water demand possible to supply at different levels of mobilization of the potentially available water.

There is however also a fifth type of predicament, which we may call the *country type V*. This type represents highly water-wasting societies with water demands exceeding some 100 H. The general situation is unsustainable to the extent that the water supply includes extraction of fossiled groundwater, implying a decreasing water table with increasing pumping costs as a consequence. The water policy chosen in SW USA (El-Ashry and Gibbons, 1986) for such cases is a legislation which forces the states to present plans for how they intend to reduce the water demands down to the renewable yield, with 2025 AD as the latest target year for achieving that goal.

The perspective that it all boils down to can be catched in the concept 'water as the ultimate constraint' to development. To date we have been to much influenced by *western thinking*, i.e. a highly water-wasting society in positions I and II, caught in mainly water pollution problems. These problems are the consequence of the spread of pollutants in a landscape leached by passing water. The effects are propagated onwards in the water cycle from land to groundwater and rivers, to water bodies, and onwards to the coastal waters. The predicament of poverty-stricken countries with rapid population growth, especially those in position I and III, however, indicates that we will have to modify our general ideas of development. We need to switch the general approach from the humid zone thinking (how much water do we need and where do we get it?) to the evident approach under water scarcity (how much water is there and how can we best benefit from that amount?).

Basically, the hydroclimate and hydrography determines the potential water availability in aquifers and rivers in a country. Only part of that amount is mobilizable in the sense that it can be made accessible for use-how much depends on topography, geology, and climate. When related to the population size, this amount can be expressed as a multiple (n) of H. The question then arises whether these n. H will suffice to supply both households in rural areas (H), in urban areas (2–4 H), and a drought-proofed self-sufficient agriculture (of the order of 20 H) (Higgins, Dielemann and Abernethy, 1988). If it is to try to achieve food security, the risk would be intermittent famines. Such famines may be mitigated by altering the food support policies and switching from food self-sufficiency to partial import of food. This import has then to be financed by export of some product that produces the foreign currency needed without consuming large amounts of water for its production.

One consequence of increasing population pressures on water, particularly in rapidly growing urban areas, is the spreading of wet and dry waste from human activities. The risk produced is contamination of water sources, followed by increased incidence of water-borne diseases, escalating both morbidity and mortality. Also, the waste from industries contributes to this situation although the type of pollutants may differ.

Crucial measures to minimize these risks included

— retarding population growth by satisfying the demand for child spacing;
— mobilizing an increased fraction of the potential water availability by water resources development structures;
— hygiene education to mitigate the risk for water source contamination;
— improving waste handling, both of dry waste and wastewater (sanitation, wastewater treatment, control of dry waste deposits); and
— changing food policies.

CONCLUSION

It has been shown that water is at the core of both environmental and development problems. The basic cause of environmental problems is human activities in the landscape: either in order to get access to food, fodder, water, fuelwood, timber, energy, or to dispose of sanitary waste, dry waste, and wastewater. It has also been shown that environmental preconditions of poverty-stricken countries involve a particular vulnerability: hydroclimatic water scarcity (A, B); vulnerable soil surface (C); and increasing population pressure on a finite water availability (D).

Consequently, it is urgent to bridge the gap between the environmental lobby, preparing for the Brazil Conference, and the water specialists acting from an inherited platform of water knowledge to which Ven Te Chow skilfully and abundantly contributed and which he also competently summarized and described in a sequence of classical works.

It is moreover fundamental, in order to cope with these parallel difficulties, to develop a conceptualization that integrates societal demands, the landscape as the scene for human livelihood activities, and water's support functions in the life support systems (biomass production, societal supply), and water as a unique solvent on continuous move above and below the ground.

Finally, it is important that to develop balancing skills so that the necessary manipulations of the landscape can be balanced against the desired societal benefits. Balancing criteria should include three sustainability principles: a commonsense principle of protected potability of the groundwater/edibility of the fish/productivity of the land; a biodiversity principle; and the principle of non-overexploitation of renewable resources.

REFERENCES

Tolba, M. K. (ed). 1988 *Evolving Environmental Perceptions. From Stockholm to Nairobi.* United Nations environmental Programme. Butterworths, London.

Brouwer, F. and Falkenmark M. 1989. 'Climate-Induced Water Availability changes in Europe.' *Environmental Monitoring and Assessment*, No. 13, pp 75–98.

El-Ashry M. T. and Gibbons, D. C. 1986. *Troubled Waters, New Policies for Managing Water in the American West.* World Resources Institute, Study 6.

Falkenmark, M. 1986. 'Fresh Water-Time for a Modified Approach'. *AMBIO*, Vol. 15, No. 4.

Falkenmark, M. 1989. 'The Massive Water Scarcity Now Threatening Africa—Why Isn't It Being Addressed?' *AMBIO*, Vol. 18, No. 2, pp. 112–18.

Falkenmark, M. 1991. *Regional Environmental Management: The Role of Man-Water.* The World Bank, Environment Dept., Divisional Working Paper No. 1991–21. Washington, D.C.

Falkenmark, M. Lundqvist, J., and Widstrand, C. 1989. 'Macro-Scale Water Scarcity Requires Micro-scale Approaches. Aspects of Vulnerability in Semi-Arid Development.' Natural Resources Forum, Vol. 13, No. 4, pp 258–67.

Higgins, G. M. Dielemann P. J., and Abernethy, C. L. 1988. 'Trends in Irrigation Development, and their Implications for Hydrologists and Water Resources Engineers.' *Hydrological Sciences Journal*, Vol. 37, No. 1–2, pp 43–59.

Preparatory Committee for the UN Conference on Environment and Development, 1991. United Nations A/CONF 151/PC/14

Preparatory Committee for the UN Conference on Environment and Development, 1990. United Nations A/CONF 151/PC/WGII/L2/Rev 3.

Rogers, P. 1991.Concept Paper for World Bank. Comprehensive Water Resources Management Policy Paper. Memorandum. Cambridge, Mass.

Szesztay, K. 1979. 'Evapotranspiration Studies for Estimating Man-Influenced Streamflow Patterns under Arid Conditions. The Hydrology of Areas of Low Precipitation'. Proceedings of the Canberra Symposium, December 1979. IAHS-Publ. No. 128, pp. 197–204. IAHS Press, Wallingfrod.

UNEP. 1988. 'Environmental Perspective for 1990's and beyond'. Annex in: Tolba, M. K. (ed). *Evolving Environmental Perceptions. From Stockholm to Nairobi.* United Nations Environmental Environmental Programme. Butterworths, London, pp. 15–46.

II / Water Resources Policy

5 / Policies for Water Resources Management in Arid and Semi-arid Regions

MOHAMED T. EL-ASHRY

INTRODUCTION

Many of the freshwater problems of the twenty-first century will arise from increasing demands for water which stem from rapid population growth, urbanization, industrialization, and irrigation. The growing demand for water is being exacerbated by the excessive pumping of groundwater aquifers, some of which hold 'fossil' (i.e. ancient) water, and by the deteriorating quality of both surface water and groundwater supplies. When it comes to the role and the fate of water resources—despite the many differences socially, politically, culturally, and economically among regions around the globe—many similarities actually exist. This chapter broadly reviews some of the formidable worldwide pressures on water resources and examines, in some detail, how these issues manifest themselves in arid and semi-arid regions, specifically, western USA, especially the Central Valley of California; northwest Mexico, especially the Comarca Lagunera and Costa de Hermosillo; and the Aral Sea region of the Central Asian Republics. These case studies show that, in order to improve water management and water use patterns, we must learn from past experience, utilize available information effectively, and avoid repeating mistakes.

If we look back at human history, we find that the first great civilizations were nurtured on the banks of major rivers—the Nile in Egypt, the Tigris-Euphrates of Mesopotamia, the Indus in Pakistan, and the Hwang He of China. We also know that some civilizations collapsed when water supplies failed or were mismanaged. The decline of the Sumerian civilization of Mesopotamia, for example, is believed to be due to poor irrigation practices which caused the build-up of salt in the soil.

Stewardship of water resources is at the heart of the increasing worldwide concern for the environment. More than ever before, we now need to correct our appraisal of freshwater ecosystems. The exploitation of river basins beyond their capacity threatens to limit future economic development in many countries. Efforts to make the desert bloom deplete water resources, and subject surface water and groundwater to serious pressures. Experience has shown that a comprehensive and integrated approach to water resources management can protect the integrity of river basin ecosystems and aquifers and their ability to function in perpetuity. This is essential because rivers, and the water they contain, play an indispensable role in our lives. However, in many places man is pushing the capacity of this vital resource to dangerous limits. Water scarcity no longer refers to shortages alone. It applies also to situations of abundance where pollution forecloses beneficial uses. If we hope to succeed in meeting present and future demands for water, we must address the fundamental issues that are taxing water resources today.

CHALLENGES TO SUSTAINABLE DEVELOPMENT

We begin the last decade of this century still facing daunting challenges to long-term sustainable development: rapid population growth; increasing demands for water to satisfy people's needs, both in agriculture and in expanding urban centres; failing water quality and pollution; health impacts; groundwater depletion; conflict over shared water resources; a growing worldwide energy imperative; and the uncertainties of global climate change.

Population Growth

The first and most pressing challenge is *exponential population growth*. Under the most optimistic scenario, our numbers will grow from 5.4 billion today to approximately 8 billion 35 years from now. In many regions where most of that growth will take place, both the quality and the quantity of water are already under severe pressures. Increasing demand for land is pushing farmers onto steep slopes and into watershed and forested areas. As land and water get more scarce, the potential for conflict—including armed conflict—over water resource issues will also intensify.

In many places, population pressures and increasing water demands have pushed river ecosystems to the point where they cannot fulfil their basic ecological services. In Bangladesh, for example, deforestation of watersheds, combined with excessive rainfall, has resulted in disastrous floods and human suffering. In the Aral Sea region of the Central Asian Republics, extensive environmental degradation, which has been described as an ecologic disaster, is manifesting itself in both social and economic terms. While we strive to reduce population growth, we must also mitigate environmental impacts through conservation, greater resource efficiency, and better management of both surface water and groundwater systems.

Irrigated Agriculture

An old nemesis to the environmental health of river basins is *irrigated agriculture*. An important component of food production for thousands of years, irrigation continues to be practised in some form in every country of the world today. Chile and Peru derive 50–55 per cent of their agricultural production from irrigated land, China 70 per cent, Pakistan 80 per cent, and in Egypt 98.6 per cent of the croplands are irrigated. Irrigation is extremely water-intensive, and most irrigation practices are grossly inefficient. Worldwide, only 37 per cent of irrigation water is consumed by crops, while most of the rest is wasted, contributing to salinization and waterlogging where drainage is inadequate. Salinization causes 'sterilization' of some of the world's best and most productive farmlands. Salinity now seriously affects productivity on about 20–30 million hectares (about 7 per cent) of irrigated land around the world. And it is a persistent problem in the plains of eastern and western China, the Indian subcontinent, the Central Asian Republics, southeastern Europe, the Middle East, North and West Africa, and Australia. In other words, salinization has become commonplace wherever irrigation is practised on a large scale.

Pollution

Pressure on river resources comes also from other forms of water *pollution*. Three main culprits of water contamination are domestic waste, industrial effluent, and land-use runoff. In many developing countries, failing water quality has rendered the water supply unfit for human consumption. Organic pollution from untreated domestic wastewater jeopardizes the health of rural and urban populations. High infant mortality rates have been linked to viruses, and bacteria found in contaminated water supplies. Organic pollutants also upset natural biological systems, leading to overfertilization or eutrophication of lakes and coastal lagoons and destroying fisheries and aquatic habitats. The Chao Phraya River, in Thailand, has been anaerobic for some time, with oxygen-depleting wastes leaving no dissolved oxygen in the water to support aquatic life.

Failing water quality is also rooted in the industrial process. Industrial wastewater, still strongly polluted with chemicals and heavy metals, is often returned to the water cycle. The accumulation of unsafe levels of metals and inorganic residues in fish and other aquatic life create serious health risks for people who look to rivers and estuaries for their livelihood and food supply. River contamination in East Asia, for example, has become a critical problem. Concentrations of heavy metals in Thailand's industrial effluent are now reaching the Gulf of Thailand, a shallow and heavily fished body of water. Abu Quir Bay, in Egypt, is a case in point.

Runoff from agriculture and land clearing further adds to the stress and contamination of water sources. New technologies and demand for greater agricultural productivity have led to a sharp escalation in fertilizer and pesticide use. The resulting runoff has become one of the most widespread and critical of all water quality problems. Today, pesticides and other synthetic organic chemicals are a common ingredient in rivers around the world.

In watersheds and forested areas, land clearing leads to soil erosion, choking rivers and reservoirs with sediment—sometimes more than a hundred times the normal sediment load. In Colombia, build-up of silt behind the Achincaya Dam has reduced the dam's anticipated 50-year capacity to only 12 years. In Sudan, the capacity of Khashm El Girba Dam has been reduced from 1.3 billion m^3 to 718 million m^3 in 1976, and is expected to drop to 500 million m^3 in 1997 due to siltation. Extensive erosion can also disrupt regional hydrology while the leaching of soil nutrients impairs soil fertility to the detriment of cropland productivity.

Conflict over Common Resources

Many countries depend heavily on inflows of water from outside their borders. When we consider issues relating to international river basins, we face questions of *competing national interests* over allocation and water rights, issues of conflict management, and environmental degradation. Who owns the water? How should it be apportioned? How do downstream riparians protect themselves from upstream pollution? How should disputes be resolved? These questions are not insignificant since

40 per cent of the world's population occupies international river basins. An important aspect of the interdependence of countries within river basins is that one nation's industrial and agricultural development becomes the proper concern of another. If upstream countries export pollution, siltation, and depleted fisheries, they impose environmental risks and economic burdens for those downstream. International water problems may also involve groundwater. There are a number of cases where aquifers cross international boundaries, and pumping in one country interferes with another country's stream flows. Further, water diversions in one country to recharge an aquifer or for interbasin transfers can reduce the quantity and quality of stream flows in another country. As countries sharing water resources have to deal with increasing scarcity and failing water quality, they will have to move toward closer collaboration or face escalating conflict over resource allocation.

Energy Imperatives

Also directly impacting river basin resources is the growing *global demand for energy*. People in developing countries cannot accept declining standards of living indefinitely—nor should they— and their growing economies will demand more energy. A key question is: what type of energy? We are aware of the risk in choosing non-renewable resources. Fossil fuels and nuclear energy pose major environmental risks which are difficult to avoid or cheaply mitigate. Among the renewable resources, so far only hydropower has the capacity to satisfy energy needs today on a larger scale. With strict attention to social, environmental, and economic issues, hydropower may be a reasonable alternative in an energy package that is feasible and affordable for many countries. This does not imply that hydropower is not fraught with potential environmental problems. Recent history is replete with examples that are evidence of poor planning and inept management. Among the many challenges of hydropower development, the issue of involuntary resettlement is one of the most complex. With the creation of reservoirs behind dams, people are forced to leave their land, their homes, and their livelihoods.

With transparency of planning and pluralism in decision-making, with credible environmental analysis, decentralization of management, and participation by all affected people, much of the potential adverse impacts of dam and reservoir projects can be avoided. An integrated environmental assessment of projects is key to ensuring that hydropower projects become regional projects—integrating objectives with catch-ment area management and rural development. If energy development is designed in the context of an overall river basin and regional develop-ment planning, the potential for unanticipated cumulative adverse envi-ronmental effects and intersectoral problems can be checked.

Climatic Changes

Finally, complicating the picture for water planners and managers in arid and semi-arid regions are the long-term *climatic changes* expected to result from the build-up of carbon dioxide in the atmosphere and the accompanying global warming. Scientists are predicting that tempera-ture changes could have profound effects on precipitation, soil moisture, evapotranspiration, water runoff, and regional hydrology. For example, the warmer and drier climates associated with global warming could reduce net river basin runoff by as much as 20 per cent in the case of the Great Lakes in the United States. Moreover, shifts in mean temperature would affect also the frequency and severity of climatic events such as droughts, floods, and frost. Atmospheric scientists are now debating not whether there will be such a warming but when and at what rate it will occur.

MAKING THE DESERT BLOOM—CHALLENGES OF WATER USE IN ARID AND SEMI-ARID REGIONS

Increasing pressures on water resources make their presence felt in arid and semi-arid lands no less than in other regions of the globe. In fact, overexploitation of precious water resources has now reached a crisis point in some semi-arid regions.

A common feature of all semi-arid lands is the sparse and variable rainfall. Another typical trait is the relatively high rate of population growth, whether in sub-Saharan Africa, India, or Southern California. It is estimated that, by the end of the century, 20 per cent of the additional 1.1 billion people in the world will be in arid and semi-arid regions. In a bid to contend with the pressure of these combined forces, irrigation has become a primary source of stress on river basin systems and under-ground aquifers in these zones.

Globally, irrigated agriculture accounts for about 73 per cent of de-veloped water used in arid and semi-arid regions. Irrigation's direct con-tribution to world agricultural growth has been substantial, because both the irrigated area and the yield from it have expanded rapidly. From 1950 to date, cropland under irrigation has increased by about 3 per cent per year, from 94 to 270 million ha. Today, about 18 per cent of the world's cultivated land is irrigated, but it produces 33 per cent of the total harvest.

Irrigation requires enormous amounts of water. It takes about 1000 tonnes of water to grow one tonne of grain, and 2000 tonnes to grow one tonne of rice. In Asia, irrigation comprises 82 per cent of total water withdrawals; in the USA, 41 per cent; and in Europe, 30 per cent. Water withdrawals for irrigation can have serious environmental effects, as in the case of the Aral Sea, the Central Valley of California, and Lake Baiyangdian in North China, among others.

Despite the high priority and massive resources invested in water resources development, the performance of large public irrigation systems has fallen short of expectations, in developing and developed countries alike. Crop yields and efficiency in water use are typically less than originally projected and less than reasonably achievable. Poorly planned and badly executed irrigation projects generate large quantities of salts and other chemical compounds, resulting in critical salinization problems. The frequent decision to postpone the construction of expensive drainage systems to a later stage of an irrigation project means that short-term financial constraints get transformed into long-term, even more expensive, resource degradation problems. It is interesting to note that regions experiencing high rates of population growth, and the need to increase agricultural production, suffer most acutely the effects of salinization and waterlogging. A half of all affected irrigated cropland is in South Asia, with Pakistan and India being the most serious victims. According to various estimates, 30–60 per cent of Pakistan's 15 million ha of irrigated cropland suffer from salinity and waterlogging. In India, about 7 million ha, out of a total of 40 million, are prone to salinity and waterlogging. In Egypt, salinization and waterlogging now affect 28 per cent of all farmland, and average yields in such areas have fallen by about 30 per cent.

Of the many similarities in the role and the fate of water resources in semi-arid environments, the distinctive ones are:

1. Favourable weather conditions substantially boost development and growth which is seen by some as desirable and necessary, and by others as unsustainable. The concern, especially in the last two decades, is for what these regions may become; the phenomenal growth

is failing to keep pace with the environmentally-undesirable by-products of that growth. Consider, for example, the congestion and air
pollution in Cairo, Delhi, and Los Angeles.

2. Poor management practices, inefficient water use, and failure to
place a high economic value on water result in resource degradation
by waterlogging, soil and water salinization, and pollution of aquifers.

3. Irrigated agriculture now accounts for about 73 per cent of developed
water put to use around the world, but soaring population growth and
increasing demand for water for other uses are leading to rapid mining of aquifers, water shortages, and to competition and conflict.

4. The outlook for developing significant new surface water supplies to
meet growing demands is questionable, given limited financial resources, escalating construction costs, and increasing environmental
opposition.

The following case studies examine, in some detail, how these features
manifest themselves in three geographic regions: western USA, especially the Central Valley of California; northwest Mexico, especially the
Comarca Lagunera and Costa de Hermosillo; and the Aral Sea region of
the Central Asian Republics.

Western USA

As far back as 1902, federal programs establishing irrigated agriculture
in the desert relied on massive projects to harness and move water when
and where it was needed. Things seemed to work well. But today, use
exceeds average stream flow in nearly every western subregion, causing
water quality degradation, groundwater mining, and depletion of in-
stream flows. As a result, competition over water is increasing among
different economic sectors and among neighbouring river basins.

Soil salinity and salinity of water supplies pose a major threat to agriculture in the American West and may worsen as saline water is used
for irrigation, or as poorly drained lands get waterlogged. Each year,
salinity costs millions of dollars in damages to agriculture, as well as to
industrial and municipal water users, and these costs are escalating.

The largest irrigated area in the USA is the Central Valley of California. The basin is roughly 805 km long and 195 km wide and constitutes
more than one-third of the entire area of the state. The San Joaquin
Valley, which occupies the southern half of the basin, has about 2.8 mil-

lion ha of irrigable land, of which about 1.6 million ha are currently developed. Water for irrigation is brought from the northern basin of the Central Valley in several canals. The other source of irrigation water is groundwater, which accounts for 45 per cent of the water supply. Because of the interrelationship between surface water and groundwater, conjunctive use is practised to maximize water supplies and protect groundwater sources from rapid depletion. None the less, yearly groundwater utilization in the Central Valley includes approximately 1.5 million acre-feet of overdraft. Some parts of the valley have been designated as critically overdrawn.

Irrigated crop production in the Central Valley is currently facing problems of both water quantity and water quality. In some areas, groundwater mining might continue for many years without reaching the point of economic exhaustion of the aquifer. But other areas are already nearing that day, and eventually groundwater pumpage will have to be decreased. Because of the difficulty, for political and economic reasons, of obtaining new surface water supplies, the Central Valley's need for more water could be alleviated by improving irrigation efficiency and the mobility of supplies. This could be accomplished through trade or transfers within agriculture or between agricultural and urban areas. The valley floor is criss-crossed with canals, and many such transfers are physically feasible. Clearly, an increase in trading would improve the overall efficiency of water use in the Central Valley. If a farmer stood to gain more from selling or leasing his water than from irrigating low-value crops, that water would move to another use of higher value. For such arrangements to work properly, however, a system of property rights and pricing mechanisms is a prerequisite.

Interstate competition over water in the Colorado River Basin mirrors that between the cities and the farms. The Colorado River Compact apportions the flows of the Colorado between the states of the Upper and Lower Basins. The Upper Basin has been much slower to develop and put all its water share to full use. On an average, an estimated 2.8 million acre-feet of water flow out of the Upper Colorado River Basin unused each year. These flows produce recreational opportunities and generate hydroelectric power as they travel down to Arizona and California, where they are finally used for irrigation, municipal, and industrial purposes. But these values accrue to Lower Basin states, and the Upper Basin does not share in any of the benefits. Concerned over the eventual loss of such water, the Upper Basin states, while continuing to use water inefficiently, are taking the path of preemptive development, promoting water projects that are economically and environmentally unjustifiable.

Considering the overall increases in water demand throughout the Basin and the potential for increased interstate conflict, the states need to work together to divide the costs and benefits of Colorado River water use more equitably. The states need to reorder their water development priorities, improve the current fragmented and inefficient management of this valuable and scarce resource, and devise comprehensive basin-wide schemes for addressing current and emerging water quantity and water quality issues. Interstate water markets and leasing arrangements should also be encouraged and fostered. These recommendations, when adapted to prevailing political, social, cultural, and economic conditions, could contribute to increasing the productivity of water and land resources in other geographic regions as well.

Northwest Mexico

On Mexican irrigated farms, especially district farms, large subsidies destroy incentives for water conservation, and water is treated essentially as a 'free' good. As a result, water is wasted in overly large field applications, unmaintained canals, and deteriorating conveyance infrastructure. At the same time, the level of technical preparation and education of farmers is low, and Mexico's extension service has not efficiently upgraded the technical competence of farmers using irrigation.

The government's failure to control groundwater exploitation is leading to serious water depletion and contamination in several northern areas and is permitting sea water intrusion into coastal aquifers in the northwest. If current trends continue, Mexico faces intractable problems of water scarcity and water quality in important population centres and agricultural areas—notably in the Comarca Lagunera area, Costa de Hermosillo, and in Baja, California.

The reliance of Mexico's irrigated agriculture on groundwater has increased markedly over the past three decades. In the 1950s, less than 5 per cent of irrigation water was obtained from groundwater sources. By 1980, that share had risen to about 35 per cent—some 15.8 billion m^3 per year. Pumping out groundwater faster than an aquifer can recharge has already become a serious problem in the Comarca Lagunera and Costa de Hermosillo regions: annual pumping exceeds annual recharge by 139 per cent and 122 per cent, respectively. Crop intensities in the Comarca Lagunera regions could not have increased if groundwater had not been tapped, but these gains have accrued at a price. The water table has been falling by some 1.5 metres per year over the last 25 years. As a result, costs are mounting and the fear of aquifer contamination or exhaustion is growing.

In the Costa de Hermosillo, extensive aquifer mining in the early 1970s resulted in surface subsidence and the encroachment of brackish sea water into the aquifer. Initially, the government considered a massive south-to-north interbasin transfer of some 1 billion m³ of water, but the plan was abandoned for economic and technical reasons. Instead, the government established strict quotas for groundwater pumping and levied stiff charges. These efforts helped reduce mining from 850 million m³ in the early 1970s to 427 million m³ in 1983. Such reduction was also helped by a change in cropping patterns to less water-intensive crops.

Aral Sea Region

The Aral Sea, a large desert lake in south-central Asia, is fed by two mountain streams—the Amu Darya and Syr Darya. The Aral Sea and surrounding regions are experiencing extensive environmental degradation with major economic consequences in the five republics that share the basin: Kazakhstan, Uzbekistan, Kirghizia, Tajikistan, and Turkmenistan. The area of the Aral has been reduced by 40 per cent and its volume by 66 per cent in 30 years. Total river runoff into the Sea has dropped from 40 km³ in 1960 to 5 km³ in 1989, while salt content has increased from 10–28 g/l during the same period.

Rapid development of irrigated agriculture, combined with high population growth rates, has triggerred the region's problems. Early in the 1960s, an ambitious plan for agricultural development of this semiarid region was put into effect by the Soviet central government. Irrigated land doubled to 7 million ha; a half of the land produces cotton, and the other half produces rice, corn, vegetables, fruits, and forage for livestock. With the rapid expansion of irrigated lands, the total inflow of water to the Aral decreased sharply and the Sea's level dropped from 53.3 m in 1960 to 39.0 m in 1989. The exposed sea bottom of the Aral is becoming salt flats and a source of constant windblown silt and salts, mainly sulphates and chlorides. As a consequence of the physical changes, the Aral Sea has also lost most of its productive fisheries. Increased salinity and dried-up spawning grounds have caused 20 of the 24 commercial fish species to disappear.

In recent years, the state of the environmental deterioration of the

Aral Sea has received much attention regionally, nationally, and internationally. A number of solutions to the 'Aral Crisis' have been proposed.
These include: diversion of Siberian rivers to increase water supplies;
improving irrigation and drainage; developing irrigation efficiency; conjunctive use of surface water and groundwater; retirement of marginal
lands; and a return to the traditional agriculture practised early this century. One conclusion, however, is clear: restoring the hydrologic, ecologic, and economic integrity of the region will not be possible without
the full participation and cooperation of the five republics that comprise
the region.

POLICIES FOR WATER RESOURCES MANAGEMENT

Resolving these critical water resource issues will require a shift in attention from the development of water resources to their management.
Basin-wide, comprehensive solutions are needed with actions on the
political, economic, social, and environmental fronts. Nothing less than
a multidisciplinary approach will do. Water resources management is no
longer the prerogative of one discipline. An effective water management
plan must be part of a broader, regional economic development plan that
takes account of other sectoral dimensions—agricultural, manufacturing,
ecological, and health-related needs, among others. Careful analysis of
all available options and alternatives is essential if we hope to find lasting, cost-effective solutions, and if economic development is to be sustainable.

Three factors are critical to a comprehensive approach to water management. These are:

— Integrating land and water management in river basins.
— Linking management of surface and subsurface water resources.
— Considering both water quality and water quantity in water planning
  and management efforts.

These three 'keys' are simply common sense based on lessons learned
from around the world.

Building institutional capacity is also integral to the comprehensive
approach. Institutional arrangements need to be developed that encourage agencies with jurisdiction over water resources to exchange information and communicate with one another on a regular basis and engage
in joint planning. Local actors should be given greater responsibility for
water management at the local level, and they need to collaborate with

governmental institutions in the creation of an overarching development strategy and framework. Few developing countries have the resource inventories and data bases necessary to design, monitor, and support water policies. Nor do regulatory and legal frameworks exist to enforce them. Building these capacities is integral to addressing water allocation and reallocation, protection of surface water and groundwater supplies, establishing water markets and price reforms, resolving conflict over water rights, and for designing resource-use policies based on the interaction between land and water systems.

Environmental protection and health must also be viewed within the broader context of an integrated approach whereby environmental considerations are addressed early on and as part of planned water resources management. Pollution is without question a major cause of water quality degradation, but pollution control and clean-up is only one important component of any water management policy. Prevention is central. This means ensuring adequate sanitation, wastewater collection, and industrial waste disposal facilities, and promoting environmentally-sound technologies.

The traditional strategy of responding to water shortages in semi-arid regions by increasing water supplies through capital-intensive water transfer or diversion projects has clearly reached its financial, legal, and environmental limits. Reform of water pricing policies is critical to arrest the overexploitation of water resources and extreme drawdown of surface and groundwater sources. Many opportunities exist for improving the efficiency of irrigated agriculture which would release water for other sectors, reduce conflicts, and in the process improve agricultural productivity. In the American West, for example, improving agricultural irrigation efficiency (which averages about 55 per cent) by just 10 per cent would double the amount of water available for urban residences and businesses. A 10 per cent increase in water efficiency in the Indus region of Pakistan (which averages less than 40 per cent), on the other hand, would release enough water to irrigate another 2 million ha or to be used for other purposes, thus reducing the pressure for further development of water supplies. Unfortunately, incentives for water conservation in agriculture are few, and disincentives are numerous. Neither water prices nor visible opportunity costs encourage the farmer to invest in the technology and management expertise needed to conserve water.

One of the most obvious disincentives to conservation is the low cost of water for agriculture. This problem is particularly striking in semi-arid regions, where public investment has provided huge price subsidies for irrigation water in both developed and developing countries. In California, for example, the US government is spending more than $534 million a year (while collecting only $58 million) to provide cheap irrigation water to western farms, many of which are producing surplus crops that qualify for additional federal farm subsidy. In Mexico, while the law requires water users to repay part of all capital costs associated with water development projects and all operation and maintenance costs, water users in Mexico's irrigated agriculture sector pay only about 11 per cent of the full cost, implying an 89 per cent subsidy.

Reforming water pricing policies, regardless of the prevailing climate, must be part of a more comprehensive agricultural policy which also addresses government regulation of agricultural prices that farmers receive, as well as politically-popular policies in many countries for providing low-cost food and fibre to consumers. Higher-cost inputs in conjunction with low, fixed-output prices could place farmers in a vice. If water-pricing schemes are to be used to foster greater efficiency in water use, agricultural price policies in general have to be re-examined.

On the global front, the 1992 Earth Summit, the U.N. Conference on Environment and Development in Rio de Janeiro, offers the world an opportunity for long-awaited actions by resolving to meet certain goals by a specific date. From a water resources perspective, three goals can be singled out:

— Guaranteeing every individual, almost three billion, access to clean water and sanitation. This requires targeted investments and better educational services to ensure that water of acceptable quality is available at affordable cost. Special attention must be focused on community involvement and the role of women.
— Feeding the hundreds of millions of hungry people in a sustainable manner. This means adopting integrated strategies for reducing land and water degradation by addressing the interactions among soil, water, and vegetation on the one hand, and land-use and government policies affecting natural resources on the other hand.
— Stabilizing world population at sustainable levels. The strain of rapid population growth on social services, on rural and urban environments, and on political systems is already immense. Investments in education, health care, and family planning seem modest when compared with the possible costs of not curtailing present population growth rates.

In all three areas, addressing the important question of financial resources is paramount in the minds of developing countries.

CONCLUSION

Despite all the progress achieved in this century, the waters of the world and the people who help manage them for the benefit of all whose lives depend on them still face major challenges. The lessons from the past are clear. Without integrated approaches and without appropriate policies and institutional capacities for comprehensive water resources management, no technical or engineering fix will succeed. In fact, such fixes may well create the need for additional expenditures to mitigate environmental degradation. Solutions are needed to address today's challenges and priorities. Better management and more equitable allocation of water resources will go far to help countries sustain economic prosperity without undervaluing or destroying the fragile natural capital of water resource ecosystems.

6 / Water Policies for Sustainable Development

MAYNARD M. HUFSCHMIDT

INTRODUCTION

The emerging challenge to water management in the twenty-first century is how to achieve sustainable development in the face of continued expansion of population and economic activity and the pervasive problems of poverty and environmental degradation. In the arid and semi-arid regions of the developing world, water is already extremely scarce, but even in the sub-humid and humid zones, competition for readily-available supplies is strong and rapidly increasing. The time has passed when abundant supplies of water were readily available for development at low economic, social, and environmental cost. Now we are entering the period of the 'maturing water economy', with increasing competition for access to fixed supplies, a growing risk of water pollution, and sharply higher economic, social, and environmental costs of development. The shift is from a supply orientation to emphasis on demand management. These trends necessitate a new look at water policy, especially in developing countries.

No matter how effective existing water policies may have been in guiding water resources management over the past decades, they are not suitable for meeting the challenges of the maturing water economy of the future. Yet, the last comprehensive look at water policy for developing countries was 14 years ago at the United Nations Water Conference in 1977 (Biswas, 1978). A recent resurgence of interest in the subject has included a study of water resources policy in Asia (Ali *et al.*, 1987), a report on water supply policies for developing countries (Munasinghe, 1990), and a policy paper on sustainable water development and management (UNEP, 1989). In addition, the World Bank is currently undertaking an in-depth study of water resources programmes and policies in developing countries to provide a factual basis for revising Bank policies, strategies, and programmes on water resources management. Finally, a United Nations Intersecretariat Group for Water Resources has been preparing a comprehensive report on a proposed water strategy for the next decade.

These studies and reports can serve as useful inputs toward developing a comprehensive water policy for sustainable development. This chapter is offered as an additional contribution to this end. Focusing on the topic of water policy at the national level, it presents a framework for water policy for sustainable development, and shows how water policy is linked to policies in other sectors, including public finance, agriculture, energy, industry and commerce, health, human settlements, transport, and the environment. The intent is to identify the essential elements of a national water policy, while giving only incidental attention to what the content of that policy should be. This attempt may provide some insights to those concerned with formulating new or revised water policies for sustainable development.

PROPOSED FRAMEWORK FOR WATER RESOURCES POLICY

The term *policy* is used here to mean a general rule or guideline for decisions or actions in specific cases. For example, a typical water resources allocation policy would be one that gives priority to domestic water uses in the event of a water shortage. Case-by-case decisions on water allocation would then be guided by this policy. Water policies may show up in various forms: constitutions, laws, administrative regulations, long-range plans and programmes, and budgets. Rarely are such policies neatly codified so that they can be readily identified. Therefore, formulation of the specific elements of a water policy is an essential prerequisite to an assessment of its adequacy and completeness. To this end, a framework for policy analysis is presented here, based on the interrelationship of the three systems shown in Fig. 1.

The first of these, the *natural water resources system*, entails the hydrologic cycle, with its components of precipitation, evaporation, surface runoff, and groundwater flows, as well as the broader 'hydrologic continuum', defined by Leopold (1990) to include the soil, biota, and atmosphere as well as water. In the aggregate, this system is the water and water-related natural resources endowment (or 'supply') available for human uses.

The second is the human *activity system* which is composed of the many human activities that affect, or are affected by, the natural water resources system. At one extreme, as in the Nile Valley, people have

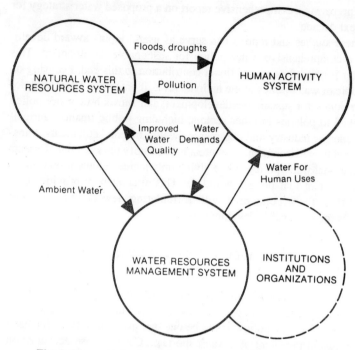

Fig. 1. Proposed framework for water resources policy

extensively modified the natural system by constructing storage reservoirs, diversion works, and canals to meet their irrigation needs. At the other extreme, as in Bangladesh, those inhabiting the floodplains of major streams such as the Ganges and Brahmaputra rivers are at the mercy of natural forces. Between these extremes are works such as stream recession irrigation in West Africa. In the aggregate, these human activities comprise the 'demand' side for water uses such as irrigation, domestic water supply, waste disposal, navigation, hydroelectric power, fisheries, and recreation, and for reduction in damages from flooding, water pollution, and drought.

Finally, the *water resources management system* embodies the activities and relationships in the public and private sectors concerned with harmonizing the supply and demand sides so as to achieve the objectives of society. In this context, *demand* includes both uses for water such as for irrigation and domestic needs, and adverse impacts such as pollution arising from human activities, while *supply* also includes adverse impacts, such as natural floods and droughts, imposed by the water resources system on human activities. As shown in Fig. 1, an essential support to the water resources management system is the institutional and organizational framework for management.

In the sections that follow, we will identify those elements of a national water policy that are relevant to each system. An effective water resources policy includes specific elements which (a) preserve the integrity of the natural water resources system, and (b) provide water and water-related services to people in an economically efficient, equitable, environmentally sound, and sustainable manner.

NATURAL WATER RESOURCES SYSTEM

Maintaining the integrity of the hydrologic continuum, as proposed by Leopold (1990), is essential to the sustainable use of the natural water resources system. Policies concerned with achieving a scientific understanding of the hydrologic continuum, and the use of such understanding in water resources assessment and planning, are relevant. Examples include:

1. Establishing and maintaining an effective national hydrologic data system; coordinating this system with other specialized public and private data systems; establishing open access to these data bank systems; participating in a national geographic information system combining data series on land, water, and other resources; and promoting the highest scientific standards in all of these activities.
2. Sustained support for research on the natural water resources system and its linkages with other natural resources and the human activity system.
3. Adopting appropriate spatial units for water resources assessment and planning, such as the river basin or groundwater aquifer, so as to incorporate major land-water-ecosystem interactions.
4. Adopting conjunctive management of quantity and quality of surface water and groundwater to maintain the integrity of the hydrologic system and achieve efficient use of these water resources.
5. Managing water resources for multiple purposes in order to capture complementaries and to reduce competition and identify trade-offs among uses in the natural water resources system.
6. Integrating environmental impact assessment into water planning, including the effects of development on aquatic and terrestrial ecosystems, on humans, and on the built environment.

HUMAN ACTIVITY SYSTEM

Policies of special relevance to the human activity system are those concerned with (a) specific water demands for human activities, such as irrigation water for agriculture, potable water for domestic use, and water for industry, electric power generation, waste disposal, navigation, fisheries, and recreation; (b) human adjustments to water-based natural hazards such as floods and droughts; and (c) human-caused degradation of natural systems, such as pollution, sedimentation, and salinization. In general, these policies are concerned with influencing human activities so as to reduce adverse impacts on the natural water resources system and minimize economic and social losses from natural hazards.

Demand for Water Services

1. Adopting demand management as an integral part of water management, including formulating and evaluating demand reduction methods and strategies as complements to and substitutes for supply augmentation projects, in order to bring projected demands for and supplies of water into balance.
2. Using prices as a tool for demand management, including volumetric pricing of supply or wastewater on the basis of marginal supply or disposal costs, along with increasing block rates. Where appropriate, seasonal pricing and temporary drought surcharges would be imposed.
3. Implementing efficient technical measures for curtailing urban water use and transmission losses in the supply system. This includes changes in plumbing codes to require water-saving plumbing fixtures, programmes of leak detection and control, and sustained operation and maintenance.
4. Opting for recycling and other technical means to reduce withdrawal rates for water for industry, especially for cooling.
5. Using technical means for controlling irrigation water use, including drip irrigation, sprinkler irrigation, land levelling, canal lining, along with institutional means such as modifying water rights systems to encourage efficient use of irrigation water.
6. Utilizing lower-grade water for certain domestic, commercial, industrial, and agricultural purposes. The use of brackish water and treated wastewater for non-potable purposes often involves installation of dual water supply systems.

Human Adjustments to Floods and Droughts

1. Controlling human occupancy of flood-prone lands to minimize flood risks. This involves effective enforcement of regulations encouraging compatible land uses, such as recreational, agricultural, and some commercial uses, while restricting non-compatible uses.
2. Adopting a loss-minimization strategy for flood management, including flood-proofing structures and adopting flood insurance, flood warning systems, and evacuation and restoration plans.
3. Basing redevelopment programmes following flood disasters on risk-minimization land-use controls and management strategies. Public investments, and subsidies and controls on private investment for redevelopment, would be in accordance with such essential human adjustments.
4. Planning for human adjustments to drought based on specific rules for reducing water withdrawals to achieve efficient and equitable sharing of limited water resources, through pooling of available supplies, allocation to uses of the greatest social value, with appropriate compensation to losers.

Reduction of Pollution from Human Activities

1. Reducing generation of pollution at the source, through changes in production processes, by-product recovery, and wastewater reuse, making use of technical advice, regulation and enforcement, pricing policy, and tax incentives.
2. Adopting a polluter-pays policy, including the levy of effluent charges adequate to achieve desired reduction of pollutants, and earmarked to finance the clean-up costs of residual pollution.
3. Installing basic sanitation facilities in rural and low-income urban areas, including community involvement in planning and installing and maintaining low-cost facilities meeting minimum standards.
4. Reducing water pollution from agricultural, grazing, and forestry activities by lowering sedimentation from soil erosion, cutting down discharges of pesticides and fertilizers, and reducing the saline content of irrigation return flow. Tools that may be used are subsidies (where appropriate), removal of perverse subsidies, changes in property rights, tighter regulation of forestry activities, and enforceable stipulations on types and methods of application of agricultural chemicals.

WATER RESOURCES MANAGEMENT SYSTEM

Policies relevant to water resources management are those that guide the planning and implementation of public and private programmes and strategies for harmonizing the supply of and demand for water to meet the efficiency, equity, and sustainability objectives of society. Examples of such policies are:

1. Establishing unified national objectives and priorities for water resources management, including setting guidelines for resolving the inevitable conflicts between national economic growth and self-sufficiency, regional development, equitable income distribution and social impacts, environmental quality, and sustainability of the resource base.
2. Developing constructive international agreements on water management, which entails equitable sharing of benefits and costs of development/management of international river basins, and clear definition of rights and responsibilities of affected nations.
3. Guiding national investments in water resources development by means of capital investment budgets and programmes, national-local cost-sharing, international or bilateral grants and/or loans, cost-sharing by provincial, local, and private agencies, and private investment.
4. Adopting project formulation and evaluation criteria involving benefit-cost analysis, risk-assessment analysis, and multiple objective (including environmental impact) analysis—to be used for project and program feasibility studies and monitoring and evaluation of performance.
5. Establishing a better balance between *development*—the creation of new projects, such as dams and irrigation systems—and *management*, focusing on more efficient use of existing facilities.
6. Planning for involuntary resettlement from development projects, such as storage reservoirs, so as to minimize economic and social dislocation, promote development opportunities, and mitigate adverse effects in an equitable manner.
7. Adopting workable approaches to deal with water conflicts that emphasize negotiation and mediation rather than confrontation.
8. Formulating procedures for allocation of water and waste assimilation capacity that take account of interdependency of water uses and the role of pricing policy. Alternative approaches are via water mar-

kets with clear property rights versus allocation via planning; or some combination of these two.

9. Establishing standards on centralization versus decentralization of water planning and implementation; for example, reliance on a highly-centralized national irrigation or power agency versus regional or local irrigation agencies.

10. Promoting public involvement/local participation in project planning and implementation, especially for irrigation, upstream watershed management, and rural and urban water supply and sanitation projects.

11. Providing for adequate funding of project operation and maintenance, e.g. from user charges, especially for projects to be turned over to local water users for operation and maintenance.

12. Planning for effective monitoring and ex-post evaluation of projects.

INSTITUTIONS AND ORGANIZATIONS

Policies concerning national institutions and organizations provide an essential basis for effective water resources management. These policies are ordinarily incorporated in national legislation and the organizational structure of government.

1. Establishing a national water code, which may involve private ownership of surface water and groundwater rights (riparian or prior appropriation), full government ownership, with rights to use (including limitations) granted by government, or mixed public-private rights to water use which recognize water as a collective good. The code should include a water rights system which recognizes the hydrological realities of surface water—groundwater and return flow linkages, and the stochastic nature of precipitation and stream flows.

2. Formulating an approach to organization for water resources management, including integration of activities of different agencies at the planning and implementation stages, spatial integration by river basin, water resources demand region, or political jurisdiction, and division of responsibilities for water resources management among national, provincial, local public, and private sectors. The activities involve water allocation, regulation of use and abuse, development, preservation, and operation of water supply and treatment facilities.

POLICY OVERLAPS

The preceding discussion on the major elements of a national water policy was without reference to the specific locus of these elements in the national governmental structure. In fact, water resources management is typically divided among a number of governmental sectors. This means that water policies are not the exclusive domain of a water resources sector but overlap with other sectoral policies, as illustrated in Fig. 2. For example, in many countries, the Ministry of Agriculture has purview over irrigation, and many policies concerning this extremely important water use are established by this agency. Similarly, other water uses such as hydroelectric power and navigation are the policy domain of the ministries of energy and transport. Urban and rural water supply and sanitation are often the concerns of the ministries of health and human settlements, while environmental agencies establish policies for water quality and preservation of natural aquatic ecosystems, and forestry agencies are often involved in watershed management activities which have major repurcussions on water resources. In addition, national

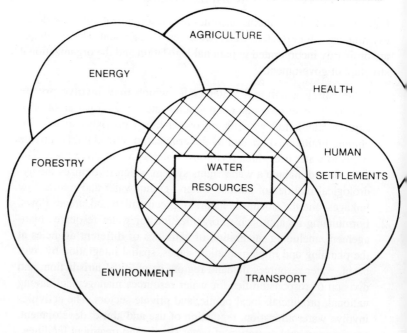

Fig. 2. Policy overlaps: water resources and other national sectors

macro-economic policies on finance, budgets, and trade can have important impacts on water resources management.

This feature of policy overlap in water resources has been discussed in some detail by Munasinghe (1990). He points to the need for analyzing the links between water and other sectors of the economy, including those in agriculture, industry, transport, energy, and health. In his conceptual framework, an overall national water policy entails (a) policies covering the water resources sector as a whole, (b) policies relating to specific subsectors of water resources, such as potable water and irrigation, and (c) policies concerned with other sectors (e.g. energy) that affect water resources.

CONCLUSION

Based on the framework presented here, the important elements of a water resources policy can be developed on a comprehensive and consistent basis for any specific use. Though our focus is national policies, the approach can be applied also to local, provincial, and international levels.

ACKNOWLEDGEMENTS

I am grateful for the helpful comments and suggestions of Blair T. Bower, Regina Gregory, and James Nickum.

REFERENCES

Ali, M., Radosevich, G. E., and Khan, A. A. (eds). 1987. *Water Resources Policy for Asia*, A.A. Balkema, Rotterdam.

Biswas, A. K. (ed). 1978. *United Nations Water Conference: Summary and Main Documents*, Pergamon Press, Oxford.

Leopold, L. B. 1990. 'Ethos, Equity and the Water Resource', *Environment*, vol. 32, no. 2, March, pp. 17–20; 37–42.

Munasinghe, M. 1990. 'Water Supply Policies and Issues in Developing Countries', *Natural Resources Forum*, vol. 14, no. 1, February, pp. 33–48.

UNEP (United Nations Environment Programme). 1989. 'Sustainable Water Development and Management', *International Journal of Water Resources Development*, vol. 5, no. 4, December, pp. 225–51.

7 / Surface Water Management: A Perspective for the Twenty-first Century

GERT A. SCHULTZ

INTRODUCTION

As we approach the end of the twentieth century, the development of water resources management is based on new methodologies (e.g. operations research, expert systems), new hardware (computer main frames, PCs, work stations, automatic control devices), and new data acquisition systems (e.g. laser and ultrasonic devices, remote sensing, remote data transmission). Most of these modern techniques are applied mostly in an isolated fashion. Extrapolation of the trends of these developments into the future, including modern water management practices as well as scientific developments, allows the postulation of scenarios of surface water management systems that may become operational in the twenty-first century.

INFORMATION SYSTEMS

Efficient water management depends largely on the availability of adequate hydrological and other data. For design purposes, long-time series of data with high resolution in time and space are required. For operation of water resources (WR) systems, the relevant data have to be provided in real-time, i.e. without delay.

Conventional Data Acquisition and Remote Data Transmission

In the twenty-first century, all hydrological data will be collected in data banks with access possibilities in real-time or off-line. Conventional measurement devices (rain gauges, river gauges, etc.) will continue to be in use in the twenty-first century since they are simple and inexpensive.

These devices will, however, be connected with WR management control centres (e.g. of a water authority), thus being available in real-time (e.g. for flood-control purposes). The data transmission will then be achieved with the aid of telephones, wireless, or by data-collection platforms, using satellites in space as relay stations (e.g. Meteosat).

Real-time Monitoring from Satellites

For hydrology and water management geomorphological conditions, land-use, vegetation cover, and other information in a river catchment are highly relevant and can be obtained from satellites (Schultz and Barrett, 1989), e.g. Landsat (USA) or Spot (France). The new Earth Observation System (EOS) launched by NASA, ESA, and NASDA, expected to be operational at the beginning of the next century, will provide multispectral satellite data with high resolution in space and time. It is hoped that these data will allow a permanent real-time monitoring of water quantity (floods, lake levels, snow conditions) and water quality (sediments, pollutants, temperature, etc.) even if clouds are in the atmosphere. This information will allow more efficient water management of large river and lake systems.

Weather Radar and Satellites

Weather radar of the C-band type (Europe) or S-band (NEXRAD in North America) allows rainfall measurements of a large area at one point (radius ca. 100 km). Since the resolution in time and space is very high, radar is eminently suitable for flood forecasting in real-time as basis for the operation of flood storages (Fig. 1).

It may be assumed that at the beginning of the twenty-first century the joint European radar network—at present under construction—as well as the North American and the Japanese radar systems will be operational. Also, data obtained from certain satellites (at present Meteosat, GOES, GMS) will facilitate rainfall estimation. Data such as that obtained from the EOS will be in more suitable spectral bands (e.g. from the Canadian Radarsat) and with better spatial and temporal resolution. Combination of radar data with satellite data will provide the opportunity to forecast rainfall, which will make for more accuracy in flood forecasts and flood management.

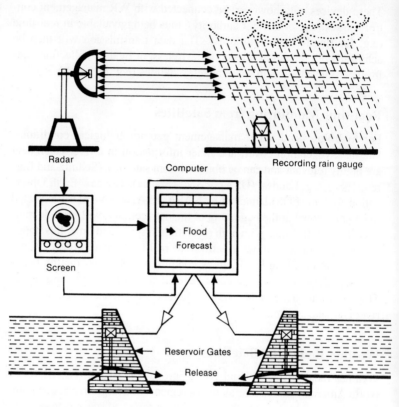

Fig. 1. Reservoir operation based on real-time flood forecasts with aid of radar rainfall measurements

Data Banks and Control Centres

Integrated management of all elements in a multipurpose multi-unit WR system requires a sophisticated monitoring and control system. In a control centre (e.g. of a water authority), a computer will contain a Geographic Information System (GIS) with all relevant system information, a data bank for historical and real-time hydrometeorological and other data, a program library with all computer routines of a DSS (decision support system) and expert knowledge. Here, management decisions can be made in real-time and in an optimum way on the basis of all relevant data, and expert knowledge stored in the computer's 'knowledge base'.

DECISION SUPPORT SYSTEMS (DSS)

The responsibility for decisions is now and—hopefully—will continue to be always with man and not with machines. Although a completely automatic process—one that provides water management in some 'optimum' way—is conceivable, it is advisable that all available 'high tech' be geared to provide the manager, i.e. a qualified person, with decision support as efficiently as possible, but not to 'free' him from decision-making. The ultimate decision should rest with man—otherwise undesirable consequences cannot be excluded.

Modern Theoretical Methods for Water Management

The application of 'Operations Research' techniques in water management (e.g. optimization, simulation) has wide coverage and is extensively used. A discussion here is therefore unnecessary. The euphoria about optimization techniques in the 1980s has given way to a recognition of the dubious meanings attributed to 'optimum' in specific cases as, for example, in a multipurpose WR system where several competitive or non-commensurable objectives have to be met. Literature offers multi-objective decision-making (MODM) methods, which generate a unique optimum solution. The problem with MODM methods is, however, the fact that the decision-maker (DM) has to specify 'weights' for each objective *a priori* or *a posteriori* or in a dialogue. This makes the generation of the optimum solution by no means easy or transparent. At present, research is being conducted on improved MODM methods such that the DM will find *his* optimum solution without being overcharged by specifying parameters, the implication of which he cannot anticipate (Laabs and Schultz, 1991). Such efforts pave the way for the capability, after the year 2000, for optimum multi-objective decisions, even when more than one DM is involved.

Among the new theoretical techniques needed for future water management, forecasting techniques will play an important role. It can be expected that hydrological variables (e.g. floods) can be forecast with high reliability, e.g. on the basis of remote sensing data in combination with stochastic techniques.

However, water management requires also forecasts of other variables, particularly for planning purposes, for instance, water demand, expected environmental quality, and economic interest rates. In such cases, a multidisciplinary effort is still a requisite.

Operation of Water Resources Systems

Today, most WR systems are operated according to operating rules that are fixed in principle but depend on the actual systems conditions, e.g. reservoir levels, discharge, demand, etc. A comparatively more sophisticated operating policy would entail the use of adaptive operating strategies which compute different decision information for each individual situation (e.g. each specific flood), ensuring a more efficient use of water or better protection from water. Such adaptive control strategies, which will be applicable to the more complex WR systems of the future, require the forecast of flows (floods, low flows, etc.) which may be obtained with the aid of remote sensing devices.

Another problem, which will have to be faced in the next century, is the artificial separation of water quantity management from water quality management. This separation will not be possible any more in the future because it often means inefficient use of the available precious water resources. Therefore, techniques that optimize the management of water quantity and water quality have to be developed. This means that the operation of storage reservoirs in a river catchment cannot be performed independent of the operation of sewage treatment plants. The optimum integrated operation of all elements in a water resources system—storage reservoirs, sewage treatment plants, water supply systems, hydropower, and irrigation systems—is at present an unsolved problem. Several research activities all over the world have, however, the promise that components for this complex task will be available in the near future. Research entails not only the difficult combination of water quantity and water quality mathematical models but also the incorporation of information obtained from such models into decision-support models based on MODM techniques.

A new technique is being researched which may become useful in solving such difficult WR management problems in the future, namely, the so-called 'expert systems' representing a special branch of AI (artificial intelligence).

Objectives of Water Management

During this century, the main objectives in surface water management were: drinking water supply, irrigation, industrial water supply, flood protection, navigation, and hydropower.

In the twenty-first century, drinking water supply will still have top priority, including improved water quality for protecting people's health. Due to the soaring world population, irrigation as also flood protection will gain considerable importance. In many countries, the growing awareness of environmental dangers will lead to an increasing significance of low flow augmentation for dilution of pollutants, for improvement of the reliability of drinking water supply from bank infiltration, and for groundwater level stabilization (required for agriculture and drinking water supply).

Other objectives are losing importance: the necessity for reduction of industrial water use and for recycling of water (due to environmental impact and water shortage) leads to lower industrial water demands, at least in many developed countries. Since in many regions groundwater resources are exploited, drinking water demand increase will be met not by groundwater sources but rather by surface water reservoirs.

WATER MANAGEMENT BY EXPERT SYSTEMS

In theory, many powerful techniques were developed (e.g. MODM and adaptive control methods), the practical use of which is currently hampered by the fact that the methods are too complex and difficult to apply. 'Expert systems' allow the use of expert knowledge together with conventional data for decision processes. The operation of WR systems in real-time represents a problem requiring the application of an expert system. For the operation of a multipurpose multi-unit reservoir system, such an expert system is being developed by the institute of hydrology and water management at the Ruhr University in cooperation with a German water authority. This will be briefly presented as an example (Fisher and Schultz, 1991). The idea is that the dispatcher at a control centre of the water authority shall make the necessary operating decisions in a computer dialog with the aid of the expert system stored in the computer (Fig. 2). The 'user' (Fig. 2) is the dispatcher of the main reservoir (no. 1).

The main difference between 'normal' computer programs and expert systems is that the latter contain a so-called knowledge base in which the expert knowledge is stored separate from the problem solver program (or inference engine). This way the knowledge base can be changed or 'learnt' from experience without a change in the inference engine. Figure 3 shows the basic structure of an expert system. Such an expert system may contain not only observed data (water levels, rainfall rates) but also expert knowledge and complex computing techniques such as MODM

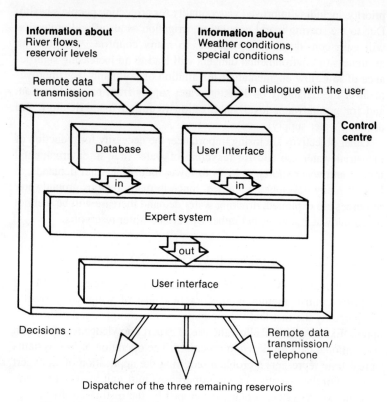

Fig. 2. Flow of information into and from the expert system

methods. A dispatcher with average engineering qualification would then be able to make decisions based on the knowledge of an expert. It is estimated that by 2000 AD expert systems for very efficient real-time operation of WR systems will not only be available but also be used in practice due to their relatively easy application.

FUTURE SCENARIOS

Scenarios of surface water management relevant to the twenty-first century will have to consider two different developments:

— the introduction of new information systems, and decision support systems, including expert systems for the optimum management of WR systems as discussed above;

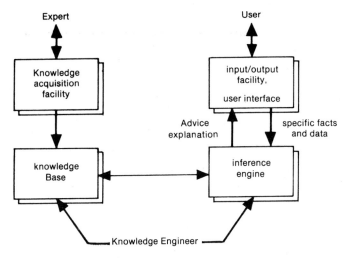

Fig. 3. Basic structure of an expert system (Feigenbaum and McCordruck, 1983)

— natural and man-made long-term modifications of WR systems caused, for example, by land-use changes or climatic changes.

Impact of Land-use Changes

Obviously, the water resources systems in the next century will differ from the prevailing ones. Many parts of the world will be confronted with land-use changes due to urbanization and industrialization, with increase or reduction (e.g. in Europe) in agriculture, dying forests, or desertification. These changes will influence the efficiency of water management practices. Mathematical models currently under development (applying GIS and satellite data) allow anticipation of such changes as far as the consequences for reliability of water resources systems are concerned. Such models will provide information necessary for the timely adaption of our water systems to future situations. It can be anticipated that industrial and urban developments current in many parts of the world, leading to an increased imperviousness of the catchment area, will give rise to more severe floods (higher peaks, shorter time to peak) and to more severe low flows (lower discharges, longer low flow

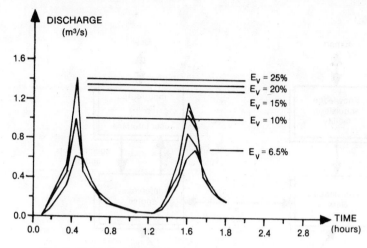

Fig. 4. Flood aggravation due to increased imperviousness of catchment area (Historical flood in a catchment in Germany)

periods). Figure 4 shows the impact of increased imperviousness on a specific flood in a German catchment (Richter and Schultz, 1988). It was proven that there is a general linear rise in flood peak values with increased imperviousness of the catchment.

Impact of Climate Change

The permanent increase of CO_2 and other trace gases in the atmosphere tend to influence not only climatic changes but also hydrology. This, in turn, will give rise to potential failure of our water systems (e.g. due to increased low flow periods, floods, or different interannual distribution of flows). The combination of Atmospheric General Circulation Models (AGCM's) with macro-scale hydrological models (as intended in the GEWEX program) will allow the computation of such expected changes in hydrology and water resources for the twenty-first century. On the basis of this knowledge, precautions can be taken to avoid jeopardizing the well-being of human society by adapting our water resources systems to the new conditions as early as possible.

Although all predictions of future climatic and hydrological patterns are still rather uncertain, some qualitative changes can already be predicted. The hydrological changes will not be uniform in time and space; some areas will profit from improved conditions, but extensive regions

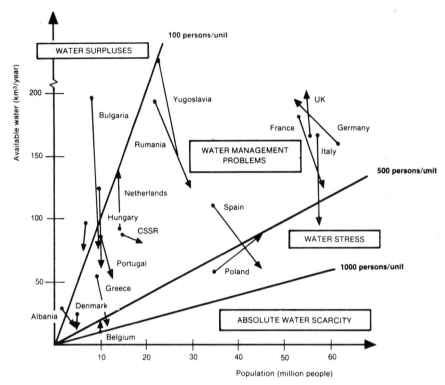

Fig. 5. Indicative shifts in relative water availability (based on
UKMO-model) of European countries in response to climate change
and population growth (From Falkenmark, 1989)

of the world will suffer from unfavourable changes. Figure 5 shows the
expected changes for Europe, where the southern region will be afflicted
with major problems as this area will be much drier: see the lines for
Greece, Spain, Italy, all of which move from the 'water management
problems' zone into the 'water stress' area. This will certainly lead to
water supply problems and to food shortage due to a reduced irrigation
potential. Timely recognition of this threat, together with planning and
management of improved water resources systems, should allow, however, the alleviation of such distress in the twenty-first century. Crossing
lines in Fig. 5 indicate the water competition index in number of individuals per one million cubic metre of water per year.

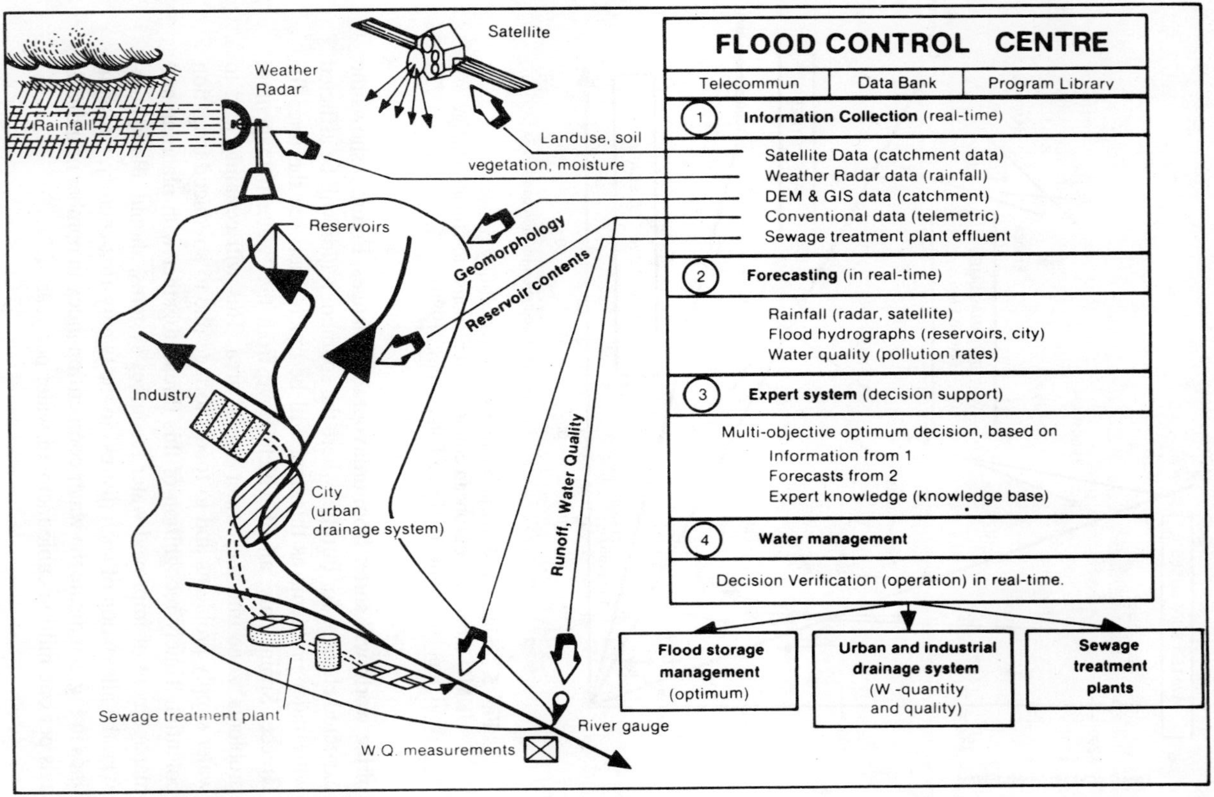

Fig. 6. Water resources system management during floods: scenario for twenty first century

FLOOD CONTROL CENTRE

Telecommun	Data Bank	Program Library

1 — Information Collection (real-time)

Satellite Data (catchment data)
Weather Radar data (rainfall)
DEM & GIS data (catchment)
Conventional data (telemetric)
Sewage treatment plant effluent

2 — Forecasting (in real-time)

Rainfall (radar, satellite)
Flood hydrographs (reservoirs, city)
Water quality (pollution rates)

3 — Expert system (decision support)

Multi-objective optimum decision, based on
Information from 1
Forecasts from 2
Expert knowledge (knowledge base)

4 — Water management

Decision Verification (operation) in real-time.

Flood storage management (optimum)

Urban and industrial drainage system (W-quantity and quality)

Sewage treatment plants

Satellite
Landuse, soil vegetation, moisture

Weather Radar

Rainfall

Geomorphology

Reservoir contents

Reservoirs

Industry

City (urban drainage system)

Runoff, Water Quality

Sewage treatment plant

W.Q measurements

River gauge

Adaption of Water Resources Management to Future Conditions

If all components relevant to future WR management are combined, an integrated systems operation would be an opinion approach incorporating:

— Data from maps, GIS, satellites, and DEM for catchment state description to be updated permanently;
— Data from weather radar, satellite, and conventional sources for event-dependent information (rain, snow, soil moisture, water quality, etc.)
— Expert system developed for a multipurpose multi-unit WR system, allowing the operator to find compromise optimum decisions in a computer dialogue. Here, conjunctive use of groundwater and surface water, as well as the combined water quantity and water quality management, will be considered. Assessment of the knowledge base of the expert system allows also consideration of forecast extreme conditions (low flows, floods).
— Real-time systems operation in a most efficient way without time delay since data arrive in real-time, and computing time for decision support will be close to zero with the new computer generations.

As an example for such future WR management, a vision scenario for the twenty-first century is given in Fig. 6 for the operation of a WR system during flood conditions. The figure, which is self-explanatory, integrates all the elements discussed in this chapter.

CONCLUSION

The main features of surface water management in the twenty-first century will most probably comprise:

— data acquisition from satellites, weather radar, GIS, and conventional telemetric systems;
— management of the entire WR system organized in a control centre containing computers, remote data transmission systems, data banks, image processing, GIS, and computer program libraries;
— DSS providing the decision-maker with management suggestions based on multi-objective compromise optima considering all relevant water quantity and water quality conditions (this decision support is

based on all available information and forecasts computed with the aid of an expert system);
— long-term effects such as climate and land-use changes computed and considered in long-term decisions of WR system management.

REFERENCES

Falkenmark, M. 1989. 'Climate-Induced Hydrological Shifts in Europe and their Implication Spectrums', Proceedings *Conference on Climate and Water*. The Academy of Finland, 9/89, Helsinki: Government Printing Center.

Feigenbaum, E. G. and McCordruck, P. 1983. *The Fifth Generation: Artificial Intelligence and Japan's Computer Challenge to the World.* Addison-Wesley Publishing Company, Wokingham, England.

Fischer, H. and Schultz, G. A. 1991. 'An Expert System for Real-Time Operation of a Multipurpose Multi-Unit Reservoir System', Proceedings IAHS Symposium *Hydrology of Natural and Man-made Lakes*. Vienna, IAHS publication no. 206.

Laabs, H. and Schultz, G. A. 1992. 'Reservoir Management Rules Derived with the Aid of Multiple Objective Decision-making Techniques'. Special issue: Multiple Objective Decision-making in Water Resources, *AWRA Water Resources Bulletin*, USA.

Richter, K. G. and Schultz, G. A. 1988. 'Aggravation of Flood Conditions due to Increased Industrialization and Urbanization', Proceedings International Symposium: *Hydrological Processes and Water Management in Urban Areas*, Unesco, Duisburg, April, pp. 495–503.

Schultz, G. A. and Barrett, E. C. 1989. 'Advances in Remote Sensing for Hydrology and Water Resources Management', Technical Documents in Hydrology, Unesco, Paris.

8 / Biomass Strategy for Watershed Development

J. LUNDQVIST, K. R. DATYE, AND M. FALKENMARK

TWO PARADIGMS BASED ON SIMPLIFIED WATER PERCEPTIONS

Free Water and Missing Water

For people in the arid and semi-arid parts of the world, the prospects of sustained and high production of water supply are invariably described as gloomy. Conventional thinking about options for people in such areas rests on two alternative paradigms, one optimistic and the other primarily negative.

The optimistic paradigm assumes high external inputs in terms of water, fertilizers, pesticides, and high-yielding varieties. The type of resource use emanating from this paradigm has created two interlinked types of challenges. The economic viability of the high input agriculture is in question and it can be sustained only through heavy subsidies. The resource management associated with the 'optimistic paradigm' has a limited applicability, mainly to plains with comparatively easy access to exogenous water and other inputs.

The paradigm with a negative outlook concentrates on what is lacking in dryland farming. As opposed to the optimistic paradigm—where water is perceived as a free resource—,water is typically missing according to this line of thought. For the hundreds of millions of people who depend on dryland farming, the future is supposed to be sought in terms of outmigration or alternative employment rather than in improving the livelihood situation *in situ* (see, for instance, FAO, 1989).

A New Focus of Attention

Both paradigms are based on a simplified understanding of water in local production systems. Attention is usually focused on the total quantum of rainfall and the high potential evapotranspiration, thereby ignoring the pattern of rainfall and also the dynamics of various fractions of water in connection with partitioning, that is, evaporation, transpiration, infiltration, etc. By emphasizing the imperfect rainfall pattern, the perception illustrates the stance that 'Everybody complains about the weather, but nobody does anything to correct it.'

Local water resources management should be considered from the point of view of food security and income stability. Local water needs could then be divided into an assured and a variable component. The assured component would have to be estimated from a baseline rainfall that is available with a high degree of dependability, say, 80 per cent. Part of this water could be provided by water harvesting of rainwater over nearby non-cropped areas, storing it and making it accessible for protective irrigation of the land earmarked for food security. Over and above the assured supply, a variable component would be accessible in those years with better-than-average rainfall. This water could be used for tree crops and yield augmentation in the tree plot or the food plots, as also for commercial crops. Evidently, the assessment of assured water and requirements for basic needs has to be site-specific. The assured water should be treated as a scarce resource and be distributed equally to attain sustainable livelihood and food security for local farming communities in vulnerable areas. The surplus water could be distributed as a free market good and be used for commercial cropping or desired alternatives.

It therefore makes sense to focus more on those aspects that can be manipulated and relate them to resource management options. The possibilities for adjusting land-use to water-scarcity situations through variation in cropping pattern and geographical extent are, surprisingly, overlooked. For people in large parts of dry climate tropics and subtropics, it is necessary to carefully design land-use, so as to make optimum use of available water from local rains.

Productive Conservation

Experience from different parts of the world suggests that production can be substantially enhanced in semi-arid regions without high external inputs (IUCN, 1988; Young, 1988). The strategic role of limited but well-timed water applications has, however, not been systematically considered in development strategies for semi-arid areas. The main element of the strategy is optimal use of scarce water resources by an integration of various categories of land-use within the watershed for multiple purposes: tree crops for fuelwood and construction material; timber and organic material for soil amelioration; and seasonal crops and horticulture for food security and cash. With such integrated resource use, human needs can be met concurrently with a concern for the environment. It is also logical to review petrified concepts which convey a sense of uselessness of certain parts of the resources base. 'Wastelands', for instance, play a role within a watershed as supplier of organic inputs to cropped areas and as a recharge area of water. This view adds a new dimension to the concept of integrated rural development.

PRODUCTION THROUGH LOSSES

Manipulation of Water Partitioning

In the tropics and subtropics, the water available through precipitation is subject to a rapid return flow to the atmosphere due to high potential evapotranspiration (Fig. 1). This 'loss' of water is as natural as it is necessary for the maintenance of life-support systems. The hydrological cycle cannot be stopped, and the important issue is not the fact that water returns to the atmosphere, but rather how it returns. Basically, we may distinguish between two principal return flows: one that is necessary for life-support systems to grow and be maintained, and the other that is of

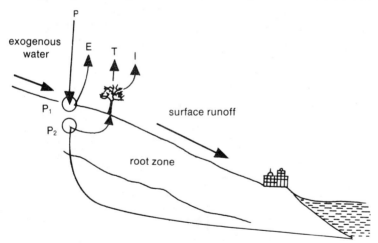

Fig. 1. Simplified model of fractions of rainwater after partitioning in P_1 and P_2

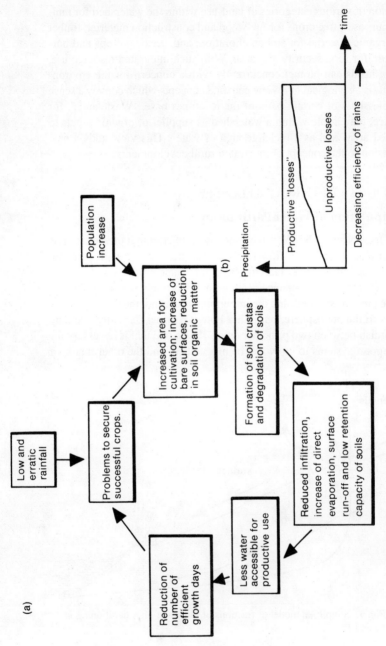

Fig. 2. (a) Dynamics and main components of a 'vicious circle' and (b) consequences for relative share of productive and unproductive losses of rainwater

no direct significance in this regard (Fig. 1). Transpiration through plants or other biological material is an example of the first type, and direct evaporation from wet surfaces an example of the latter.

The fraction of rainwater that infiltrates the ground and the amount left on the surface for direct evaporation and runoff are very much dependent upon land-use. In addition, soil structure and constituents or organic matter are important for water-holding capacity and retention time of water in the root zone (Jackson, 1988). Water balance for the Sahelian rangelands (with 100–600 mm annual rainfall) leaves only about 15 per cent of the rainwater for productive use, whereas about 60 per cent returns to the atmosphere as unproductive evaporation from the soil surface. Regrettably, the crucial distinction between unproductive evaporation and productive transpiration is seldom made explicitly.

To break the vicious circle for people in large parts of the semi-arid regions of the world today (Fig. 2), a strategy is urgently needed that ensures that the locally-accessible water is allocated such that it satisfies various needs of the communities without endangering the environment.

'Carryover Benefits' through Strategic Land-use

Tree crops have a distinct advantage over seasonal crops in areas where moisture-deficit conditions are rampant. Through their perennial life-cycles, trees have the ability to tide over periods of water stress. Apart from the initial period after planting, the yield from trees is not exclusively dependent upon single seasons of good or bad weather conditions but is rather the accumulative and average result over a number of yields. Apart from this type of 'carryover benefit', residue from trees and bushes may be collected and used in other parts of the watershed for soil amelioration and water conservation purposes. Benefits from the complementarity of trees and seasonal crops relate both to the environmental and socio-economic aspects (Ostberg, 1988; Chambers and Leach, 1989). Seasonal crops are typically much harder hit by water shortage and stress, leading to severe socio-economic and environmental consequences. The task is to develop a land-use strategy where perennial tree crops are combined with seasonal crops.

Potential Biomass Production per Water Unit

The knowledge on water productivity in terms of potential biomass production per unit of accessible water does, unfortunately, seem to be rudimentary. Information from studies based on small plots with an experimental design is of limited significance. Hydrological studies, on the other hand, focus on the return flow to the atmosphere and its two main components: evaporation losses from moist surfaces as opposed to productive losses. Based on zonal data from Lvoich (1979), the amount of biomass production in natural ecosystems per unit of water returned to the atmosphere tends, in dry and hot climatic conditions, to be in the order of 1 tonne/1000 m^3 of water (Falkenmark, 1986).

In an area of 500 mm precipitation, the total amount of rainfall water is 5000 m^3/ha, which corresponds to a theoretical biomass potential of 5 tonnes/ha or 10 kg/mm/ha. The calculation refers to natural vegetation, which generally implies an optimal use of accessible water, as seen on a year-round basis. For humid climate, the productivity per unit of water may be much higher and may amount to the order of 1 tonne/200 m^3 of water, in other words, 25 tonnes/ha, or 50 kg/mm/ha, that is, five times higher water productivity than under dry conditions.

The figures from Lvovich refer to an average productivity without human interventions in terms of land and water management. He also presents a comparison between managed (a barley field) and non-managed (virgin) conditions on the USSR steppe. The results indicate a productivity increase of the order of around 40 per cent. The question that arises is, therefore, what may be achieved if, for instance, land and water use is committed to certain segments in the landscape and to certain crops carefully scheduled for specific periods of the year?

WATER REQUIREMENTS FOR SAFE YIELDS

Model for Judicious Use of Water

A basic requirement for the model outlined below is estimation of the critical amounts of applied water that are necessary for food security, that is, the amount of water that has to be provided in excess of precipitation water.

The water requirements of a rural family may be divided into three main components: (a) domestic needs, including cattle, (b) agricultural lands, and (c) nurseries and recently-planted seedlings, that is, tree crops.

Domestic Needs

Based upon an assumption of a daily per capita requirement of 100 litres, the needs of a family of five would be about 200 m³/year. This level would allow for certain losses and use-at-source. The cattle would need an equivalent amount, placing the total domestic need at around 400 m³/year per family.

Agricultural Lands

It is estimated that a grain requirement of 1.2 tonnes per year for a family of five is sufficient for food security. On-farm experiments carried out in the semi-arid parts of Maharashtra show that grain yields in the order of 3 tonnes/ha are realistic, provided that small amounts of fertilizers, compost, and applied water are available. Biomass inputs would raise land quality, and possibly increase the potential yield. A holding of about 0.4 ha would thus be a reasonable requirement for attaining food security. To safeguard the required yield, it is assumed that an applied amount of 150 mm, or about 750 m³ per year, would be needed for agricultural land. In water-short years, a minimum of 600 m³ should be just sufficient for the cultivation of 0.4 ha (0.4 × 3 tonnes/ha = 1.2 tonnes).

Nurseries and Recently-planted Seedlings

Tree crops are needed for various purposes. Surveys on actual consumption patterns of firewood and fodder per family show that 2 tonnes/year and 5 tonnes/year, respectively, are required. Another crucial component is the biomass needed for compost to improve soil in the agricultural portion. Recommendations on the amount needed vary considerably from or between 5 tonnes/ha to 10 tonnes/ha and above. Biomass inputs of 5 tonnes dry matter per hectare are found to be adequate in the field trial of farmer systems in Maharashtra. The recorded annual biomass increment has been in the order of 11–16 tonnes/ha three years after initiation of the trials. A level of 15 tonnes/ha per year would therefore seem realistic with proper species selection and management with three initial waterings.

A water balance is presented in Table 1 for a fairly typical holding of 1.2 ha of which 0.4 ha is grain area. Assured water availability of 1400 m³/family is assumed for a good year, and 800 m³/family for a bad year, to cater for food security and domestic needs. During years with low rainfall, domestic water use must be curtailed to a minimum, and nursery and planting activities must be stalled.

A calculation was carried out on water availability on these assump-

Table 1. Water requirements in addition to rainwater*

Requirement of Assured Water (m³)	Good Year	Bad Year
Food security	750	600
Domestic water	400	200
Establishment of plantations	250	
Total amount required	1400	800

*Harvest rainwater productively utilized: 300 mm × 1.2 ha = 360 ha m = 3600 m³

tions for one severely and one mildly drought-prone area of Maharashtra for their respective rainfall series for all available years from 1901. It showed that exogenous water was required for the mildly drought-prone area in only three out of 76 years (for which data were available) and for nine out of 86 years in the severely drought-prone area. It also showed an average availability of 880 m³ variable extra water per family per year over and above the provision of assured water for a severely drought-prone area of 500 mm average rainfall.

The on-farm experiments, described in more detail in Datye and Paranjape (1990), suggest that the biomass production per unit of water may be increased to 35–40 kg/mm under semi-arid conditions. This corresponds to a productivity increase by about four times the natural water productivity in the semi-arid region as opposed to two times in the humid tropics. The figures indicate that the potential for increased production in semi-arid areas is quite significant. The implication is therefore that not only can direct evaporation losses be reduced but also that the crucial management component is crop selection and concentration of land-use in segments of the landscape.

Water requirements, yields, and food security are based on experience gained through on-farm experiments in a number of villages in Maharashtra. Provided that the extra water estimated above can be made available, the model indicates that food security and sufficient supplies of fuelwood and fodder for a family of five can be achieved within 1.2 ha. In drought-prone areas of Maharashtra, the per capita family watershed areas (PFWA) is, on average, about 2 ha (allowing 3 ha for wastage), as calculated in the Subramaniam Committee Report 1988 (Datye and Paranjape, 1990). The percentage of agricultural land would thus be about 20–25 per cent of the total land area within the watershed, thus leaving 75–80 per cent of the area for perennial tree crops, commercial cropping, and other land-use requirements (compounds, roads, etc.)

Water harvesting is of crucial importance. The techniques and storage methods in the area vary from locality to locality, the main ones being check dams, earth bunds, and shallow wells.

SCALING UP INDIVIDUAL SUCCESS

Community Dynamics

The on-going efforts in Maharashtra's villages show results that, though not conclusive in terms of the general viability of the 'biomass strategy', indicate the ecological soundness of the strategy and its potential for enhancing production in drought-prone regions. The challenge of implementing the strategy is therefore not limited to the technological aspect but has scope for scaling it up to groups and communities. Unless the communities are involved and the process is replicated on a larger scale, the success of the strategy is of limited significance. Some principles can be presented in this regard.

Human resources and institutions of impoverished village communities, at the brink of environmental disruption, are not adequate for the creation of a new order within a reasonable period of time. External support is vital for the chances to turn the tide, but it can never substitute for the commitment and energies of the local communities.

The negotiations for usufruct rights and realization of yields from plantations often take ten years or longer. By matching the external support with internal preferences, this period can be substantially curtailed. Water rights for the landless, along with availability of bulk biomass for value added through usufruct rights on common land and land tenurial arrangement on private land or produce-sharing price agreements, are therefore crucial for the success of the strategy. Development of process technologies for bulk biomass (wood, bamboo, fibre) and creating market linkages thus become other important prongs of the strategy.

Livelihood Needs and Profitable Crop Production

One of the dilemmas of community-based development is the conflict of interests within the community. The poor and disadvantaged would need access to resources while the enterprising and resourceful farmers would demand and benefit if avenues are kept open for profitable commercial production. With limited amounts of arable land and a scarcity of water and other resources, the conflicts are obvious. But there must be no

choice between the two goals. Both are important for a sound development, but they require persuasive skills of community-based voluntary
organizations and adjustments in tenure and usufruct rights on common
properties.

An important experience from the efforts to stimulate a biomass
strategy in Maharashtra is that there seems to be no other way of realizing the creation of assets for the resource poor than the separation of
water rights from land rights. Given the fluctuation in water supply from
year to year, the strategy is to distinguish between an assured and a
variable component of water as described above.

Having access to water without access to land is, of course, of limited
interest. Various measures have been attempted to overcome this dilemma. Two options are of interest. One is to persuade landowners to allocate land to the landless and disadvantaged sections for part of the year.
Through water harvesting and post-monsoon cropping with supplementary irrigation, this would be possible. The other alternative is to utilize
the common land, that is, government land. The challenge is then to
reverse the negative effects of encroachment and to negotiate with the
officials for usufruct rights.

The separation between property and water rights and allocation of
basic minimum quantum of water to each family has proved to be an
effective means of gaining the confidence of the resource poor and socially disadvantaged. The allocation must be determined through a par-
ticipatory process and the community must be enlightened about
resource constraints and the possibilities of sustainable livelihood.

REFERENCES

Chambers, R. and Leach, M. 1989. 'Trees as savings and security for the rural poor'
    World Development, vol. 17, no. 3, pp. 329–42.
Datye, K. R. and Paranjape, S. 1990. 'Sustainable Agriculture in Semi-arid Regions:
    Opportunities for Small and Marginal Farmers'. *Wasteland News*,
    August–October 1990, New Delhi.
Falkenmark, M. 1986. 'Freshwater-time for a modified approach', *Ambio*, vol. 15, no.
    4, pp. 192–200.
FAO. 1989. *Sustainable Development and Natural Resources Management*,
    Twenty-fifth Session, 11–30 November, Rome.
Jackson, I. 1988. *Climate, Soils and Agricultural Development in the Tropics*,
    Longman, Harlow, UK.
IUCN. 1989. *The IUCN Sahel Studies*, IUCN Office of Eastern Africa, Nairobi.

Lvovich, M. J. 1979. *World Water Resources and Their Future.* Translation by the American Geophysical Union, Litho Crafters Chelsea, MI.
Young, A. 1989. *Agroforestry for Soil Conservation*, ICRAF, Nairobi.

9 / Macro-Engineering: Super-scale Water Resources Development

HIROSHI HORI

INTRODUCTION

In order to achieve sound global progress, it is believed that we should carefully choose and promote, in various parts of the world, the development of a number of super-scale infrastructure projects which would exert decisive influences over extensive areas, while cautiously making efforts to develop smaller-scale projects in each region to meet its immediate pressing needs. In this context, what has been sought for the future balanced prosperity of mankind is an ideal called the Macro-Engineering concept, i.e. well-coordinated multidisciplinary planning and execution of the project, followed by careful, deliberate management of its maintenance and operation, as proposed by Professor Davidson. However, it is evident that the application of this idealistic concept to the development of a gigantic water resources project is not practicable. For its success, the first requirements are regional socio-economic stability, strengthened by a politically-stable international and domestic climate. In addition, substantial funds should be provided for the implementation of the project. Even more important is that, from the earliest planning stages on, all kinds of key input data have to be made available, including natural, social, economic, and other data. Unfortunately, this necessity has often been neglected, or given short shrift, by decision-makers. It is apparent that a long planning period is a prerequisite to any super-scale infrastructure project.

JAPAN'S ODA

It has been recognized, both in Japan and overseas, that Japan ought to help developing countries by investing her capital funds and also by rendering extensive technical services in appropriate and effective ways.

To respond to the expectation, the Japanese government's fiscal budget for the official development assistance (ODA) has been increased year after year, touching some US $10 billion in 1990. This amount is roughly 20 per cent of the world total, ranking it number one, surpassing even the contribution of the United States. In parallel, Japan's private sector's overseas investment has also been progressively increasing.

The recent Gulf War, which has demonstrated that it is easier to destroy than construct civilization, has highlighted the importance of the spirit of international cooperation. It is now almost unanimously believed among the Japanese who are responsible for the functioning of the ODA that such international collaboration should be extended for constructive rather than destructive purposes.

In order to restore peace in the Middle East, the Japanese government had passed some US $9 billion to the United States during the Gulf War. With the cessation of the War, it is expected that the balance of this fund would be returned for utilization by Japan's ODA for the most befitting purposes.

NEW WAVES IN JAPAN

Global Infrastructure Funds Research Foundation

In 1977, a movement to set up the Global Infrastructure Fund (GIF) was initiated by Japan's private sector with the noteworthy aim of eradicating poverty and hunger worldwide and promoting a peaceful construction of the global community. Many people in Japan and elsewhere supported the movement. As a result, the GIF Research Foundation Japan was established in Autumn 1990, with the support of the Federation of Economic Organizations of Japan.

At the GIF Tokyo Conference held in March 1991, several topics on the GIF concept were addressed, all of which were large-scale development schemes riddled by difficulties in their planning and implementation.

Recent Opinions in Japan's Official Circles

In parallel with the above-mentioned motion, official circles in Japan have initiated several research groups for the development of super-scale infrastructure projects which had been disregarded, even by the people involved, as daydreams and completely impracticable.

While the Ministry of Agriculture, Forestry and Fishery initiated the ambitious greening-of-the desert concept in West Africa, the Ministry of Construction established in 1988 an *ad hoc* committee named the Global Super Infrastructure Project Study Committee. The Committee, composed of officials and scholars related to the ODA, decided to select projects that fulfilled the following criteria:

— the influence of the development should extend to either a number of countries or to a very broad area;
— its realization is considered to be beyond the capacity of the countries concerned due to economic and/or technical handicaps;
— the scale of the project should approximate several billion US dollars;
— the project should not cause any drastically detrimental environmental effects;
— the local government(s) should necessarily be in favour of the Japanese government's cooperation.

In the light of the above criteria, the following projects were selected as the most appropriate examples:

— the Ganges–Brahmaputra water storage, diversion and long transmission project;
— the Kra Isthmus canal project in Thailand;
— the Gibraltar Strait interconnection project between Spain and Morocco;
— the improvement of the environment in desert areas.

Of these four projects, the first and the fourth are related to the large-scale water resources development. A brief explanation of the Japanese development concept on the Ganges-Brahmaputra Super-scale Project follows.

GANGES–BRAHMAPUTRA WATER STORAGE, DIVERSION AND LONG-DISTANCE WATER TRANSMISSION PROJECT

The two gigantic rivers that traverse the Indian peninsula, vertically and horizontally, connect at their downstream and penetrate Bangladesh. The western and the southern parts of India often suffer from a water shortage, while the eastern part is frequently flooded. The Global Super Project Committee has formulated a massive development scheme by which this present maldistribution of water may be overcome and, at the same time, make available a huge hydropower generation. The scheme envisages the erection of two large dams at the Assam gorge on the Brahmaputra River for storage of a substantial volume of flood water and generation of power of some 10 million kW, and the construction of a long canal interconnecting the Brahmaputra at Dhubri city and the Ganges at Patna city; and furthermore, the transfer of the river flow of the Ganges towards rivers in the west and also towards rivers nearby Madras city, in the south of India, through super-scale, long waterways.

The major problem of this ambitious scheme is, of course, that it requires massive investment. In addition, the foundation of the proposed two dams would be vulnerable to frequent earthquakes, and the trapping of sediment by the dams would cause undesirable influences in the river channel. In addition, seawater intrusion at the estuary would be aggravated. Moreover, resettlement may affect some three million people, while those residing in the downstream area of the two rivers may suffer from a water shortage during the dry season after the completion of the long-distance canal.

In 1990, the Japanese Ministry of Construction dispatched to India a civil engineer who had played a responsible role in the programming of the project to ascertain the reaction of the Indian government. The latter elucidated that the preference for building the Dihang Dam, instead of the two proposed dams, just upstream of the Assam Valley was intended to decrease the number of expected resettlers. The Indian government also expressed its need for Japanese assistance in the development of the Koshi High Dam Project on the Koshi River, a tributary of the Ganges, located within the territory of Nepal, rather than for the Assam Dams Project as proposed by the Japanese. With regard to the planned long-distance canal projects, the Indian government conceded that both the interconnection of the two large rivers and the construction of a long canal along the Indian Ocean—which waterway must transit many rivers such as the Mahanadi, the Godavari, the Krishna, the Penner and join the Cauvery at its end—would be possible, but emphasized that the project, which aimed to transfer the flow of the Ganges and the Brahmaputra to the west of India, could not be considered.

Based on this feedback, the Japanese Ministry of Construction has been continuing the study of the requested alternative projects with the GIF Research Foundation group. The Japanese civil engineer's report also revealed that whereas the Indo-Bangladesh Joint River Commission had been established in July 1972 and the Indo-Nepal Joint Commission

Table 1. Merits and demerits of Ganges–Brahmaputra project

Project	Construction of dams on the Brahmaputra
Plan	Construction of two large fill-type dams, each 40 m high, at the Assam Valley (gross storage 250 billion cu m) to store the flood flow of the Brahmaputra
Merits	It will be possible to generate some 90 billion kW/year with the installed capacity of 10 million kW
	The two reservoirs may cut down the peak flood from 100,000 cu m/sec to 60,000 cu m/sec, thus contributing to mitigation of flood disasters in Bangladesh
	Advantages of irrigation could be expected in two countries
Demerits	The proposed dams may suffer from earthquake risks
	Some 3 million people may have to be evacuated. Meanwhile, some 15,000 km^2 of land along the Brahmaputra in Assam will be inundated
	Expected trapping of sedimentation by the dams may cause undesirable influences to the river channel
	Seawater intrusion at the estuary will be aggravated
	Many socio-economic maladies may arise
Project	Construction of diversion channel and long-distance water transmission system in India
Plan	Construction of a long diversion channel between Dhubri (Brahmaputra) and Patna (Ganges)
	Construction of an ultra-long distance canal, 2600 km long, between Patna city and the Cauvery River at the south of Madras
	Construction of a branch water-channel between the above-mentioned Ganges–Cauvery Canal and the Narmada River nearby Ahmedabad
Merits	Discharged flow from the above-mentioned dams would ensure the supply of irrigation water in the deep Indian peninsula; drinking water will also be secured
Demerits	When the Plan is realized, it may become difficult for Bangladesh to ensure living and irrigation water at the downstream of the diversion site, especially during the dry season
	Bangladesh may exert her veto rights against the Plan with various other serious reasons
	Many unforeseeable detrimental socio-economic effects may arise in both Bangladesh and India

in August 1988, the Permanent Indus Commission had been active since 1960, and that it would be imperative for the Japanese government to first contact such well-established commissions for initiating any action

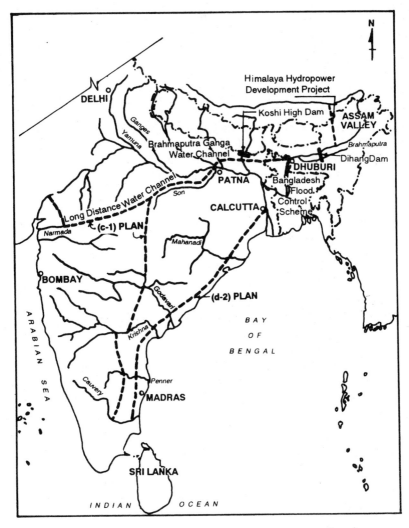

Fig. 1. Location map of Ganges–Brahmaputra water storage, diversion, and long-distance transmission project

with regard to cooperative ventures in the planning and execution of any super-scale development project in the region.

The Super-scale Infrastructure Project Study Committee then concluded that Japan should adopt a positive but prudent stance in future decisions, one that takes into account all the factors relating to any such huge development scheme programmed in the area.

CONCLUSION

Seeking the future balanced prosperity of mankind, worldwide cooperative efforts should be made to promote super-scale infrastructure projects, including water-related projects. In all such ventures, Japan should take a leading role. For unqualified success, the concept of Macro-Engineering which pursues the well-coordinated, multidisciplinary planning, execution, and management of such projects should be adequately applied.

I am convinced that both the large-scale development of water resources as also medium and small-scale projects (which would meet urgent local requirements in the developing countries) should be promoted in parallel for the sustainable well-being of humankind. At the same time, a somewhat different perspective resulted from my brief trips to Fez and Marrakesh, both well-known, ancient Moroccan cities. What deeply impressed me there was the traces of traditional, even medieval, times that may be witnessed in the local people's livelihood. It seemed to me (a complete outsider passing through) that the people in the cities and in farm villages in Morocco continue to revel in quiet, tranquil, even poetic, lives, their traditional culture merging with the trends of western civilization. There, the water and air seemed untainted and the sky was clear.

Reflecting on the busy and clamorous life which I had left behind in Tokyo, I began to question the meaning of 'civilization' which Japan has pursued since the Meiji era some 120 years ago. In pursuit of modern amenities, the Japanese people seem to have almost completely lost the calm of their erstwhile community whereas the people in Morocco continue to enjoy the tranquillity of the homestead. Moreover, the Japanese have been constantly dogged by frustration and irritation!

I had been convinced of the necessity of planning large-scale water resources development among extremely primitive societies, such as in the Lower Mekong River Basin and East Africa. Yet, suddenly, I came to reflect anew on the merits and demerits of our 'civilization', our 'modernization', and our 'value judgement'. How important it is to protect ourselves against the destruction and devastation of the 'good, old spiritual soil' while promoting large-scale development! By arriving at this conclusion, I remembered the advocacy of Professor Davidson on

'Macro-Engineering' and, for the first time, I felt that I had grasped the essence of the spirit of his credo.

Nowadays, there is much talk about 'preservation of the environment'. However, defining ways to 'cautiously protect and uplift the human mind, while trying to sustain the prosperity of our global society as largely and firmly as possible' seems equally important in securing a bright future for mankind. This should be the guiding principle of the twenty-first century.

REFERENCES

Davidson, F. P. 1978. *Macro-Engineering and the Infrastructure of Tomorrow*, Westview Press, Boulder, USA.

Hiroshi, Hori. 1990. 'Macro-Engineering: a view from Japan', *Technology in Society*, vol. 12, Pergamon Press, USA.

Ministry of Water Resources. 1988. *Water Resources of India*, CWC Publication No. 30/88, New Delhi, India.

Ministry of Water Resources. 1988. *Major River Basin of India—An overview*, CWC Publication No. 50/89, New Delhi, India.

Ministry of Water Resources. 1990. *Storages in River Basins of India*, CWC Publication, New Delhi, India.

Manabu, Nakagawa. 1982. *Here Comes Era of Large-scale Engineering in Challenge of Macro-engineering*. PHP Research Institute, Japan.

Verghese, B. G. 1990. *Waters of Hope, Himalaya-Ganga Development and Cooperation for a Billion People*, Oxford & IBH Publishing Co. Pvt. Ltd., New Delhi , India.

10 / Importance of Dams for Water Supply and Hydropower

JAN A. VELTROP

INTRODUCTION

Without water, life is impossible. Yet the record of this life resource is not reassuring. Even though during the past decade safe drinking water was made available to an additional 1.3 billion people, some 1.2 billion of the present world population of 5.2 billion are still without safe water. There is neither a water supply system for 65 per cent of the world's rural population, nor for 35 per cent of the urban population (UNDP, 1990). By the year 2000, 50 per cent of the world's population is expected to live in cities, with ten cities having 10–15 million inhabitants each, and the urban population in Africa is predicted to increase from 20 per cent in 1980 to 42 per cent. Urban water supply in Africa actually dropped from 83 per cent to 74 per cent, despite an increase of more than 50 per cent in absolute numbers served (*World Water*, 1989). Factors contributing to the pressure on water resources are: unprecedented growth in world population, rising expectations for economic development, improvements in standards of living, and vast expansion of irrigated agriculture.

Worldwide, water use and population both doubled between 1940 and 1980. A further doubling of water use is expected between the years 1980 and 2000, with a population increase of 1.83 billion (or 41 per cent). As early as 1975 there were 19 countries without adequate renewable water resources for domestic and irrigation uses (*New York Times*, 1989). Population forecasts for the coming century (shown in Fig. 1; Sadik, 1990) can be expected to worsen the damaging effects on the earth's natural resources, perhaps critically. Clearly, mankind faces the onerous task of increasing water supplies on a sustainable basis. Because water is not evenly distributed, this natural resource must be shared in a realistic way and managed for maximum benefits at the lowest reasonable cost.

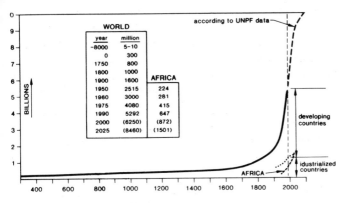

Fig. 1. World population

WATER SUPPLIES

More than 97 per cent of all water on a global scale is sea water, and only 2.665 per cent is fresh water (*Encyclopedia Brittanica*, 1987 and Gerarghty, 1990). Of this fresh water, 76.5 per cent is stored in polar ice and glaciers, and another 22.9 per cent is present as groundwater. Though the remaining quantity is rather small (stored in lakes, soil, atmosphere, and rivers), the amount available for exploitation is much larger as a result of precipitation. The total river runoff amounts to about one-third of 38,820 km^3 precipitation over the continents. Some 24,810 km^3 runs off in floods, leaving 14,010 km^3 for use. Potentially available fresh water resources are shown continent wise in Table 1 (Gerarghty, 1990 and Falkenmark, 1976).

Table 1. Available fresh water by continent

Continent (except polar areas)	Runoff, km^3 per annum total	stable portion	unstable portion	Stable Runoff as % of Total Runoff	Depth of Runoff (mm)
Africa	4225	1905	2320	45	142
Asia, except USSR	9544	2900	6644	30	356
Australia	1965	495	1470	25	249
Europe, except USSR	2362	1020	1342	43	499
North America	5960	2380	3580	40	279
South America	10,380	3900	6480	38	592
USSR	4384	1410	2974	32	197
All continents	38,820	14,010	24,810	36	297

Water withdrawals differ greatly among continents, and there are wide variations within each continent too. It is usually assumed that 10 per cent of the total annual runoff can be withdrawn without difficulty, that thorough planning is necessary to increase withdrawal to 20 per cent, and that larger withdrawals impose limits on social development. Allocation of water for domestic/municipal, industrial, and irrigation uses is influenced most strongly by the importance of irrigated agriculture in a nation's economy.

Though very large quantities of water are available on a global scale, there are distinct variations in its availability in time and location:

— Great imbalances exist between regions: one-sixth of the total river flow of the world is in the Amazon; and annual per capita runoff ranges from over 100,000 m^3 in Canada to less than 1000 m^3 in Egypt.
— Significant variations occur in regional precipitation and stream flow.
— Water is often unavailable at times and places when needed: e.g. the three-month monsoon season in India is followed by nine dry months.
— Flood runoff is frequently not economical to develop, because it occurs as large flash floods in a short period.
— Much of the groundwater is at great depth or occurs in sparsely populated areas.
— Populations have grown, and regions have been developed, where readily usable water supplies were inadequate (Los Angeles). Populations continue to grow fastest in some of the most water-short regions (Postel, 1984).

The depth of total water runoff in Africa is the lowest in the world (see Table 1). Furthermore, this limited amount of water is unevenly distributed across the African continent as well as throughout the year. About 50 per cent of the total runoff occurs in the Congo basin (UN, 1977). In large areas, rivers exist only intermittently, occasionally flushed by powerful and sudden floods of water. Only three areas have a water surplus: the Congo basin with tropical rainforests, the southern coast of Nigeria and the Cameroons, and the expanse between Ghana and Guinea. Fourteen countries in Africa have 85 per cent of their land in zones of sparse rainfall (Falkenmark, 1976), and most of Africa has a water deficit, i.e. vegetation needs more than precipitation supplies. The development of irrigation facilities is progressing very slowly. There is

little flexibility in the use of land, which is mostly cattle farming, resulting in a single ecosystem.

Natural factors influencing these conditions are: droughts (the Sahel
suffered severe droughts between 1907 and 1915, and again from 1968
to 1973), a dry climate (deserts), unfavourable agricultural conditions
(poor soils and soil erosion), temperature extremes and highly capricious
rainfall (often dry rivers). Effects due to human actions are: fast rate of
population growth, relatively dense populations in the dry zones of
North, East, and South Africa, and faulty treatment of the soil which
erodes nature's own recuperative capacity.

WATER WITHDRAWALS

Worldwide, withdrawals for consumptive use have increased from 100
km³ in 1700 to 3528 km³ in 1975 (Fig. 2; White, 1988). Consumptive
withdrawal is expected to increase to 4640 km³ by the year AD 2000.
Table 1 shows this increase of 1112 km³ as being available from stable
runoff, provided water is captured, stored, and distributed when and
where needed. The ratio between the stable and unstable portions of river
runoff is influenced by man's management of land surfaces and changes
in vegetation, or by withdrawals and artificial storage.

By 1986, irrigated areas in the world had increased to 265 million ha
and provided about one-third of the food produced. The Third World is

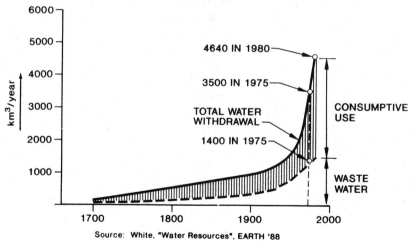

Source: White, "Water Resources", EARTH '88

Fig. 2. Water consumption and waste

Table 2. Water withdrawals by continent (in litres/capita/day)

Continent	Acutals for 1980				Projections for 2000			
	D/M	Indus-try	Irriga-tion	Sub-total	D/M	Indus-try	Irriga-tion	Sub-total
Africa	47	30	558	635	96	106	514	716
Asia	82	110	1215	1407	152	250	1138	1540
Australia/Oc.	432	148	1686	2260	562	274	1826	2602
Europe	265	1066	608	1939	300	1338	669	2307
North America	440	1960	2200	4620	504	2045	2185	4734
South America	236	295	687	1218	299	784	672	1755
USSR	223	1137	2526	3886	309	1281	2651	4241
World	144	415	1205	1764	203	546	1147	1896

largely agrarian, with irrigated agriculture using 80–90 per cent of the developed water resources. In Egypt, agriculture uses 90 per cent of water supplies, employs one-third the population, and contributes 25 per cent to the Gross Domestic Product, yet food imports in 1975 exceeded 65 per cent of total requirements (Falkenmark, 1976). Egypt depends on the Nile for 95 per cent of its water supply (Hamman, 1990). On a global scale, approximately 70 per cent of total water consumption is used for irrigation of crop lands, 23 per cent for industry, and the remaining 7 per cent for domestic and municipal purposes. The uses of water vary greatly among countries, depending on natural climatic conditions, availability, accessibility and quality of water resources, and their economic and social development.

The variations in water use among continents are demonstrated in Table 2 for the three major requirements—domestic/municipal, industrial, and irrigation—which make up about 95 per cent of total use. Water uses for domestic/municipal (D/M) purposes range from an average of 47 litres/capita/day for Africa to 440 litres/capita/day for North America. The variations for industrial uses are even greater.

INCREASING WATER SUPPLIES

In the 20th century, large water resource projects have been developed to supply water for agricultural expansion and economic growth. By the 1960s, the accelerating pace of water withdrawal was being affected by the changes in socially-acceptable patterns. These changes placed a heavier emphasis on non-structural measures and on patterns of resource development involving greater harmony of technological and environmental aspects. Alternatives to developing additional sources of water supply are frequently mentioned in the literature and by the media, such as: to use water efficiently, to conserve it, to improve irrigation practices, to enhance the yield of reservoirs (Wurbs, 1990), to recycle wastewater, to desalinate sea water, and to pump groundwater. (Outside the polar regions, 94 per cent of all fresh water is stored as groundwater.) In arid regions (e.g. Riyadh, Saudi Arabia), groundwater is often the only stable indigenous supply (Ambroggi, 1980). There is pressure in large arid and semi-arid areas of Africa to base development on supplies of fossil groundwater. However, permanent communities cannot be established on this basis. Temporary use of fossil groundwater can be envisaged while other permanent sources of water supply are developed (e.g. Phoenix, Arizona). Artificial recharge of suitable aquifers is receiving increased attention in the United States (Bouwer, 1990).

Better management of irrigation practices is needed to prevent the detrimental effects of waterlogging and salination, to reduce seepage losses, to improve water distribution among farmers, and to control the amount and timing of water application to the fields. Between 200,000 and 300,000 ha of irrigated land in the world are lost every year as a result of salination and waterlogging (Falkenmark, 1976). It is estimated that a total of 20–25 million ha have been severely damaged by salination. This is about 7.5–9 per cent of the irrigated area in the world. Upgrading is also needed in about 150 million ha (Postel, 1985). Operational efficiencies can be doubled from the 30–40 per cent range to as much as 75–80 per cent.

The four major sources available for increasing water supplies in the African continent are:

1. capturing the uneven and inadequate precipitation;
2. storing more water from the four large rivers: Congo, Niger, Nile, and Zambezi;
3. tapping groundwater resources, especially from rainfall in the mountains; and
4. desalinating seawater.

IMPORTANCE OF DAMS

Existing water shortages and increasing demands for water cannot be met by the above-mentioned measures, even when they are conjunctively applied. More surface reservoirs are needed to modify the uneven distribution of precipitation in time, and together with aqueducts to remedy the uneven distribution in space (Los Angeles water supply). Dams have a multi-purpose role. When storing water for human consumption and agriculture, dams create head for hydroelectric power generation, provide space for storing floods, deepen channels for water-based transportation, and support lakes for recreation and fishing.

River runoff needs to be regulated and river waters will need to be diverted into arid areas on an unprecedented scale in the immediate future. This necessitates human intervention in the water cycle, which causes changes in the quality of surface water and groundwater. Management of water should include countering adverse effects when water is used as a recipient of sewage and other effluent which could act as a medium for infection. Naturally, water management must also ensure reduction in the destruction of life and property due to flooding and the damage upon the habitat of wildlife as a result of drainage or reclamation of wetlands.

For at least 5000 years dams have enabled civilizations to flourish by assuring a dependable supply of water for domestic purposes and for irrigation. Many civilizations have disappeared with the loss of the ability to construct, maintain, and repair dams. Over the past century, engineers have introduced major new technologies to increase the ability to withdraw, transport, and purify water and to supply and transmit electrical energy. Significant advances in the design and construction of dams have also been achieved, partly as a result of evaluating dam failures and near-failures, but mostly due to broadening the scientific base of geology, hydrology, and the properties of natural and man-made materials, as well as a better understanding of the loadings to which a dam is subjected, new analytical methods, powerful computers, quality control during construction, and instrument observations of the structural behaviour of dams. Factors of safety have been refined, human errors reduced, and design criteria have found international consensus. Steps are being taken to strengthen older dams against possible failure due to earthquakes or floods. Independent reviews of designs are carried out routinely, and monitoring of dam behaviour has become standard practice. The modern well-designed and constructed dam presents a negligible risk to the public.

Dams have both detrimental and beneficial effects. Voluminous literature deals with numerous examples of adverse environmental, cultural, social, and economic impacts created by dams. The three most important, and often most difficult, issues to resolve are: (a) resettlement of indigenous, politically inexperienced populations, (b) salination and waterlogging of irrigated fields, and (c) health issues resulting from water-related diseases. The noteworthy positive environmental effects of dams are: they regulate and augment low flows of rivers, decrease erosion, control floods, minimize water waste, and cultivate deserts. An effort must be made to quantify adverse and beneficial environmental and social impacts, so that these costs can be incorporated as part of the economic evaluation of a project. At the same time, it is necessary that all those directly affected participate in the conceptual development of dams and hydroelectric schemes.

Prior to 1890 there were about 427 dams, as reported in the World Register of Dams-1988 Updating (ICOLD, 1989). A phenomenal increase in the number of dams took place after the middle of the twentieth century, as shown in Fig. 3. Over 85 per cent of 36,000 existing dams over 15 m high were built in the last 35 years (ICOLD, 1989). The number of dams, continent-wise, is shown in Table 3.

More than 78 per cent of these 36,237 dams are between 15 m and 30 m high, with fewer than 26 dams exceeding a height of 200 m (Fig. 4). At present, reservoirs behind dams store some 6000 km^3 of water, of which about two-thirds is available for use, the rest being dead storage.

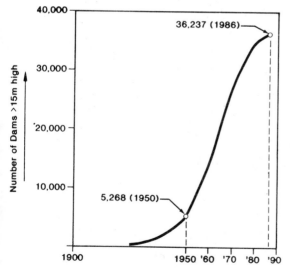

Fig. 3. Number of dams

Table 3. Number of dams over 15 metres high (1986)

Continent	1950	1982	31 Dec 1986	Under Construction
Africa	133	665	763	58
Asia	1554	4194	4569	430
Australia/Oc.	151	448	492	25
Europe	1323	3961	3982	204
North & Central America	>2099	>7303	6595	39
South America			884	69
USSR	incl.Europe	incl.Europe	132	18
Sub-total	5260	16571	17417	843
China	8	18,595	18,820	183
World	5268	35,166	362,37	1026

This amount of 4000 km³ adds about 30 per cent to the stable portion (14,010 km³) of annual river runoff in the entire world (Table 1). Over 200 dams were completed in 1989, of which 80 per cent were <30 m and 1 per cent >100 m. Also 12 very large dams were either over 150 m high,

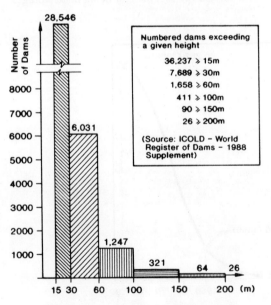

Fig. 4. Number of dams by range in height

or contained a volume of over 15 million cu m, or had a reservoir capacity over 25 km³, or had a power installation of 1000 mW or more. Some 45 more of these very large dams were under construction in 1989, and 48 in 1990 (Mermel, 1991). This number has been nearly constant over the past five years.

A variety of constraints often delay or prevent the construction of new dams and hydroelectric power installations. These include physical impediments (quality of site and inundations); financial, institutional, and market constraints; environmental, social, cultural, and economic impacts; political conflicts where rivers are shared: and adjustments of western-gained experience to conditions in developing countries. These must be understood and overcome.

HYDROELECTRIC POWER

In 1988, the world's hydroelectric plants produced 2,000,000 GWh, i.e. 20 per cent of the world's total electric energy production of 9,965,000 GWh (2,100,000 GWh in 1989). In Africa, hydropower generated about 16.8 per cent of total electric energy. The installed capacity in the world in 1988 was 549 GW (Mermel, 1989), which increased to 567 GW in 1989. An additional capacity of over 100 GW was under construction in 1988 in 71 countries, with significant expansions in China, Asia, South America, and the USSR.

Hydropower, a clean source of energy and a well-established technology, provides large, concentrated quantities of electricity to run factories and to light cities. Small-scale and micro hydroelectric plants provide power to isolated, sparsely populated communities and agricultural processing plants. To reduce energy shortages in today's world, conservation, improved efficiencies, and expanded use of renewable resources are environmentally the most acceptable solutions. Hydropower is renewable because it is powered by the hydrologic cycle. Future opportunities for hydroelectric power development are indeed bright: it is a vast potential resource in the developing countries where less than 10 per cent of the technically usable potential has been developed to date—in Africa, only 3.1 per cent. On a worldwide basis in 1988, only 13.5 per cent (14.5 per cent in 1989) of potential hydroelectric generation was developed, as shown in Table 4 (Mermel, 1989).

Data for dams, stable runoff, hydroelectric generation and potential are combined in Table 5 and shown on a per capita basis, using 1990 population data.

Table 4. Potentials for hydroelectric generation in 1988 (in GWh/yr)

Region	Potential (1)	Generated in 1988 (2)	(2) as % of (1)
USSR	3,831,000	219,800	5.74
South America	3,189,300	330,558	10.36
S. Asia/M.E.	2,280,700	170,937	7.49
China	1,923,304	109,177	5.68
Africa	1,153,600	35,775	3.10
Canada and USA	968,982	536,127	55.33
Western Europe	910,000	436,269	47.94
Central America	346,000	32,242	9.32
Australia	202,000	36,945	18.29
Eastern Europe	163,000	49,107	30.13
Japan	130,524	87,384	66.98
World total	15,099.310	2,044,296	13.54

Table 5. Populations, dams, stable runoff, and hydropower

Continent	Population in 1000s per dam	No. of dams per km^3 of stable runoff (1986)	Hydroelectric generation kWh/cap (1988)	potential hydropower kWh/cap	(1) as% of (2)
Africa	849	0.4	55	1782	3.1
Asia	432[1]	1.6	118	1395	8.5
Australia/Oc.	54	1.0	1395	7628	18.3
Europe	75	3.9	975	2156	45.2
North America	65[3]	2.8	1943	3512	55.3
South America[2]	336	0.2	810	7891	10.3
USSR	2182[4]	0.1[4]	763	13,302	5.7
World total	239	1.2	386	2,853	13.5

(1) Excludes China, which has 18,820 dams or 60,000 people per dam.
(2) South America includes Central America and the Caribbean unless otherwise indicated.
(3) Includes Central America and the Caribbean.
(4) The number of dams is grossly understated, because dams for domestic water supply and agricultural purposes are not included.

The number of pumped-storage plants is rapidly increasing because owners of power systems have found these to be the most economical way of storing surplus electricity for use during peak demand hours. In addition, pumped storage brings dynamic benefits to a utility system: capabilities for voltage, frequency, and power factors correction, and the

Table 6. Number of pumped-storage projects

Africa	3
Asia	49
Australia/Oc	6
Europe	217
North America	38
South America	11
USSR	2
Total	326

opportunity to minimize cycling of thermal plants. The number of these plants in the world is shown in Table 6 (Mermel, 1991).

Many countries, particularly in the Third World, are installing small plants (<15 MW) at the village level to provide decentralized power on a sustainable basis. Aside from economic benefits, these installations have also improved the quality of rural life. Small-scale hydropower generation totalled nearly 10,000 MW worldwide in 1983, and is estimated to reach 29,000 MW by 1991. Small-scale hydro has the benefit of using indigenous labour and materials, thereby helping developing countries to break the cycle of impoverishment and dependence. During 1989, some 170 small hydro contracts were awarded in 30 countries (Mermel, 1991).

Broad application of small hydro has not occurred because of lack of inventory of suitable sites, lack of standardized off-the-shelf units, lack of technical expertise, tendency for western-trained engineers to overdesign and, lastly, the continuing bias of many Third World utilities and governments towards large projects (Flavin, 1986). Progress however has been made since 1980 in developing appropriate indigenous approaches. In this regard, China's experience is unique in that it has used these benefits, together with its own capital and technology, to build tens of thousands of small hydro facilities. Because of its usefulness, small hydro is destined to receive wider attention and more funding.

CONCLUSION

By comparing the estimated population increase (Fig. 1) with water consumption (Fig. 2) and the number of dams (Fig. 3), it is evident that there has been a common trend of rapid increase since the beginning of the 20th century. The exponential growth is true also for the total area of irrigated cropland and the generation of hydroelectric power. Available natural water resources can, and must, be developed to meet the needs of exploding populations. As a consequence of the population growth now current in Africa (647.5 million in 1990 to an estimated 1581 million in 2025), food demand, especially in the rapidly growing urban areas, is fast intensifying. Reliable water supplies are needed to improve the state of health and to increase productivity, especially of food. The development of water resources is basic to the survival of human and animal life, and is a prerequisite for the growth of Africa's agricultural and industrial potential. The development of hydroelectric power is important for industrial and mineral development. These developments and their management require close interregional cooperation. In the case of water supply and hydroelectric power generation, this means capturing, storing, and releasing more water from the stable portion of the runoff through the construction of more dams and reservoirs. Such developments must be environmentally acceptable, and conducted on a sustainable basis and with respect for people and their culture. The ultimate purpose of dam-building and of water resource planning and management is to serve and enhance the well-being of people. The acute need for increasing water supplies on a sustainable basis is not only a challenge for engineers, but also for the world's statesmen.

REFERENCES

Ambroggi, R. P. 1980. 'Water', *Scientific American*, September.

Bouwer, Pine, and Goodrich. 1990. 'Recharging Ground Water', Civil Engineering-*ASCE*, June.

Encyclopedia Britannica, 15th edition, vol. 20, 1987. 'The Hydrosphere'.

Falkenmark, M. and Lindh, G. 1976. *Water for a Starving World*, Westview Press, Boulder, Colorado.

Flavin, C. 1986. 'Electricity for a Developing World: New Directions', *Worldwatch*, Paper 70, June.

Gerarghty and Miller. 1990. *The Water Encyclopedia*, 2nd edition.

Hamman, S. 1990. 'A Report from Egypt', *Journal of the Institution of Water and Environmental Management*, vol. 4, October, pp. 494–96.

ICOLD. 1989. 'World Register of Dams—1988 Updating', *International Commission on Large Dams*, Paris, June.

New York Times. 1990. '115 Nations Consider a Water Supply Crisis', September 11.

Postel, S. 1984. 'Water, Rethinking Management in an Age of Scarcity'. *Worldwatch*, Paper 62, December.

Postel, S. 1985. 'Conserving Water—The Untapped Alternative', *Worldwatch*, Paper 67, September.

Sadik, N. 1990. 'The State of World Population 1990', United Nations Population Fund, New York.

United Nations. 1977. 'Water Development and Management', Proceedings of the Conference, Part 2.

UNDP. 1990. 'Global Consultation of Safe Water and Sanitation for the 1990s', UN Conference, New Delhi, India, 10–14 September.

Mermel, T. W. 1989. 'The World's Hydro Resources', *International Water Power and Dam Construction*, September.

Mermel, T. W. 1991. 'The World's Major Dams and Hydro Plants', *International Water Power and Dam Construction*, Handbook 1991, pp. 52–62, UK.

White, G. F. 1988. 'A Century of Change in World Water Management', *EARTH '88—Changing Geographic Perspectives*, Proceedings of Centennial Symposium, National Geographic Society.

World Water, 1989, 'The Decade under Analysis', December.

Wurbs, R. A., Carriere, P. E., and Johnson, W. K. 1990. 'Management Strategies for Increasing Reservoir Yield', *Water International*, vol 15, no. 3, September.

11 / Integrated Water Management in the Netherlands: Myth or Practice?

C. B. F. KUIJPERS

INTRODUCTION

The location of the Netherlands has made water management a priority activity since the Middle Ages. For instance, without the dunes and dikes, 65 per cent of the Netherlands would be flooded at high sea and river levels. Initially, water management was directed primarily towards flood control. Although this task is still crucial, the pollution of surface water and groundwater, as well as the protection of the ecological function of water, calls for more attention.

This is, of course, not only so in the case of the Netherlands. Environmental problems in respect of water resources are of grave consequence all over the world (WCED, 1987; McDonald and Kay, 1988). Yet, many industrialized and most developing countries carry huge economic burdens from inherited problems such as severe water pollution, depletion of groundwater, and heavily polluted sediments. These problems do not cease at local, regional, and national borders, nor can they be solved by any one organizaion or within the responsibilities of any one policy area. Problem-solving needs an almost overwhelming interagency coordination at all stages of the policy-making process.

Integrated water management is worldwide seen as a sound policy strategy in coping with this need for coordination (OECD, 1989; Mitchell, 1990). However, the question that arises is whether there is enough provision for the achievement of a more integrated approach towards water resources problems. By which arrangements is this goal hindered or stimulated? The relevance of this question is shown from the experiences with the implementation of integrated water management in many countries. The third National Policy Document on Water Management of the Netherlands (Ministry of Transport and Public Works, 1989) states, for instance, that administrative and legal conditions are not yet satisfied. Mitchell (1990) makes clear that, despite the general acceptance of the strategy of integrated water management, progress in actual implementation has been limited.

In this chapter, a representative example of water resources problems in one Dutch water system, called the *Naardermeer*, is used to clarify the need for an integrated approach to water management in the Netherlands. This is followed by some brief comments on the focus of integrated water management in the Netherlands and the institutional problems confronting the authorities concerned. Finally, the conclusion is confined to speculatory remarks on the future of integrated water management.

THE WATER SYSTEM OF NAARDERMEER

The Naardermeer, a natural lake located in the central Netherlands, about 20 miles east of Amsterdam, is a famous bird sanctuary and of highly botanical value (Wassen, Barendregt, Bootsma, and Schot, 1989). One of the oldest protected nature reserves in the Netherlands, this 700 ha area of lakes and marshes and some pasture land has been put on the list of internationally important wetlands.

Nature conservation and management in the Naardermeer is related mainly to hydrological factors (see Fig. 1). Groundwater flow is directed to lake Naardermeer from the higher grounds in the eastern part of this lake, while in the western part infiltration occurs as a result of low water levels in the adjacent polders. This infiltration, as also a diminished supply of groundwater caused by withdrawals in the recharge area for drinking water, steadily reduced the water levels in lake Naardermeer. Initially, surface water from outside the Naardermeer (lake IJ) is supplied during summer to prevent parching and mineralization. Although a better quantitative situation was reached, the phosphorous-rich suppletion water causes many qualitative water resources problems, such as eutrophication, which threaten the ecological function of the lake.

In the past, attempts to solve the problems of dehydration and eutrophication temporarily arrested the suppletion. Nowadays, the suppletion water is subjected to dephosphorization, and many other measures which have the common drawbacks of being mainly sector-orientated and unsuccessful in altering the hydrological situation—the primary cause of the water resources problems for the lake.

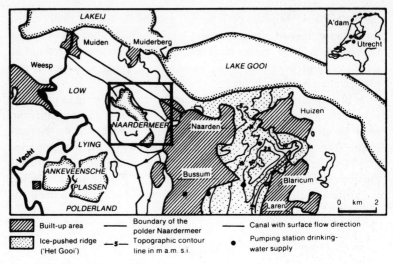

Fig. 1. Location of the water system Naardermeer (Schot, 1991)

Recently, a more integrated approach has been developed. The main characteristic of this approach is that more attention is given to the surroundings of lake Naardermeer and the typical hydrological situation. For example, it is suggested that discontinuing groundwater extraction in the adjacent Gooi area will strengthen the groundwater flow. Another proposal is to raise the groundwater levels in the low-lying polderlands in the west part of lake Naardermeer in order to minimize the infiltration. If these measures are accepted, the water companies would have to seek new sources of water supply, and the spatial use of the polders would have to be changed from intensive agriculture use towards extensive use or nature conservation.

The integrated approach for lake Naardermeer has to be achieved and implemented in a fragmented policy network which includes more than five largely autonomous administrative bodies. Each of these bodies represents different interests and is responsible for only one function or aspect of the water resources problems in this region. For instance, the responsibilities for quantitative and qualitative surface water management and groundwater management are divided among three public agencies. Furthermore, the requisite measures have, for one part, a hydrological character, but involve also activities in respect of physical and environmental planning and nature conservation. The integrated approach can therefore be achieved only by coordinating the policy-making of the different actors and policy areas involved.

TOWARDS INTEGRATED WATER MANAGEMENT

The Naardermeer is only one example of many more water systems, all of which reflect, more or less, the need for a more integrated approach in Dutch water management—not as an end in itself, but as a means to improvement of the effectiveness of water resources management strategies. This has only recently been recognized in the Dutch policy-making process related to water resources problems.

Over the years, water management in the Netherlands has passed through different stages (Ministry of Transport and Public Works, 1989). The first period, commencing early in the Middle Ages, was distinguished by protection against flooding. Drainage and water supply, central issues during the second period of water management (beginning at the end of the nineteenth century) are vital elements of Dutch water management even today. In this period, a series of canals was dug, drainage was improved, and with the help of a hydraulic infrastructure water levels were regulated to some extent. Since the seventies, the pollution of surface water and groundwater became a major task for the water authorities. In the third period of Dutch water management, many sewage treatment plants were planned. Due to these efforts, the pollution of surface water, mainly for oxygen-consuming substances, was curtailed. Nevertheless, the reduction of nitrogen and phosphate was still too limited; and the reduction of heavy metals and organic micro-pollutants was not yet achieved.

Kuijpers and Glasbergen (1990) typify Dutch water management as an on-going process of rationalization. Though the Dutch dependence on the vagaries of water, which was characteristic of the Midddle Ages, is strongly reduced, some serious qualitative problems still remain. To resolve these problems more effectively, water management in the Netherlands will have to give more attention to the relations between surface water, groundwater, shorelines, and hydraulic infrastructure, as also to the relations between the management of water resources and the management of land-use. For instance, many of the present water resources problems, such as the dehydration of land and the eutrophication of lakes, can be solved only through changes in the use of land and fertilizers and the methods of production and consumption. This idea determined Dutch water management in the eighties, marking the fourth period of Dutch water management.

IMPLICATIONS OF AN INTEGRATED APPROACH

Since 1985 the main focus of Dutch water management is a more integrated care for the condition and use of water systems—comprising the media water, beds, and banks or shores—with their physical, chemical, and biological components, in relation to their relevant surroundings. The philosophy of integrated water management was presented in the memorandum 'Living with Water' (Ministry of Transport and Public Works, 1985). This document formed the background to the steps taken in the years that followed. It presents a scenario of the main lines along which policy with regard to the water regime could develop in the long term. Essential in this policy is the water system approach, which combines the different elements in integrated water management (Glasbergen, 1990):

— the hydrological system, with its morphological and ecological characteristics, its inherent value, and autonomous development, all of which contribute to setting preconditions for reacting to intervention;
— the societal functions and vested interests, which exert demands and influence upon hydrological systems;
— the administrative policies and management which, directly or indirectly, influence both the hydrological systems and their functions.

The system approach to water management views water more in the context of its environment. This may be the direct surroundings such as shores and beddings, but it could cover also relations over a much larger area. The example of the Naardermeer showed that to resolve the problems of this water system it is also necessary to take into account the groundwater extractions in the adjacent Gooi area and the spatial use of the polders.

The integrated approach has far-reaching implications (Mitchell, 1990). Questions arise with regard to the information needed to assist in planning and management decisions: how to involve the general public in the process; identifying financial sources for support of the integrated initiatives; the consequences for the administrative activities of the various governmental agencies and public organizations that impinge upon a water resource system. In this respect, it is relevant to realize that the integrated approach in the Netherlands must be implemented not only within the reality of a complex hydrological and societal situation but also within a diverse institutional context (Koudstaal, Pennekamp, and Wesseling, eds, 1988). The example of the Naardermeer illustrated that the Netherlands has a fragmented administrative structure in respect of water management.

In general, at least five ministries are involved at the national level. Where water is not under state control, the 12 provincial governments and about 150 water boards are responsible for water resources management. The provinces determine their own policies for regional waters within their territory and exercise control over the water boards. These boards concentrate on matters concerning either qualitative or quantitative aspects of surface water management whereas the provinces cover the management of groundwater. Such responsibilities involve not only many organizations, but all the legal and financial powers of these organizations are also embodied in more than 20 different statutory regulations.

The interdependence between all these parties, which is highlighted by the water systems approach, requires innovative organizational measures to integrate policy and management (Glasbergen, 1990). An interdependent water system demands an integrated administrative system where activities are coordinated by the participants who are involved in mutually influential tasks. In order to stimulate such integration, the Department of Public Works (of the Ministry of Transport and Public Works) instructed the Department of Environmental Sciences to investigate the institutional conditions determining an integrated approach to water management. The term *institutional* is meant to include those legal, political, financial, and administrative structures and processes influencing decisions in respect of water resources management (Ingram, Mann, Weatherford, and Cortner, 1984). The results of this research were recently published (Kuijpers and Glasbergen, 1990; Glasbergen, 1990).

Institutional Barriers for Implementation of Integrated Water Management

The research showed that though the authorities in the Netherlands realize that an integrated approach to water and land will resolve the complexity of water resources problems, the strategy of integrated water management is still, as in many other countries, mainly a policy at the strategic level. Experiences with an integrated approach at the operational level are limited.

The research showed also that the Dutch institutional framework is not yet adapted for implementation of an integrated approach in a short term. The gap between integration at a strategic level and at the operational level is still insurmountable. Not any one aspect of the institutional context can be attributed the entire blame. A combination of a complex administrative structure, the many statutory regulations, as well as the funding system of water management hinder integrated problem-solving and nurture a process of decision-making on separate aspects, forms, or functions of water systems. For instance, the firm division of labour, regulations, and financing between surface water management and groundwater management or between issues relating to quantitative and qualitative water resources favour a more sector-orientated approach. However, not only the different elements of water management but also the policy areas of water management, environmental preservation, and physical planning often operate too independently. This is a consequence of an encapsulated administrative system and the absence of an integrated system of funding and regulations.

Some recommendations, which aim to improve the conditions for integrated policy-making, have been broadly adopted by policy-makers. The recently published third National Policy Document on Water Management states, for instance, that the extremely limited task interpretation by some water authorities hinders the implementation of an integrated approach. There is also agreement on the fact that the legislation on water management is still insufficiently harmonized and integrated; and although many funding problems arise out of boundary problems between levels of government, among agencies, or among divisions of departments, they are also caused by too strict regulations in respect of levies, subsidies, and other funding sources.

A Multi-track Approach as Answer

Partly due to research and policy recommendations, the implementation of integrated water management in respect of the institutional aspects is nowadays stimulated along three tracks.

The first track is to simplify the administrative structure of water resources management in the Netherlands. The state, which has a preference for setting up district water boards per catchment area or parts of catchment areas, would exert, as far as possible, to bring quantity and quality management of surface water under the singular control of the water boards. The provinces are responsible for the implementation of these plans. At least five provinces intend to decrease the number of water authorities. However, the stout opposition to these plans places their effectiveness in jeopardy.

A second track is related to the legal conditions of integrated water management. Statutory regulations have been partly implemented, and other changes are still to be studied. A recent achievement is the introduction of the Water Management Act, 1989 which provides a legal basis for a more integrated planning structure—one that incorporates the previously separate planning obligations concerning aspects of surface water and groundwater into a single plan. The significance of the planning regulations encompassed by this Act is that the whole field of water management is covered: management of quantity and quality of both surface and groundwater. At the same time, the coordination with the policy areas of environmental management and physical planning on the regional level is explicitly arranged, with the aim of integrating water legislation compactly.

Finally, the implementation of an integrated approach is improved by project-based and the more-or-less spontaneous and non-legal activities of the water authorities. These integrated activities, often sponsored by the state, can be subsidized—as is that of the Naardermeer—up to 50 per cent of the total investment costs. The aim of such subsidy is to stimulate the development of integrated projects and to develop skills for the agencies engaged in coordination work. Such projects can also have an important catalytic function for other initiatives in the region. A more fundamental change in the financial structure remains to be studied.

CONCLUSION

The institutional analysis is often neglected or is nothing more than an annotated listing of public agencies, statutes, regulations, and decisions. The Netherlands experience has revealed that more attention to the institutional aspects of integrated water management is essential. The development of an integrated approach to water resources problems on the strategic and operational level requires a revaluation of the institutional analysis as an adult part of the research.

Our research has also highlighted that the success of the integration process depends to a significant extent upon the cooperation of the actors. People who are enthusiastic supporters can often make a poor system work well. Conversely, a well-designed system may falter if the actors are determined not to pool their efforts. Therefore, it becomes necessary to change an institutional culture that encourages public agencies to serve their own interest before societal welfare. Unfortunately, there are usually few explicit incentives for cultural integration. Educational programmes, specific instructional programmes for administrators, and the establishment of a reward system for integral behaviour are a few of the potential incentives which are applied in the Netherlands.

Equally important as the organizational matters, regulations, and ways of financing is the 'human dimension' of an integrated approach. The uncertainty about the future of integrated water management clearly reflects the status of integrated water management in the Netherlands and many other countries: we are still learning as we proceed. Hence, it is very useful for nations to exchange data on experiences of how an integrated approach to water resources problems is facilitated, the hindrances encountered and how these can be tackled.

REFERENCES

Glasbergen, P. 1980. 'Towards a policy network approach to integrated water management. Experiences in the Netherlands', *Water Resources Development*, vol. 6 no. 3, September, pp. 155–62.

Ingram, H. M., Mann, D. E., Westherford, G. D., and Cortner, H. J. 1984. 'Guidelines for improved institutional analysis in water resources planning', *Water Resources Research*, no. 20, pp. 323–34.

Koudstaal, R., Pennekamp, H. A., and Wesseling, J. (eds). 1988. 'Planning for water resources management in the Netherlands', Delft Hydraulics/Institute for Land and Water Management Research, Wageningen.

Kuijpers, C. B. F. and Glasbergen, P. 1990. 'Perspectieven voor integraal waterbeheer', *SDU Uitgeverij, 'S-Gravenhage.*

McDonald, A. T. and Kay, D. 1988. *Water Resources Issues and Strategies*, Longman Scientific and Technical, New York.

Ministry of Transport and Public Works. 1985. 'Living with Water: Towards an Integral Water Policy', Public Works Survey Department, The Hague.

Ministry of Transport and Public Works. 1989. 'The Third National Policy Document on Water Management: Water in the Netherlands: a Time for Action', Ministry of Transport and Public Works, The Hauge.

Mitchell, B. (ed). 1990. *Integrated Water Management: International Experiences and Perspectives*, Belhaven Press, London and New York.

Organization for Economic Cooperation and Development. 1989. *Water Resource Management, Integrated Policies*, OECD, Paris.

Schot, P. P. 1991. *Solute Transport by Groundwater Flow to Wetland Ecosystems*, Geografisch Instituut Rijksuniversiteit Utrecht, Utrecht.

Wassen, M. J., Barendregt, A., Bootsma, M. C., and Schot, P. P. 1989. 'Groundwater

chemistry and vegetation of gradients from rich fen to poor fen in the Naardermeer', *Vegetatio*, no. 79, pp. 117–32.
World Commission on Environment and Development. 1987. *Our Common Future*, Oxford University Press, Oxford and New York.

12 / Economics of Irrigation Water Allocation under Uncertain Conditions

NORMAN J. DUDLEY AND
WARREN F. MUSGRAVE

INTRODUCTION

Irrigation development in the uniform and summer precipitation areas of the lower latitudes in Australia has focused attention on the uncertainty environment in respect of water management. This is because of the very stochastic nature of both the supply and the demand for irrigation water in those zones. The probability of storages being full at the beginning of the irrigation season is considerably less in those latitudes than in the higher latitudes, while the more significant, but typically highly variable, summer rainfall, underpins the stochasticity of both water supply and demand. Uncertainty of the outcomes of water resources decision-making is much greater for water systems in those latitudes than in the winter precipitation areas of higher latitudes (Dudley, 1990a). These contrasting experiences have led to a better understanding of the problems of irrigation water management in uncertain environments, of modelling them, and of policy options for coping with them. The question of reliability or robustness of supply is brought sharply into focus, as too is the concern of irrigators that policies with respect to those attributes of supply should be as explicit and stable as possible.

Because so much of the literature dealing with water allocation is based on experience in higher latitude, less uncertain environments, some sharing of this Australian experience should be of interest to those concerned with the management of irrigation water in more uncertain environments. Apart from serving to discuss the Australian experience, the purpose here is to review policy options in the context of uncertain environments leading to a discussion of the concept of capacity sharing (CS)—an institutional arrangement which has a number of appealing features in most water environments but particularly in those that are of immediate concern in this analysis.

AUSTRALIAN WATER DOCTRINE AND ATTENUATION OF RIGHTS

In contrast to, say, the western part of the United States where irrigation, involving property rights to unregulated stream flows, was well established before the construction of major storages, the arid and unstable Australian environment meant that major headwork dams had to precede significant irrigation development. What is more, the size of storage necessary to ensure (politically) acceptable security of supply was so great that funding was beyond the capacity of the private sector. The result was the establishment of an irrigation industry with storage, reticulation, and drainage largely funded by the public sector, and with control of the storage (water supply) in the hands of public agencies separate from the individuals who used water released from the storage for irrigation (water demand). This history led to a doctrine of water use property rights growing up around regulated water supplies and being defined in terms of stored water in Australia, whereas in western USA such rights are defined mainly in terms of stream flows before these are regulated (Dudley, 1991).

This doctrine was dubbed 'a temporal non-priority permit system' by Davis (1968), in a comparison of water law in Australia with that in the United States, to distinguish it from the prior appropriation system of western USA. The doctrine is based on the premise that each user is entitled to a certain volume of water per season, which is specified at the start of the season, and usually expressed as a share of a target water allocation, or entitlement, which is constant across the years. The probability of the seasonal volume meeting the target allocation depends on the reliability of the total irrigation system. This, in turn, depends on the size of the storage, the extent of irrigation development, and the stochasticity of stream flow and irrigation demand. The volume to be released to each irrigator is determined by a central administering authority (Musgrave *et al.*,1989). That is, the initial allocation or entitlement, and the annual volume to be released, is determined by this authority. Though these decisions are not necessarily carried out in a vacuum, and there is typically some interaction between users and the authority, 'it is not too gross a simplification of reality to say that reliability is determined independently of the preferences of users . . . (and) in this sense the reliability decision is exogenous to the use decision'. (Musgrave *et al.*, 1989, p. 176).

Clearly, the state water agencies have considerable powers in determining the timing as well as the quantity of irrigation water use. What is more, users' property rights in water are highly attenuated,* in the sense that the agencies typically do not contract to deliver water according to some pre-specified reliability. Attenuation is exacerbated by the fact that title to entitlements is relatively short while, until recently, their attachment to specific parcels of land meant they were not transferable. Such attenuation of rights is not conducive to the most efficient use of water, and the creation of water markets is seriously impaired. In particular, if markets are to exist at all, transferability of entitlements must be permitted—in which cases, the persistence of other forms of attenuation could seriously impair the efficiency and effectiveness of the resulting market.

Emergence of the circumstances, now widely described as characterizing a mature water economy, has led to a search by Australian water managers for ways to improve the efficiency of water use. This has resulted, at least to some limit, in attempts to reduce the degree of discretion left to central administering authorities and the extent of the attenuation of user rights. The most distinctive of the initiatives has been the introduction of transferability of entitlements. This move, which permits exchanges of entitlement through a water market separate from the land market, has been undertaken somewhat tentatively (Pigram and Hooper, 1990). While implementing this radical development, most Australian states have adopted a cautious, staged approach. Though initial apprehensions over the consequences of the reform have generally proved to be unfounded, a number of difficulties, typically associated with third-party effects, have given rise to the need to constrain transferability in many circumstances. In particular, transfers between agriculture and other sectors of the economy are ruled out, and the spatial scope of transfers tends to be limited. These limitations have restricted the impact of the reform and, while significant undesirable third-party effects may have been avoided as a result, certain desirable efficiency and environmental benefits may not have been attained. Overall, the devel-

---

*Property rights are said to be attenuated if they are incompletely specified, they are not exclusive (that is, costs and benefits are not borne by those who create them), they are not enforceable or enforced, and they are non-transferable (Randall, 1981).

opment has apparently facilitated efficient water use and enthusiasm, as indicated by its general occurrence in the industry (Delforce *et al.*,1990).

Despite this reform, significant attenuation of water rights remains, particularly with regard to length of title and the probability distribution of water supplies associated with entitlements. While transferability permits trades in water to occur and, therefore, markets to exist, reduction of this remaining attenuation would improve efficiency in the operations of these markets and lead to more efficient water use. Such problems and their resolution are discussed in the context of a number of alternative institutional arrangements (Dudley, 1990a): capacity sharing (CS), and arrangements under which volumes allotted to users and the reservoir carryover are determined by

(a) pre-set system operating rules: or
(b) some mix of: administrative and/or political discretion: and consensus among water users.

Capacity Sharing (CS) is a system whereby users are allocated long-term or perpetual rights to percentage shares of reservoir inflows and percentages of empty reservoir capacity or space for storage of their inflows. It is as if each user owns a small reservoir on his own small stream. Thus, individual reservoir management operations will determine individual supply reliabilities, and a high level of consumer sovereignty is attained (Dudley and Musgrave, 1988).

There are other ways of tackling these problems of attenuation. For example, if users had knowledge of aggregate reservoir inflows and the reservoir was operated by known, pre-set, unalterable release rules, with individual users having fixed shares in those releases, they could again calculate their supply reliabilities (Dudley, 1990a). If shortages were managed by allocating different priorities for delivery in such circumstances, then we may call the system priority sharing (PS). The relative inflexibility of most such systems makes them unattractive when compared with capacity sharing. All are superior to systems such as the present one, however, which confers a high degree of discretion on the supplying agency where there is no clear unequivocal assurance that release rules will not be changed and where consumer sovereignty is seriously eroded.

Given that transferability is now possible, albeit in a limited way, concern in the study of water use in the lower, high risk latitudes in Australia has turned more explicitly to the consideration of the reliability of supply and the attenuation of reliability rights. The fact that water may be uncertain in supply does not mean that such rights need inevitably be attenuated. Both CS and PS are water allocation systems which confer non-attenuated property rights. The prior appropriation system in western USA, for all its faults, has the virtue of conferring on water users a system of non-attenuated reliability rights. Concern now turns to the elucidation of what should be the preferred characteristics of a system of ownership of water which confers on the owner a set of non-attenuated reliability rights. CS is shown to possess these characteristics to a greater extent than any other alternative.

EFFICIENT DECISION-MAKING UNDER UNCERTAINTY

To make efficient decisions about water use, including transfers, users need to be extremely confident in their information on the probabilities of supply. In the high latitude, winter precipitation areas, where beginning-of-season storage levels (and catchment snow-pack) reasonably well set supply for the forthcoming season, such confidence is readily established with probabilities being implicit only. In the low latitudes, however, where the situation is more complex and probabilities are not so readily established, information needs to be explicit if decision-making is to be efficient. Knowledge about the probabilities of supply has to be combined with a corresponding grasp of the probability of demand in some type of formal or informal decision model; this enables the selection of plans of action which are consistent with the irrigator's preferences concerning cash flow, the variability of income, the likelihood of going broke, and the like. The greater the uncertainty about the various probabilities, the less is the likelihood of efficient decisions. Increasing the uncertainty and complexity of decision problems may lead decision-makers to resort to rules that restrict their behaviour to a 'limited repertoire of actions", instead of optimizing from the total set of options available (Heiner, 1983). Wright (1984) has argued that farmers operating in highly 'turbulent' environments may fare better by using traditional rules of thumb, with all their inflexibility and restrictiveness, than formal analytical decision aids. If institutional arrangements for the allocation and ownership of water improve the ability of irrigators to estimate the probability distributions of random variables associated with their tactical and strategic managerial decisions, then the turbulence of their environment is reduced and the prospects of them being able to make decisions from the full range of options available are increased.

Central to such institutional arrangements is the need for security of tenure in rights determining or associated with such probability distributions. In particular, users need to know that the probabilities of supply, over their planning horizons, will not be changed by legislative or administrative fiat, or by private action (such as the acquisition of rights), without what they judge to be sufficient compensation. This point is analogous to that made by others with regard to the efficiency and environmental benefits flowing from long-term security of landholder property rights (Roth *et al.*, 1989; Feder and Onchan, 1987). Other writers have pointed to the need for security of tenure in water rights in general as characteristics of desirable resource allocation mechanisms (Howe *et al.*, 1986; Chechio and Colby, 1988). Following Roth *et al.* (1989), security of tenure is defined as the owner's perception of a zero likelihood of losing a specific right in property without acceptable compensation. In the case of land, such rights could include the right to cultivate, graze, fallow, transfer, or mortgage. In the current context, concern is with a perceived zero likelihood of reduction in the reliability with which sufficient quantities of water will be supplied at specific times without adequate compensation.

While arguing that security of probabilities of supply is necessary for efficient water utilization, the possibility of divergence between the optimum for the individual irrigator, the region, or for society as a whole must be acknowledged. Efficiency in an uncertain environment is determined by decision-maker attitudes to risk as well as by such considerations as technology and prices. Divergences between the optima for the various levels of society having a 'stake' in irrigation will therefore arise if attitudes toward risk vary in any significant way between those levels. There are suggestions that such differences in attitude may exist, with Arrow and Lind (1970) arguing that the nation as a whole may be *risk neutral* even while individuals in the society may be *risk averse*. Regardless of the possible existence of such conflicts and their implications for resource management, the argument is that security of probability of supply to users would improve the overall efficiency of resource use. A corollary of this argument is that moves to adjust institutional arrangements so as to lower the confidence in water supply will impose costs through reductions in the efficiency with which users allocate their water. Consequently, such adjustments should create benefits that compensate for these costs.

With this discussion as background, attention is now turned to the assessment of possible types of institutional arrangement. Guiding the assessment is the capacity of arrangements to provide the security of probabilities of supply which is a relevant determinant of efficient water use, particularly in irrigation environments such as are found in the lower latitudes in Australia.

COMPARISON OF SOME INSTITUTIONAL ARRANGEMENTS

The institutional arrangements considered are viewed as being arrayed in three dimensions: one, the range from a completely centralized administrative system to a completely decentralized market system; another, a range of centralized types from one using invariant, pre-determined rules to one where decisions are made through time without such pre-determined rules: and the third, an array ranging from systems wherein decisions are made by an administrative or political process to ones where they are made by representatives of the users. As illustrated below, there is some intersection of these dimensions.

In Fig. 1, the first dimension is represented by the line YZ, where Y denotes a completely centralized system and Z a completely decen-

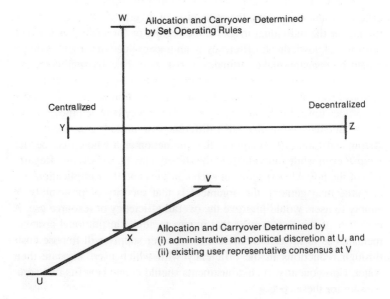

Fig. 1. Spectra of water resource decision-making

tralized system. The second dimension is represented by the line WX which, of course, must intersect YZ at a point close to its centralized end. At W, set operating rules prevail while at X, decisions are made through time without any pre-set rules. This last type of arrangement is called *discretionary and consensus allocation* (DCA). The third dimension is represented by the line UV encompassing the range from administrative or political decision-making at U to user consensus at V. CS is located at Z because, following the initial distribution of rights, water allocation is by market process only. Abstracting from the difficult ethical and political questions associated with the question of the initial allocation of rights, even that could be done through an auction or tendering process. Under CS, because of the sovereignty the water user is able to exercise over release and allocation decisions, the probabilities of (non-transfer) water supplies can be calculated directly from historical or synthesized stream flow data alone.

Arrangements such as PS would be located towards W on the WX spectrum. As with CS, supply probabilities can also be calculated, given knowledge of the operating rules and of stream flow data. The calculation is more complex, however, because it involves both stream flow data and the operating rules.

Efficient demand-side decision-making is also possible at V if the users, whose representatives are making the decisons, are reasonably homogeneous in terms of their uses of water, their technological and climatic environment, and their attitudes towards risk, and so have had similar water supply reliability preferences. This is because the users, due to their homogeneity, should be able to make quite accurate forecasts of the decisions made by their representatives. These forecasts, when coupled with stream flow data, should enable reasonably accurate forecasts of water supply probabilities. This is less likely to be the case the less homogeneous the users are.

In contrast, movement away from V towards U, giving a remote administration or political entity increasing voice in allocation and carryover decisions, would impart an unpredictability to decision-making which would reduce the confidence of users in any estimated supply probabilities. This would probably impact on user decision-making in such a way as to reduce efficiency.

The implication of this discussion is that CS is the perferred institutional arrangement for water resource decision-making of those considered above. This discussion has, however, been conducted in the context of rights to the use of water that determine the confidence with which probability distributions of water supply can be held. However, as suggested in what follows, there is reason to believe that CS has wider application and relevance.

WIDER RELEVANCE OF CAPACITY SHARING

Capacity Sharing (CS) was first developed as an arrangement for the management of water storages in order '... to enable irrigators to allocate their own water through time so as to satisfy their individual supply sufficiency requirements in a highly uncertain environment with essentially no interference from other water users of reservoir managers' (Dudley, 1991, p13). Dudley and Musgrave introduced the concept of CS and demonstrated its feasibility in the context of a surface storage supplying a population of farms of different sizes engaged in a monoculture (cotton) and whose operators displayed a range of attitudes susceptible to risk. While their concern was with the integration of the supply and the demand of irrigation water in highly uncertain environments, they noted the relevance of the concept to uses such as in-stream recreation, environmental uses, flood control, and the urban sector. Each of these uses would be represented by a user group(s) controlling a share(s) of reservoir capacity and inflows. Since then, Dudley has given more detailed consideration to the use of CS in urban supply and in common property situations such as in-stream uses for environmental or recreational purposes and the supply of irrigation communities, particularly the more traditional ones which manage water along communal lines (Dudley, 1990b, 1991). Perhaps even more significantly, an Australian state has incorporated, in new water legislation, provision for the use of CS as a water allocation mechanism.

In his discussion of the urban context, Dudley (1990b) made the point that CS could be operated in a multi-level way. The total urban sector in a valley could own a share of capacity of the total valley multiple-purpose storage system, and individual urban distributing authorities could hold individual shares in that overall sector share, and so on. In the case of common property uses of water, that is, uses that, due to some characteristics of the market such as non-rivalry or non-exclusiveness, are best managed in some collective or communal way, Dudley (1991) suggests that ownership of shares by individual common property managements could be advantageous. Thus, for any multiple-use storage, the managers of such common property phenomena as flood control, in-stream needs, and community water uses, as in many traditional societies, could each control a share of capacity. Each management could then evolve a system of management of its share which suits its objectives independent from the management goals pursued by others. The resulting individual systems could be expected to differ significantly one from the other, but the advantage of such a devolved approach to the supply of water to such a diversity of purposes over the more traditional centralized approach suggests itself, especially in view of a future characterized by increasing water scarcity.

Early in the developmental phase of CS, the Director General of the Department of Water Resources in the Australian State of Victoria, Dr J. Paterson, appreciated the potential of CS in providing a non-attenuated bundle of rights in water. He also perceived the value of the concept in the distribution of water to the generality of uses rather than just to irrigation. As part of a general review of the state's water policy, and associated legislation, the potential role of CS was assessed. One of his staff demonstrated algebraically that CS was at least as good as the traditional method of allocation, release sharing (Alaouze, 1988) in the high latitude, winter rainfall context of Victoria. Paterson reflected the acceptance of the superiority of CS in saying:

Release sharing defines entitlements in terms of *delivered* water with a given volume and reliability. The *owner/operator of the storage* decides what amount is available for release in the light of circumstances, and what 'prudential' carryover is required to meet the obligations of the *operator*. Capacity sharing allocates explicit shares of storage capacity, inflow, losses, and hence of stored water, to end users, each of whom decides, in regard to his own respective shares, what amount is available for release, and what to carry over (Paterson, 1989, p. 51).

However, the Victorian authorities favour CS for allocating bulk or 'wholesale' supplies rather than 'retail' water, apparently because the final users (e.g. irrigators) may find the cost of operating a share greater than the benefits (Department of Water Resources, 1987). This could be true in the case of users of limited amounts of water, as optimal operation within a water management system based on CS would seem to call for a sounder knowledge of and ability to analyze the hydrological characteristics of the system than would be the case with release sharing.

Nevertheless, there would be some threshold size of consuming entity above which the benefits of operation within a CS framework would exceed the cost. Moreover, the potential offered by CS could lead to the establishment of new links in the water marketing chain which could

136 / *Norman J. Dudley and Warren F. Musgrave*

facilitate operation within the system. Consultants with the necessary information and skills could be hired by users and so spread the costs of information and analysis across a number of users. A group of farmers could convert their water entitlements into capacity shares and then hire expertise (which could be the state water agency or the storage manager) to manage their aggregate share on a traditional basis. They could, however, reserve for themselves the right to direct the manager in ways that may not be possible, but desirable in terms of consumer sovereignty, under the traditional system.

CS has the capacity to encompass within it several features of traditional systems of water management while permitting scope for the pursuit of flexibility and efficiency which could not otherwise be possible.

CONCLUSION

The concept of CS was developed in response to the water management problems associated with the high uncertainty of demand and supply of irrigation water in the lower latitudes of Australia. There is strong evidence that it provides a superior framework for water allocation to most alternatives in that context. What is more, this superiority appears to extend to the more certain higher latitudes, and its appropriateness to that environment for irrigation, and other purposes, for bulk supply is demonstrated by the incorporation of provision for its use in recent legislation passed by the Victorian government. Suggestions have been made of the even broader relevance, and perhaps superiority, of CS, and a *prima facie* case could be said to have been made that CS is a simple, revolutionary, and desirable alternative to other water allocation systems.

REFERENCES

Alaouze, C. 1988. 'A Dynamic Programming Demonstration of the Optimality of Capacity Sharing over Release Sharing as Method of Allocating Entitlements to Bulk Water in Shared Reservoir Systems', Staff Paper No. 8, Victoria, Australia: Department of Water Resources.

Arrow, K. and Lind, R. 1970. 'Uncertainty and the Evaluation of Public Sector Investment Decisions', *Amerrican Economic Review*. 60(2) pp. 364–78.

Checchio, E. and Colby, B. 1988. 'Refining the Water Transfer Process: Innovations for the Western States', in *Water Marketing, 1988: the Move to Innovation*, Denver University College of Law.

Davis, P. N. 1968. 'Australian and American Water Allocation Systems Compared', *Boston College Industrial, Commercial Law Review*, 9(3) Spring, pp. 647–710.

Delforce, R. J., Pigram, J. J., and Musgrave, W.F. 1990. 'Impediments to Free Market Water Transfers in Australia' in Pigram, J. J. and Hooper, B. P. (eds), *Transferability of Water Entitlements*, University of New England, Centre for Water Policy Research. Armidale, pp. 51–64.

Department of Water Resources. 1987. 'Security for Major Water Allocations: Background Report', *Water Resource Management Series*, Report no. 8. Victorian Govt. Printing Office, Melbourne, Victoria.

Dudley, N. J. 1990a. 'Alternative Institutional Arrangements for Water Supply Probabilities and Transfers' in Pigram, J. J. and Hooper, B. P. (eds), *Transferability of Water Entitlements*, University of New England, Centre for Water Policy Research, Armidale, pp. 79–90.

Dudley, N. J. 1990b. 'Urban Capacity Sharing—An Innovative Property Right for Maturing Water Economies', *Natural Resources Journal*, 30, pp. 381–402.

Dudley, N. J. 1991. 'Water Allocation by Markets, Common Property and Capacity Sharing: Compartitons or Competitors?' University of New England, Centre for Water Policy Research, Armidale, Discussion Paper No. 2.

Dudley, N.J. and Musgrave, W.F. 1988. 'Capacity Sharing of Surface Water Reservoirs', *Water Resources Research*, 24(5). pp. 649–58.

Feder, G. and Onchan, T. 1987. 'Land Ownership Security and Farm Investment in Thailand', *American Journal of Agricultural Economics*, 69(2), pp. 311–20.

Heiner, R. 1983. 'The Origin of Predictable Behaviour', *American Economic Review*, 73(4), pp. 560–95.

Howe, C., Schurmeier, D., and Shaw, W. 1986. 'Innovative Approaches to Allocattion: The Potential for Markets', *Water Resources Research*, 22(4), pp. 439–46.

Musgrave, W. F., Alaouze, C. M., and Dudley, N. J. 1989. 'Capacity Sharing and its Implications for System Reliability' in Dandy, G. C. and Simpson, A. R. (eds) Proceedings of the National Workshop on Planning and Management of Water Resource Systems: Risk and Reliability, Australian Water Resources Council, Conference Series no. 17, Aust. Govt. Publishing Service, Canberra, pp. 176–85.

Paterson, J. 1989. 'Rationalized Law and Well-Defined Property Rights for Improved Water Resource Management', *Renewable Natural Resources: Economic Incentives for Improved Management*, OECD, Paris, France.

Pigram, J. J. and Hooper, B. P. (eds.). 1990. *Tranferability of Water Entitlements*. University of New England, Armidale.

Randall, A. 1981. *Resource Economics: an Economic Approach to Natural Resources and Environmental Policy*, Columbus, Grid Press.

Roth, M., Barrows, R., Carver, M., and Kanel, D. 1989. 'Land Ownership Security and Farm Investment', *American Journal of Agricultural Economics*, 71(1), pp. 211–14.

Wright, V. 1984. 'Farm Planning: a Business Management Perspective', unpublished Ph.D. thesis, University of New England, Armidale.

13 / Prospects for Development of sub-Saharan Rivers

RANDOLPH A. ANDERSEN AND W. ROBERT RANGELEY

INTRODUCTION

Of the many major international rivers of the world with catchment areas exceeding 100,000 sq km, 17 out of a total of 52 lie in sub-Saharan Africa. Three of these, namely, the Nile, Niger, and Zaire, are each shared by no less than nine countries—which is more than that in any other part of the world, except for the Danube in Europe. It is therefore a natural corollary that sub-Saharan Africa is largely dependent upon international collaboration for the effective development of its surface water resources.

Important features of sub-Saharan rivers are their widely-spaced geographic distribution and large seasonal variations in flow. Outside the humid zone, in and around the Zaire basin, the major rivers derive most of their runoff from highland areas. Thereafter, once they debouch onto the plains and plateaux, they pass through relatively arid zones where there is little perennial contribution of flow from tributaries. Furthermore, the nature of the climate, dominated as it is by the intertropical convergence zone, gives rise to a situation whereby, for about half the year, flows are generally inadequate for economic exploitation without provision of capital-intensive storage dams. This combination of physiographic and hydrological conditions favours large high-cost 'poles' of development for hydroelectric power and also for irrigation. The magnitude of such storages may need to be justified by optimizing benefits through integrated river basin development and by a wide distribution of outputs; otherwise they remain beyond the capacity of a single riparian country.

Groundwater has a crucial position in any balanced programme for water resource development. It is the source that largely sustains the rural communities of Africa. However, our focus is on surface waters because groundwater is less important within the context of existing international collaboration and river basin organizations (RBO). Several attempts—some successful, some less successful—have been made to adopt international programmes for the development of water resources in Africa. RBOs (seen here as any joint organization of two or more riparian states) offer the opportunity and mechanism for international collaboration in river basin development in Africa.

MAIN INTERNATIONAL RIVERS AND LAKE BASINS OF SUB-SAHARAN AFRICA

Table 1 gives the numbers of international rivers and lake basins of the world with catchments exceeding 100,000 sq km. One-third of the total, or 17, are found in sub-Saharan Africa (United Nations, 1976). Map 1 shows the 17 major international rivers (the term 'rivers' being used to include lake basins) of sub-Saharan Africa, and Table 2 lists their catchment areas, mean annual discharge, and names of countries sharing catchments.

These brief statistics demonstrate the importance that must be attached to the sharing of surface waters in Africa and to the complicated institutional and political measures that such a dispersed distribution of resources entails.

WATER RESOURCES OF SUB-SAHARAN AFRICA

Surface Waters

The major rivers of sub-Saharan Africa derive their runoff mainly from

Table 1. Major international river and lake basins (catchment in excess of 100,000 km^2)

Region	Number of countries sharing basin									
	2	3	4	5	6	7	8	9	10	Total
Africa	3	2	6		2	1		3		17
Americas		2		1		1				14
		10								
Asia	7	5	2		2					16
Europe		2		1		1			1	5
Total		11	8	2	4	3		3	1	52
	20									

Source: *Resources Naturelles*/Serie Eau No. 1, Pub. UN. New York, 1976

Table 2. International drainage basins of sub-Saharan Africa (catchment in excess of 100,000 km^2)

Name of Basin	Catchment Area (000 km^2)	Average Annual Discharge (billion m^3)	Countries Sharing Catchment Area
Zaire (Congo)	3690	1250	9–Zaire, CAR, Congo, Angola Cameroon, Burundi, Rwanda Tanzania, Zambia
Nile	2850	84	9–Egypt, Sudan, Ethiopia, Uganda, Kenya, Tanzania, Rwanda, Burundi, Zaire*
Niger-Benue	1900	180	9–Niger, Nigeria, Mali, Guinea, Burkina Faso, Cote d'Ivoire, Benin, Cameroon, Chad
Zambezi	1290	230	6–Zimbabwe, Zambia, Mozambique, Angola, Malawi, Tanzania*
Volta	390	37	6–Ghana, Burkina Faso, Cote d'Ivoire, Togo, Benin, Mali
Lake Chad	2370	IDB	6–Chad, Cameroon, Niger, CAR, Nigeria, Sudan*
Lake Rudolph	500	IDB	4–Ethiopia, Kenya, Sudan, Uganda*
Senegal	490	25	4–Senegal, Mauritiania, Mali, Guinea
Limpopo	400	NA	4–Botswana, Zimbabwe, RSA, Mozambique
Ogooue	220	NA	4–Gabon, Congo, Equatorial Guinea, Cameroon
Okavango	320	8	4–Botswana, Angola, Zimbabwe, Namibia
Orange	800	9	3–Somalia, Ethiopia, Kenya
Juba-Shebelli	827	9	2–Namibia, Angola
Ruvuma	140	NA	3–Tanzania, Mozambique, Malawi
Cunene	100	NA	2–Namibia, Angola
Awash	120	3	2–Ethiopia, Djibouti
Sabie	103	NA	2–Mozambique, Zimbabwe

*Very minor share; IDB-Inland Drainage; NA-Not available

highland areas that form the upper catchments; once they leave the hills, little inflow is contributed from tributaries other than those that emanate from the same highland areas. An exception to this generalization is the region in and around the Zaire basin where the heavier and less seasonal rainfall creates a denser pattern of perennial water courses.

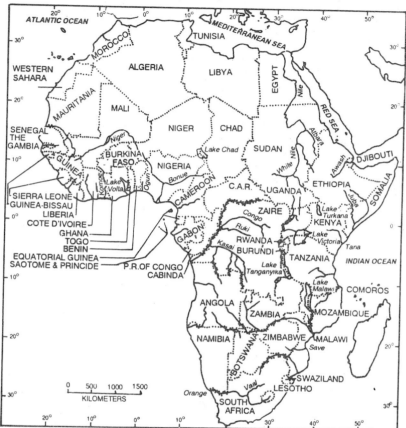

Fig. 1. Africa's main river basins

Another characteristic of sub-Saharan rivers is the highly seasonal nature of their flow and the interannual variations. To regulate the flows, large storage reservoirs are required. The geographic arrangement of perennial rivers is one with often widely-spaced 'line sources' and large river channels. This results in there being few points of abstraction for irrigation and a limited number of sites for the production of hydroelectric power. However, the sites that exist have great potential, often far beyond local needs, leading to the construction of very large dams, as illustrated by projects such as Kariba, Aswan, Akosombo, and Manantali. Each of these projects has international implications either in terms of water use or the distribution of benefits.

Groundwater

Groundwater is generally viewed more from a national than an international perspective. It is rarely seen as a resource to be shared internationally, although it may have important complementariness to surface waters. It is perhaps significant that the Helsinki Rules on the sharing of international waters neglects specific mention of groundwater (International Law Association, 1966). The International Law Commission has also deferred consideration of groundwater to a future date.

Hydroelectric Power

The hydroelectric power potential of sub-Saharan Africa is estimated to be about 300,000 MW (excluding RSA). The distribution is given in Table 3. It will be seen that about 40 per cent lies in West Africa and 80 per cent is in the first eight countries on the list. About 15,000 MW (or 5 per cent) has so far been harnessed.

Hydroelectric power has been the main purpose of most sub-Saharan major dam projects and, with the exception of the Sudan and parts of

Table 3. Hydroelectric power potential

Country	Potential Capacity 1000 MW	Country	Potential Capacity 1000 MW
Zaire	120	Cote d'Ivoire	3
Angola	23	Sudan	3
Cameroon	23	Egypt	3
Gabon	18	Central African	2
Mozambique	15	Republic	
Nigeria	13	Equatorial Guinea	5
Ethiopia	12	Ghana	2
Congo	11	Liberia	2
Tanzania	10	Mali	2
Madagascar	8	Sierra Leone	1
Kenya	6	Uganda	1
Guinea	5	Malawi	1
Zimbabwe	4	Burundi	1
		TOTAL	294

Note : Excluding the Republic of South Africa, other countries have less than 1000 MW potential and generally less than 500 MW southern Africa, this is likely to remain so. It will always be a major factor in international river basin development.

Irrigation

The opportunities to develop extensive irrigation in continental sub-Saharan Africa is very limited outside the Sudan. Vast alluvial plains, such as those of the lower Nile basin, are not found in other regions. Table 4 gives the potential irrigable areas. It will be seen that the total is no more than about 21 million ha in sub-Saharan Africa as a whole (20 million ha when Madagascar is excluded), of which about 25 per cent has been developed in varying degree. Despite its small total poten-

Table 4. Irrigation potential

Country	Irrigation Potential ('000 ha)	Country	Irrigation Potential ('000 ha)
Angola	1000*	Mali	350
Benin	90	Mauritania	150
Botswana	100	Mauritius	100
Burkina Faso	50	Mozambique	100
Burundi	50	Namibia	100
Cameroon	250	Niger	120
Central African Republic	100	Nigeria	2000
Chad	600	Rwanda	50
Congo	350	Senegal	350
Ethiopia	650	Sierra Leone	100
Gabon	100	Somalia	200
Gambia	70	South Africa	2000
Ghana	120	Sudan	3300
Guinea	100	Swaziland	90
Guinea Bissau	70	Tanzania	1500*
Cote d'Ivoire	150	Togo	90
Kenya	350	Uganda	400
Lesotho	10	Zaire	1000*
Liberia	-	Zambia	2000
Madagascar	1200	Zimbabwe	400
Malawi	300		
		TOTAL	21,010

Note: Owing to the scarcity of data, the figures for most countries are very approximate, notably those marked with an asterisk.
Sources: FAO Report III/85 CP SSA2, 1985; ICID and other sources.

tiality, irrigation is an important issue in water sharing, particularly because it involves the consumptive use of water.

Domestic and Industrial Water Supply

Rural water supplies have little impact on the sharing of the waters of the major river basins. Rural needs are served largely from groundwater and from small surface reservoirs which have insignificant effect on main river discharges. Urban and industrial water supplies, on the other hand, are often a primary consideration in arid zones such as the basins of southern Africa. Conflicts between these and other uses arise in sub-Saharan Africa, but are generally much less severe than those found, for example, in North Africa. Greater attention to efficiency and pricing might help to reduce the tensions.

Navigation

Although river navigation is an important consideration in the development of some of the major river basins, such as along the Zaire river, it has little economic importance.

EXPERIENCES IN INTERNATIONAL COLLABORATION

The various initiatives in international collaboration in river basin development have met with mixed success. As a general observation, the more numerous the member states involved, the lower the effectiveness of the collaboration.

A list of the main river and lake basin agreements in sub-Saharan Africa is given in Table 5. A number of bipartite agreements have operated successfully, including those for Kariba (Zambia-Zimbabwe); the lower Nile (Egypt-Sudan); Cunene (formerly Portugal-South Africa and now Angola-Namibia). The OMVS tripartite organization (Senegal-Mali-Mauritania) is almost unique in achieving the construction of two dams as part of a 'common works' programme. Negotiations between South Africa and Swaziland are making good progress at a bipartite level, the objective being the construction of two major dams in the Komati basin, with the agreement of Mozambique.

The Zambezi region now offers favourable opportunities for real progress in coordinated water development under the umbrella of Southern African Development Coordination Conference (SADCC)—an organiz-

Table 5. International river basins: some agreements and treaties

Name of Basin	Date of Treaty	Number of States	Functions
Niger	1963	9	Assembly of data produced by member states and planning (implementation of projects is 1986 carried out by member states).
Volta	1962	6	Provision of energy to neighbouring states, Cote d'Ivoire, Togo, and Benin. Agreements on water use with Burkina Faso, Mali, and Niger.
Mono	1964	2	Coordination of water use, planning, project implementation, and O&M for joint powr production projects.
Gambia	1981	2	Implementation by an accord relating to use of waters of Gambia river (OMVG) and navigation on its waterway. Promotion and coordination of studies and works for development of the basin. Execution of technical and economic studies at request of member states, including raising of finance. Implementation of common works and direction of agencies responsible for their O&M.
Chad	1973 (based on 1964 agreement)	4	Planning and execution of river basin projects of both regional and national character. Collection and dissemination of data. Supervision of execution of studies and works. Regulation of navigation. Preparation, execution, and O&M of specific projects. Coordination of financial planning. (Note: in practice LCBC's activities are confined largely to planning.)
Nile	1929 and 1959	2	Essentially water sharing and supervision of water allocations between two of the nine riparian states. Provisions for reduction of losses in the Sudd region with commitments to finance and to execute works so as to reduce losses. Technical collaboration through a Joint Technical Commission.
Kagera (a sub-basin of the Nile)	1977 and 1981	3	Planning with wide multi-sectoral scope, including water, agriculture, animal husbandry, minerals, wildlife, fisheries, and environmental protection. In practice does not go beyond study stage
Great Lakes Region (a sub-basin of Zaire basin)		3	Basically electric power generation under the umbrella of a regional power utility.

Table 5 (cond.) International river basins: some agreements and treaties

Name of Basin	Date of Treaty	Number of States	Functions
Cunene	1969	2	Creation of a permanent Joint Technical Commission with advisory, study, and reporting functions. Execution of works by one riparian with water sharing and financial participation by the other.
Kariba (Capc)	1963	2	Vested power previously held by Federal Power Board in the Central African Power Corporation (CAPC) with tasks of implementing new works and the general operation and maintenance of existing works. For its international (bipartite) functions CAPC is now superseded by the Zambezi River Authority.
Komati	Treaty in Draft stage	2	Aims to create a Joint Permanent Technical Committee to plan and regulate the sharing and use of Komati basin waters and to create an operating agency that will execute and operate major works on behalf of the two riparian states.

ation of nine states, including all seven of the Zambezi riparian states (Table 2). SADCC is sponsoring ZACPLAN—the Zambezi River Action Plan—which aims to promote development of the water resources of the Zambezi in an environmentally-sound manner. In other areas, progress has been disappointing, particularly in the three river basins— the Nile as a whole, Zaire, and Niger— that are shared each by seven to nine member states.

Almost all river basin organizations (RBOs) established under the various agreements suffer from shortage of both financial and skilled human resources. Some lack also political will and conviction of the member states. Possible solutions to a few of these problems are discussed in the following section.

EXISTING RIVER BASIN ORGANIZATIONS

The objectives of existing RBOs vary widely according to the existing level of planning and the political aim of the member states. For example, in the case of the Nile agreement of 1959 between the Sudan and Egypt it was possible to focus on the sharing of the available surface water resources between the two countries. The agreement recognized the building of the Aswan dam by Egypt and called upon the Sudan to carry out water-saving projects in the southern swamp lands. The only organization created under the terms of this agreement is a Joint Technical Commission with a very limited executive function.

By contrast, the OMVS agreement between Senegal, Mali, and Mauritania has broad objectives, but had a more narrow primary purpose to implement common works on the Senegal river—the now completed Diama and Manantali dams. The agreement creating the OMVG for the Gambia basin is modelled on the OMVS agreement with similar broad objectives. In both cases, councils of ministers can require these organizations to undertake almost any function relating to the development of the respective river basins.

The 1963 agreement between the then Northern and Southern Rhodesia concerning the Zambezi river started from an advanced base in that the Kariba dam project had already been implemented when the two countries were part of a political federation. The agreement is brief and essentially vests the assets and liabilities of the former Federal Power Board in a new organization: the Central African Power Corporation, which was assigned the responsibility of promoting the next phase of the Kariba project. Recently, the activities of CAPC have been divided into three agencies, one bipartite and the other two national. The bipartite organization, Zambezi River Authority (ZRA), is responsible for common works, including future dams on the Zambezi. The other two agencies are responsible for power production in the respective member states.

From these examples, and from Table 5, it is apparent that the objectives and functions of RBOs vary widely. The structure and functions of RBOs should be designed to match their specific objectives and the likely resources available to support their activities but unfortunately this is not always so. Most have some kind of planning function although in many cases it may be far removed from an integrated river basin planning approach.

From the structural point of view, most RBOs involve a Joint Technical Commission and in several cases it is supported by a Secretariat. Almost all organizations are governed by a higher authority, generally taking the form of a Council of Ministers.

In Africa, most RBOs have focused on common works, even where their mandates would permit wider scope of project activity. Exceptions are found for the Kagera and in the Lake Chad Basin Commission (LCBC) and the Authorite du Liptako-Gourma (ALG). The LCBC covers a wide range of sectoral activities, including agriculture, forestry, and transport. The ALG attempts to pursue a wide range of largely unrelated projects. Several RBOs assume a fund-raising role. The OMVS did so with considerable skill and success.

In general, the performance of RBOs in sub-Saharan Africa has been disappointing. The main problems may be summarized as:

1. excessively wide scope of activities, which is incompatible with the available human and financial resources;
2. too little autonomy provided to the RBO by its member states, or autonomy not operating in the way intended, and therefore detracting from impartiality and effectiveness of action;
3. inadequate attention to the need for prompt payment by member states in respect of their contributions to the funding of RBOs and their activities;
4. insufficient numbers of well-trained and experienced personnel, sometimes with overstaffing by unskilled personnel; and
5. heavy dependence upon external technical assistance, which, in the absence of sufficient skilled counterpart personnel, results in poor transfer of technology.

STEPS TOWARDS INTERNATIONAL RIVER BASIN DEVELOPMENT

Setting the Objectives

There is evidence that the most successful endeavours in international collaboration are based on objectives that are framed to:

— focus on well-defined, if not narrow, objectives such as water sharing (Nile Water Agreements) and the construction of specific common works (the two dams of OMVS and the Kariba Dam);
— develop projects that are of significance to the several riparian states (common works) and are not essentially national projects; and
— develop projects that are interrelated and form part of an integrated river basin plan.

Defining the Functions of RBOs

The creation of some kind of RBO forms the first practical step towards international collaboration in river basin development. The scope of an RBO's terms of reference can cover any or all of the following activities:

— data collection and processing;
— planning;
— water allocations;
— raising funds for studies and projects;
— implementation of projects;
— project operation and maintenance;
— monitoring water use, control of pollution, and preservation of environmental conditions.

The main focus should be on surface water because these resources are of greatest concern between riparians.

Data Collection and Processing

When viewed simply on a national scale, the collection and processing of hydrological data, in all its forms (including that for hydrogeology and hydrometereology) has made poor progress in much of Africa. The reasons have been lack of commitment in making long-term provision, the generally low priority accorded to the water sector as a whole, and shortages of human and financial resources. In the light of this situation, every attempt to collect and process data on a regional basis should be approached with caution. In the case of the controversial HYDROMET project, set up in 1967 to embrace the nine Nile basin countries, the final result was not successful, despite certain benefits that accrued by way of training. Wherever the project operated in practice, it tended to erode the responsibilities and initiative of the national line agencies. On balance it would seem preferable to preserve the structure and responsibilities of the national agencies and for the RBOs to derive data through them. Problems, however, occur when modern systems are employed, such as satellite-operated data collection platforms, where economy of scale demands international collaboration.

The World Bank, UNDP, African Development Bank, the European Economic Community, and the French government have sponsored a major assessment of the status of the hydrological networks and organizations of sub-Saharan Africa, covering almost all the 43 countries. Although not specifically planned on a regional basis, the study will assist countries in their efforts to enhance the quantity and quality of all hydrometric data that is a crucial requirement for the success of a collaborative effort in the development of the shared river basins.

Planning

Fundamental to the success of any RBO is the assurance of a planning capability. But planning must be perceived as a precursor to the final objective which is the promotion of the construction of river basin projects that will bring collective benefits to member states.

Development planning of a major river basin is, however, beset with difficulties—whether on a national or international scale—mostly political in nature. Planning activities are often seriously delayed because progress in planning is impossible without adopting criteria, if not decisions, that depend on political policies and strategies. This underlines the need for clear policy decisions among member states.

Problems also arise between planners in the RBOs and planners in the national planning organizations. Further, domestically, national planners do not always solicit the collaboration of national practitioners who are inevitably the final arbiters and managers. These considerations give rise to the issue of how much river basin planning should be driven by the centralized unit of an RBO, i.e. 'top-down', and how much should be 'bottom-up', starting with national practitioners and planners. In practice there is a certain degree of iterative procedure, and this underscores the importance of establishing a sound constitution and structure of an RBO, as discussed a little later.

Water Allocations

Water allocations, or the sharing of water, should be made on the basis of findings that derive from the planning process. Some of these findings may be overridden by political considerations, but that does not lessen the need for objective planning, which serves to judge the costs and benefits of the political decision.

It is not the purpose here to discuss in detail criteria for water sharing between riparian states. Suffice it to recall that the most commonly-used guidelines are the Helsinki Rules drawn up in 1966 by the International Law Association. These embrace the concept of a drainage basin as an economic and geographical spatial unit within which surface water resources are treated as the common property of all riparians. The principle of water sharing is based largely on a riparian's capability and potentiality to make beneficial use of the waters in the foreseeable future. However, there is an emerging legal framework under the auspices of the International Law Commission, a subsidiary organ of the General Assembly of the United Nations, which questions the drainage basin as the norm from which the rules of international law may be deduced.

In its mandate, an RBO should receive from its member states a clear directive on water sharing, whether this is to be based on the Helsinki Rules or on other considerations.

Raising Funds

RBOs can be effective and useful capital fund-raisers from the point of view of the member states. The very nature of their role in international collaboration and regional development has donor appeal. Grants for studies and investigations are usually made directly to the RBOs whereas funding of construction projects is channelled through the member states. Equally important, the RBOs must have well-defined procedures to assess, and to recover promptly from member states, their respective shares of apportioned capital and recurrent costs.

Implementation of Projects

Project implementation is perhaps one of the most straightforward activities of an RBO. It has the advantage that once the main objectives have been set, a construction programme should not be hindered for want of new major decisions on the part of the member states. An alternative procedure is for one of the riparians to assume responsibility for the execution of common works (as in the Cunene Agreement listed in Table 2).

Project Operation and Maintenance (O&M)

So far there are few examples of common works that involve RBOs in O&M programmes. The Kariba dam and the OMVS dams are noteworthy in this respect. There are many issues that emerge when setting up both the organizational structure and the procedures for Operation and Maintenance of common works. Among the more important are the corporate responsibility of the RBO to make decisions affecting Operation and Maintenance; the ownership of the works and the land upon which they are built; the recovery of costs from the member states and the power of the RBO to pursue regulatory matters.

Regulatory Functions

The operation of an integrated river basin development system involves a complex arrangement of water apportionment, especially where there is extensive irrigation. Water rights are established within specified limits, and steps have to be taken to ensure that they are adhered to on an equitable basis. The RBO, as an operating agency, is concerned that the rules and regulations on international water apportionment and rights are respected, but it is not appropriate for an international organization to have a 'policing' role in a member state. The regulatory powers belong to each member state, but the RBO should have a general monitoring responsibility on behalf of the member states as a whole, to ensure that water apportionments and rights are respected. The same considerations apply to pollution control and other measures that influence the efficiency of the RBO's work.

Structure and Constitution of River Basin Organizations

There are four important requirements in setting up any organization for the pursuit of international collaboration in river basin development. There should be:

— political commitment on the part of the member states;
— defined procedures to ensure interaction between the various organizations concerned;
— an organizational and incentive structure and staff that is compatible with the responsibilities it has to perform and with the appropriate legal status; and,
— financial commitment on the part of member states.

Political commitment must be related to economic need and not political whim. Experience has shown that, in most parts of the world, need provides the main driving force to international collaboration, as seen in the cases of the Indus, Nile, and Columbia (USA/Canada) basins. With political commitment there must also be the right cultural attitudes, including acceptance of a policy based on resource pricing. In fact, both governments and communities must be motivated to the pursuit of a collaborative and integrated approach to the development of the resources of a river basin.

The definition of the procedures to ensure interaction between the various organizations concerned in the river basin development involves interaction not only between member states but also within member states.

The lack of financial commitment on the part of member states is perhaps one of the major weaknesses to be overcome. As with staffing, deficiencies in finance are sometimes exacerbated by overambitious objectives. Apparent lack of financial resources to meet RBO cost apportionments could often be mitigated by member states, if they paid greater attention to cost recovery through appropriate raw water-charging systems within their own countries.

ROLES FOR EXTERNAL SUPPORT AGENCIES

External Support Agencies (ESAs) can make contributions to collaborative efforts in river basin development in several ways. Some are essentially tangible, such as technical assistance and funding. Other contributions are made by bringing independent and objective perspectives to the resolution of problems and conflicts that might otherwise be unduly influenced by political and factional constraints.

Among the main areas where ESAs can make contributions are:

— the establishment and rejuvenation of RBOs;
— river basin planning and project preparation;
— water sharing;
— raising funds; and
— project implementation.

Establishment of RBOs

Of the four main requirements for the successful establishment of an RBO stated in the foregoing section, ESAs can assist in providing technical assistance and training to ensure that the structure of the organization is compatible with the scope of its mandate. However, in respect of the other three requirements, ESAs have a less direct role to play. However, potential funding agencies should be informed on the proposed organizational structures concerned with the handling of these matters in order to avoid problems at a later stage.

River Basin Planning and Project Preparation

These are matters in which ESAs can make major and important contributions. They should be involved as much as possible at the outset in order to ensure that, in the final event, there is a clear consensus of views among member states and ESAs alike. In the planning process, competing and conflicting demands for the use of water are often identified and evaluated.

Water Sharing

While it is for the riparians themselves to agree on the allocation of the waters of a basin, the presence of a third party in the form of ESAs can help to resolve stalemate situations. By supporting sound planning studies of future needs, ESAs can bring objectivity to the analysis and to the ultimate recommendations for use of the waters.

Funding

Contrary to popular belief, obtaining funding is not one of the most difficult activities for an RBO, provided the planning and project preparation stages have been objectively carried out. There are, however, important roles here for ESAs not only in the tangible provision of funds but also in assisting an RBO in the presentation of its investment plans to an international forum.

Project Implementation

In recent years, ESAs have adopted stricter supervision of project implementation to ensure that construction works are cost-effective and built to the right quality standards. From an RBO's point of view this means that more emphasis must be placed on 'accountability'. Many water resource projects, and indeed other projects, have suffered serious cost and time overruns owing to misprocurement or accounting misdemeanours. ESAs can, through their own accountability, assist RBOs in developing appropriate accounting and financial management systems as well as sound methods of procurement.

CONCLUSION

With the numerous shared rivers that run through sub-Saharan Africa, little can be achieved in the development of surface water resources without international collaboration. Essential steps towards international collaboration are: establishment of river basin organizations (RBOs); preparation of comprehensive development plans; agreement on the sharing of waters; and implementation of 'common works' that bring benefits to several riparians.

Of the various uses of water that influence the planning of water development in the international basins, hydroelectric power is dominant, followed by irrigation and urban/industrial supplies. A few countries have significant opportunities for multi-purpose water resources development.

RBOs so far established in sub-Saharan Africa have met with mixed success. Many have suffered from lack of political conviction on the part of member states, poor financial support, and mandates that encompass activities beyond the scope of their staffing resources. To achieve success, RBOs should have well-focused, if not narrow, objectives and concentrate on projects that form common works beneficial to several riparian states. All projects should be interrelated and form part of an integrated river basin plan.

Of the various functions of an RBO, from data collection to planning, project implementation and operation and maintenance, a strong planning function is vital for success. Further, it provides the basis for reaching agreements on water sharing between riparians.

The structure and constitution of RBOs should emphasize political and financial commitments of member states; definition of procedures for interaction between agencies; and recruitment of qualified staff.

External Support Agencies (ESAs) can support international collaboration in river basin development by providing tangible financial and technical assistance and by offering independent and objective advice on matters relating to the establishment of RBOs, the preparation of treaties, the presentation of investment plans in an international forum, and on a wide range of riparian issues.

REFERENCES

United Nations. *Resources Naturelles*/Serie Eau No 1-ST/ESA/5, 1976 UN New York.

International Law Association. *The Helsinki Rules* (adopted at its 52nd Conference on 20 August 1966), International Law Association.

14 / Hydropower for Sustainable Development of the Amazon Region

MARCO ALFREDO DI LASCIO,
JUAN J. V. BENTANCURT, AND
MARIO D. ARAUJO NETO

INTRODUCTION

Statistics from the Amazon environment are a tacit statement of its staggering loss of natural resources: nearly 15,000 km^2 of forest burned each year . . . nearly 4,00,000 km^2 devastated over the last 30 years. To counter this distress, two different resolutions are often proposed. First, the *developing scenario* with the deforestation of huge tracts of land to be occupied by cattle-raising farms and mining exploitations. Second, the *conservative scenario,* characterized by the preservation of the original forest and, only in a few areas, an integrated agricultural activity, i.e. an agriculture adapted to the forest diversity. Impinging on the developing scenario are some important industrial projects in the region, specially in Manaus, Belem, Carajas, and Santarem. The official Brazilian Development Planning foresees an even greater spurt in industrialization of the Amazon region (Eletronorte, 1988). In opposition to this industrialization, conservation groups are urging the creation of a strong protective National Environmental Policy. However, its implementation has been hindered by the economic lobbies, the cultural vulnerability of local populations, and the enormous dimension of the region.

The Brazilian government planning also aims to ease economic strain by the implementation of more efficient industrial processes and by energy conservation. Eventually, conservation measures notwithstanding, most of the viable hydropower sites close to major cities will be exhausted. Therefore, the Amazon basin, with its large hydroelectric potential, must be geared to export power to the south-eastern industrial areas, located thousands of kilometres away.

Measures to curb the environmental degradation of the Amazon region should be such as to augment the cultural self-defence of the local populations, endowing them with the know-how of modern western civilization. Improvement in their standard of living, which will, in turn, reduce covetousness, is another condition that will foster conservation of the environment. In fact, it is necessary to plan a sustainable development for the region, i.e. a development that meets the needs of the present without jeopardizing the ability of future generations to meet their own needs. Regenerative agriculture and exploitation of the renewable resources, with reinvestment of the profits in the region, can be the key factor in promoting sustainable development.

Second only to the forest, hydropower is Amazonia's most important renewable resource, its capacity being bigger than necessary for the region. Thus, exportation of electricity could ensure financial support for regional integrated development with schools, colleges, hospitals, electricity, water treatment plants, etc. Due to the great environmental impact of the reservoirs, this proposition may not be enthusiastically received. Thus, it will be necessary to provide a more realistic conceptual framework to guide the studies and analysis of environmental assessments which deal with the construction of dams, one that will demonstrate the feasibility of reservoirs for the region (Di Lascio and Di Lascio, 1990). Consequently, our purpose here is to discuss a system designed to promote sustainable development in Amazonia, conserving the forest and exploiting the hydropower basically to export energy to the other Brazilian regions.

Before the above proposition can be accepted, two crucial questions must be posed: (1) how to produce electricity in the Amazon rivers, maintaining the ecosystem functioning within acceptable thresholds, and (2) how to transport this electricity without the risk of industrial dissemination because of the existence of the transmission lines. In an attempt to answer these questions, this work proposes the following measures for the mitigation of the effects of hydropower plants and the electrical transmission network within the Amazonian environment: (a) a Hydroelectric Site Evaluation Scheme (HYSES) to defect the potentialities and the limitations of the ecosystem, and the existence of preservation sites; and (b) the implementation of improvements in the hydroelectric and electrical transmission lines projects, to reduce primary and secondary environmental impacts.

AVAILABILITY OF ENERGY AND THE BRAZILIAN DEVELOPMENT

In modern civilization, electric energy is a growing part of the support structure, much like roads and public water supplies. Depending on the availability of energy, the development policy could be evaluated and living standards improved.

It is important to remember that the urbanized and industrialized south-eastern region of Brazil was plagued by shortages for 20 years following World War II. Forced outages, overloaded circuits, and excessive voltage and frequency variations were regular features of this period. In the mid-1960s, Brazil started aggressively developing its generating capacity, as shown in Table 1. Although the economy grew at an average of 6.2 per cent per year from 1970 to 1985, the electricity demand grew at 10.4 per cent. The generating capacity nearly doubled from 1968 to 1974, the years of the Brazilian 'economic miracle', when the gross national product (GNP) grew at an average rate of 11.5 per cent per year. For a long period, the electric demand growth of 6-10 per cent per year continued to be considered because of the population growth. In this context, hydropower will remain the most important source up to the year 2010 or even up to 2020. Subsequently, Brazilians will require another source, such as nuclear, coal, or other thermal power. Nevertheless, it is widely acknowledged that the only practical alternatives to meet the nation's electric energy requirements are nuclear and hydropower. Other sources such as fossil fuels and solar energy can contribute only a small fraction of Brazil's requirements. In the case of nuclear power, Brazil has had poor experience with its operating plant (built by Westinghouse) which works so sporadically that it was nicknamed 'the firefly'. However, part of the hydroelectric utilization has been reserved for four new nuclear plants which are planned for the year 2010.

Table 1. Growth of Brazilian electric energy demand and installed capacity projected by utilities up to the year 2010

Year	1950	1960	1970	1980	1990	2000	2010
Electricity demand, GW	1.8	4.5	10.4	31.2	50	86	152
Installed capacity, GW	1.9	4.8	11.2	33.2	55	92	160
Amazon hydropower, GW	—	—	—	—	4	9	46

Source: data reviewed by the authors from official figures

ATTRACTIVENESS OF AMAZON HYDROPOWER

Historically, hydropower generator stations played a major role as sources of electric energy in Brazil. It is estimated that the total hydroelectric Brazilian resources amount to about 200 gigawatts (GW). Of this, 100 GW could be taken from the Amazon rivers, confining the operation to those that would be most economic (Salati, 1990).

It is also evident from Table 1 that the increase in the electricity demand from 1990 to the year 2010 will exceed 100 GW, i.e. more than 200 per cent in 20 years. As Brazil has used its plentiful hydroelectric resources located in the developed southern region, another point illustrated in Table 1 is the importance of the Amazon hydropower for the period, with an installation necessity of more than 40 GW in the region.

The use of alternative energy sources is complicated by the high costs and environmental problems. Coal, natural gas, and oil are scarce and associated with air and thermal pollution problems. Nuclear power is expensive and the radioactive contamination is potentially important, especially in a developing country where the population is poorly educated. Related to this point it is important to remember that in the Brazilian city of Goiania, in 1987, a cesium 137 radiotherapy source was stolen from a hospital and dismounted in a junkyard, provoking radioactive contamination, and causing injuries and death to many people. These facts, allied to the increased attractiveness of the Amazon hydropower when compared with the expensive nuclear power or the rare Brazilian fossil fuels, suggest that the installation of only 40 GW in Amazonia for the year 2010 is probably a very conservative figure.

Finally, it is necessary to point out that, when an exploding population takes inventory of its resources and when alternative energy sources are not plentiful, the contemplation of such an enormous hydroelectric reserve, in Amazonia, without providing its rational use, may be judged as extremely poor engineering. Therefore, the exposed evidences corroborate the suggestion of an approach that considers a rational and integrated use of the Amazonian water power resources. Obviously, the harnessing of these resources has to include strong environmental protective measures.

SUMMARY OF AMAZONIAN EXPERIENCES IN HYDROPOWER PLANTS

Up to the present, almost all the few experiences of hydropower in Amazonia have been extremely hazardous to the environment. Actually, only five hydropower dams are in operation: Balbina (250 MW) in Amazonas state; Tucurui (4000 MW) and Curua-Una (41.2 MW), both in Para state; Coaracy Nunes (70 MW) in Amapa state; and Samuel (213 MW) in Rondonia state.

During the filling up of the Tucurui reservoir, measuring an area of 2430 km², the animal rescue campaigns resulted in nearly nothing due to the lack of knowledge about their ecology and new habitat. Once transferred to the new habitats, the animals were practically condemned to death, specially due to the competition with the existing fauna (Henriques, 1988). Also, as pointed out by Pereira, Tassin, and Mouchel (1990), the water residence time of one year along the margins and up to five years in one location influence change in the habitat, seriously harming the animals and plants. In the social context, the project doomed the old resident population to an undeniable deterioration in life quality, keeping them poverty-stricken and increasing the prostitution. In fact there are two towns near the dam: the one rich, occupied by foreigners employed in the hydroelectric plant; the other, poor and inhabited by local people. The economic aspect is another appalling situation: more than half of the energy is sold by only 35 per cent of its real cost for aluminum exportation plants (Rosa and Schaeffer, 1988).

Balbina is generally pronounced a bad dam, producing only 250 MW from a 2360 km² shallow and dendritic lake, nearly twice the early estimated 1240 km². This resulted in an average water residence period of 420 days up to several years in some places (Fearnside, 1990). The studies for Balbina were based on standard photogrammetric data which mapped the top of the forest canopy and subtracted the average tree height. Unfortunately, some of the tallest trees obscured the fact that they stood in deep ravines; thus the technique provided inaccurate topographical data that led to the formation of an almost stagnant lake.

Coaracy Nunes and Curua-Una, with their small lakes of 23 km² and 78 km² respectively, and with short water residence time of some weeks, had a negligible environmental impact which is balanced by the possibilities of recreation, fishing and electrical energy production.

Samuel, even with a 502 km², has a global positive aspect because of the valuable benefits from electricity brought to the local populations.

ENVIRONMENTAL INVENTORY AND USE OF A GEOGRAPHICAL INFORMATION SYSTEM TO PLAN HYDROELECTRIC SCHEMES

Existing endangered species and sites of historical, economical, and archaeological importance have forced postponements of power projects in the planning/construction stages. However, the occurrence of this kind of problem does not necessarily mean a costly delay of a proposed project if these species are properly considered during the initial planning stages. Mitigative measures can be recommended for the protection of the species and associated critical habitat, for example, the facilities for salmon migration in the Columbia River.

A viable solution to the proposed objective, i.e. the integrated use of Amazonian water resources, would be a Hydroelectric Site Evaluation Scheme (HYSES), before the consolidation of each hydropower plant project. Once the HYSES is accomplished, the Hydroelectric Construction Permission (HYCOPE) can be provided and the plant implemented.

The HYSES described in Fig. 1 basically entails the preparation of a biophysical inventory, including the number of threatened or endangered plant and animal species which may occur in the study area. This inventory includes not only the area of the dams but also the drainage basin and the transmission lines corridors. The idea of this approach is to emphasize primary and secondary interaction impacts and to ensure that a broad range of considerations are examined, highlighting the key impacts. Since all information has been collected on the study area, the next step will be the use of a Geographical Information System (GIS) for the integration of the data collected to define the sufficient space for growth, nutritional resources, and other requirements necessary for survival. This is, in other words, the determination of the critical habitats which will be considered as the preservation areas. Even if no imperilled species are found, the information gained during the study will be extremely valuable in extending the knowledge of the region.

INTEGRATION OF HYDROPOWER PLANTS WITH THE ENVIRONMENT

It is important to emphasize that, in the absence of adequate measures, the development of the hydropower potential of a wild free-flowing river means a complete and permanent disruption of the river valley and total turmoil in the regional ecology.

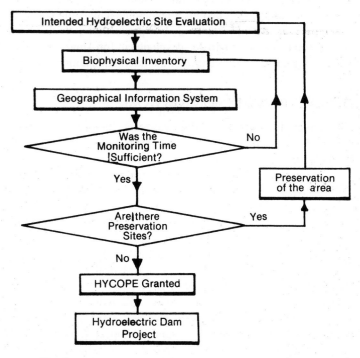

Fig. 1. Hydroelectric Site Evaluation Scheme, HYSES.

The integration of hydropower plants with the biophysical and social environments must satisfy the following conditions:

— protection of the ecosystem;
— education focusing regional problems; that is, turning the attention of schools and faculties to subjects such as tropical medicine, anthropology, biology, botany, ecology, etc.
— integrated agriculture;
— no industrial dissemination;
— exportation of hydroelectric energy (the profits accruing from this venture would directly contribute to the Amazon's development).

A review of the Brazilian economic aspects reveals that the country is in need of using trade surplus to service the debt, and to draw heavily on non-renewable resources to do so. In addition, the present social situation is very difficult due to a ten-year period of nearly stagnant growth of the economy. This extremely unsound economic status, along with a real social convulsion menace, permits a favourable bargaining position for environmentalists. If they could ally the production of hydroelectricity with a good case of sustainable development for Amazonia, they could, in exchange, request the control of the international money flow.

ELECTRICAL TRANSMISSION NETWORK

The voltage level of a transmission line determines its energy transmission capacity. By constantly increasing the voltage level, large blocks of electric energy could be transported, and the physical length of the transmission grid augmented. To evaluate the technical and economic aspects of this supply, a preliminary study was made by the utilities. The main conclusion from the study was that the HVDC (High Voltage Direct Current) and the three-phase transmission could be selected, and that the voltages will level at around 1000 kV.

The actual choice of the electricity transmission from the Amazon region has to be based upon a combination of technical, economic, and environmental factors. For this reason it is proposed here that the enforcement of the use of HVDC transmission will avoid industrial dissemination along the transmission lines. This practice will, at the same time, be responsible for minimum environmental impacts (Di Lascio and Di Lascio, *op. cit.*). The high electrical terminal costs are the major hindrance to industrial dissemination along the HVDC lines. Only very small loads can be supplied with quite reasonable costs by using the neutral circuit breaker technique developed by BPA (Bonneville Power Administration) on the west coast of USA.

The transmission corridor planning process requires continuous updating to meet changing regulatory requirements and environmental review processes established in response to the HYSES and the National Environmental Policy. For example, if it is determined that the line will adversely affect the species habitat to a significant degree, line routing modifications and adjustments will have to be made.

CONCLUSION

As a result of the knowledge of the hydroelectric experience, and environmental analysis that could be provided by the use of the GIS, it is possible to propose the following measures to achieve sustainable development in the Amazon region: elaboration of the HYSES; enforcement of the points related to the integration of the hydropower plants with the environment; and the adoption of the HVDC transmission lines.

A Geographical Information System will provide a reliable tool in the analyses of environmental data. Overlay maps and matrices will be produced in order to enable finding the best locations for the hydroelectric power plants through the crossing of biophysical and socio-economic information.

Exportation of the Amazonian hydroelectric energy will create availability of financial resources to aid regional development. Such funding will ensure more schools, faculties, hospitals, and water treatment plants for the local population.

High Voltage Direct Current (HVDC) transmission lines will be more economical, almost environmentally safe, and will avoid industrial dissemination.

Finally, it is possible to state, unequivocally, that there seems little likelihood that the Brazilians will not use the vast inexpensive Amazon hydropower even in the face of strong opposition from foreign nations. In fact, the only feasible interference in the Brazilian decisions could be an integrated sustainable project for the development of the Amazon that is tailored to environment conservation.

ACKNOWLEDGEMENTS

The authors are grateful to the National Scientific and Technological Development Council (CNPQ) of Brazil and the Brasilia University (UNB) for their support in the preparation and presentation of this paper.

REFERENCES

Di Lascio, M. A. and Di Lascio, V. L. 1990. 'A Agua Como Geradora de Electricidade: O Caso da Amazonia', International Seminar on Hydrology and Water Management of the Amazon Basin, organized by International Water Resources Association (IWRA) and Associacao Brasileira de Recursos Hidricos (ABRH), Manaus, 5–9 August.

Electronorte. 1988. 'Amazonia-Cenarios Socio-Economics e de Demanda de Energia Electrica: 1988–2010 (Amazon-Social-Economic and Electric Energy Demand Scenarios: 1988–2010)', Centrais Eletricas do Norte do Brasil-ELETRONORTE, Brasilia.

Fearnside, P. M. 1990. 'Balbina: Licoes Tragicas na Amazonia', Ciencia Hoje, vol. 11, no. 64, pp. 34–42.

Henriques, P. B. 1988. 'Salvamento ou Massacre?, Ciencia Hoje, vol. 8, no. 46, pp. 64–66.

Pereira, A., Tassin, B., and Mouchel, J. M. 1990. 'Hydrodynamic and Nutrient Budget Study of a Tropical Reservoir', International Seminar on Hydrology and Water Management of the Amazon Basin, IWRA and ABRH, Manaus, 5–9 August.

Rosa, L. P. and Schaeffer, R. 1988. 'A Politica Energetica Brasileira' in *As Hidreletricas do Xingu e os Povos Indigenas*, pp. 53–58, Sao Paulo, Zerodois Servicos Editoriais.

Salati, E. 1990. 'Modificacoes da Amazonia nos Ultimos 300 Anos: Suas Consequencias Sociais e Ecologicas' in Desafio Amazonico: o Futuro da Civilizacao dos Tropicos, pp. 25–39, Brasilia University Press, Brasilia.

15 / Water Strategies for the Twenty-first Century

IWRA COMMITTEE ON WATER STRATEGIES

INTRODUCTION

Water, which permeates life on Earth, is essential as an enabler and sustainer both of plants, animals, and humans, and of human civilization. The concern for this fundamental truth increased after NASA's Mission Mars, one of its conclusions being the urgent need to pay increased interest to the importance of the water cycle for life on this planet—the only planet where water can exist in liquid form. Water-related phenomena and functions are indeed fundamental components of any serious analysis of the relations between environment and development in general, and of development under water scarcity in particular.

The fact that we are addressing tomorrow's problems with unclear concepts and fixed mindsets from the past poses severe threats to the success of the Earth Summit. Poor data with low reliability and validity, and untested assumptions about cause–effect relationships stay in circulation. Environmental assessments continue to focus more on negative side effects of projects than on the social benefits for which they were intended. Already, the wording of the UN resolution 44/228 on the Brazil Conference ('protection of water quality and supply') indicates that water was seen only as a victim of environmental pollution or as a technical issue respectively. In past discussions on water-related problems in developing countries, the focus has been on visible water rather than on invisible water in the soil, and on man-induced environmental problems rather than on the hydroclimatically-based environmental vulnerability, which poses particular problems for human activities in these countries.

Three fundamental environmental challenges will have to be addressed in the new strategies needed for the twenty-first century:

— *multi-cause water scarcity* due to (1) population growth *per se* producing an ever-increasing population pressure on a finite water availability; (2) urban growth resulting in ever-increasing point demands for water, (3) desiccation of the landscape due to degradation of soil permeability and leading to drought-like conditions even in high rainfall areas;

— *multi-cause water pollution* due to (1) airborne emissions: (2) pollution from agricultural land-use, industrial activities, and human waste; (3) wastewater outlets (pollution from most of these sources gets caught and carried by the water cycle and ends up, often with detrimental impact, in land and water ecosystems);

— *multi-cause water-related fertility degradation* due to (1) salinization/waterlogging from poor irrigation management; (2) effects of acid rain originating from air emissions; (3) reduced water-holding capacity due to reduced use of organic fertilizers, and removal of organic matter from the soil; (4) land permeability degradation due to mismanagement of land.

To these challenges should be added the financial challenge. The widening gap between financial resources available and the escalating needs of funds for water resources development and management for the socio-economic development of the Third World region requires urgent attention. This situation forces us to find ways to get more out of less. Funds needed for investments, operation, and maintenance in the traditional water sector are estimated at up to 20 per cent of public expenditures in many countries. The debt burden in developing countries constrains their ability to invest in water projects with long gestation periods. Many countries also provide large subsidies to particular water users, which can distort water use and interfere with sustainable use of the resource.

ON THE THRESHOLD OF THE TWENTY-FIRST CENTURY

In view of the various and integrated functions which water—whether visible or invisible—plays in a number of sectors (agriculture, forestry, environment, health, energy, industry, navigation, recreation, employment, education, etc.), water-related issues are fundamentally intertwined with most sectors in the national economy. As a consequence, water cannot be seen as a sector of its own. On the contrary, water strategies have to be truly multisectoral in character and integrated with the broader economy.

Regional differences have to be given appropriate acknowledgement. Problem profiles, and thereby strategies, will exhibit fundamental differences from region to region: between already developed temperate-zone regions with mainly pollution problems on the one hand; and poverty-stricken tropical and subtropical regions with more extreme climates, rapid population growth, a significant environmental vulnerability in terms of water scarcity and/or erosion and soil degradation, and severe development problems, on the other. In the latter zone, environmental protection is a fundamental and necessary prerequisite for development.

Strategies will have to provide for the necessary balance between short-term acute needs and necessary long-term perspectives.

— Short-term strategies are necessary where sustainability of life-support systems are threatened by everyday life problems; the acute poverty factors causing the degradation of the resource base have to be immediately addressed. In large parts of sub-Saharan Africa, for instance, the environmental fabric of rural areas is almost completely broken down. Consequently, a crucial measure is a speedy solution to the energy and food needs of the households.

— The long-term strategy has to be developed and implemented in parallel, taking a multisectoral approach, and integrating water-related issues with the broader national economy. This includes population policies. The ultimate goal is a basin-wide strategy for integrated and sustainable development and management of land and water within the context of the river basin. Due attention has to be paid to upstream/downstream linkages as well as linkages between water-depending and water-impacting land-use. Attention has to be paid to the possible impacts of climate change, in particular the effects that it may have on rainfall, evapotranspiration, groundwater recharge and quality, local water tables, river flow and quality; and consequently both on water demand and land-use, on terrestrial ecosystems, and on the reliable yields from water projects. Only in a time perspective of some 50 years may water availability expansion by macro-scale projects and non-conventional technologies become more generally feasible.

A major threat in many of the most poverty-stricken countries is the parallel breakdown of life-support systems in rural areas and the increasing urban migrattion. To break this devastating trend, the agricultural sector should be seen as the primary sector for economic development, aiming at sustainable development of land productivity. In view of water's pivotal role in biomass production, *water security* has to be an essential element. Integrated soil/water management on the catchment basis should be seen as essential in order to secure the best possible use of the available rainfall. Three challenges need particular attention:

— developing ways of drought-proofing rain-fed agriculture in semi-arid marginal lands;
— developing methods for water harvesting and soil moisture management;
— rehabilitation and expansion of agroforestry systems in the humid tropics, well adapted for the poor farmers.

In water-scarce regions, efficiency in water use will become more and more crucial as population increases while water availability stays finite. Rapid population growth and scarce financial resources will make it more and more urgent to do more with less. Consequently, water has to be valued in relation to its true societal importance. The escalating costs and human effort needed for water supply projects call for the development of methods for allocation of water aiming at maximum productivity per unit of water in industry as well as agriculture. Principles for the allocation of scarce resources must, at the same time, include a guarantee for basic livelihood security of the poor and marginal social groups. Especially where a high and increasing population pressure on a limited water availability will be constraining socio-economic development, such as the North Africa and Middle East region, it is urgent to reverse the approach from the present dominating 'how much water do we need and where do we get it?' to the more productivity-oriented 'how much water is there and how can we best benefit from that amount?'

In order to meet the need to do more with less, water strategies should stimulate innovation and adaptation. There is an obvious need not only for institutional backing but also for entrepreneurship at the local level. Thus, social carriers for innovation and adaptation have to be found and stimulated to facilitate the testing and spread of new solutions such as conjunctive use of surface and groundwater, sequential reuse of treated sewage water and agricultural drainage water, irrigation scheduling (e.g. irrigation at night), etc.

Assessment of the water resources available as a base for socio-economic development is fundamental for water resources planning and strategies. Without solid and relevant data, the planning of water projects will be based on guesswork. Therefore, the extremely poor follow-up of the Mar del Plata recommendation in this regard is highly unfortunate. Instead of improving observations from basic data networks, stations have been allowed to deteriorate as a result of financial difficulties. This tendency is in contrast to the even larger data needs that follow from the particularly wide fluctuations in rainfall between years that are typical for low latitudes, and the even more rigorous criteria for ensuring that project planning incorporates the risks related to a fluctuating climate.

Shared use of water in international river basins (rivers, lakes, and aquifers) tends to present its own problems. A continuing unilateral action, caused by disparities in development and water use, is contributing to an unsound politicizing of many international river basins, blinding the people to the benefits of cooperation. The international community may have an important role to play in bridging difficulties due to differences in terms of access to information and trained personnel, and facilitate for the basin countries the benefits of a joint definition of the problems of equitable use and upstream/downstream dependencies.

HOW TO ACHIEVE THIS

It is essential to influence the attitudes to water and the environment of the next generation of decision-makers so that the present 'water blindness' is effectively mitigated. The fundamental importance of water, for both biomass production and livelihood security and quality of life, has to be widely recognized. A perspective based on an awareness of the roles of water for life, for development, and in the environment must be promoted through educational efforts at various levels:

— in pre-schools where the attitudes of tomorrow's adults are formed;
— in schools where the genesis of environmental problems can be more widely understood by benefiting from the water perspective;
— by media-oriented education efforts, including press seminars for journalists, ready-to-print articles for smaller newspapers, etc.

It is essential to ensure that management of land and water by society and by its members is founded on a basic scientific understanding of the resource base and the predicament in terms of environmental vulnerability. It is therefore expedient to bridge the gap between scientists, development experts, and politicians, and the community at large. In particular, the scientific community in developing countries has to be mobilized in order to take increased part in the water strategy process so that water-related problems in the future can be minimized. Universities, academies, and scientific societies should be stimulated to address water-related issues from a *multidisciplinary* perspective and to develop links with real problems in the field. Scientists have to be recognized as important partners by policy-makers, and a continuous dialogue has to be secured.

The Mar del Plata Water Conference included an assessment of the human resources needed for the necessary back-up of water-related socio-economic development in the Third World countries. An army of water professionals at all levels would be needed, from caretakers of local water supply schemes, including repair personnel, to the scientific, social, economic, and engineering experts needed to secure that water-related problems are correctly identified, and that societal decisions are based on a scientifically-based understanding. An educational system has to be urgently developed for adequate training of these cadres. Without such an effort, development may be seriously impeded in drought-prone or water-stressed areas with highly vulnerable environmental preconditions. Moreover, it is essential to minimize the climatic bias among Third World students, trained at universities in the North. To secure the necessary scale in professional education, major efforts should go into recurring training of trainers.

Particular weightage has to be given to capacity building within national research institutions in order to increase the capability within individual countries to address issues of sustainable development with adequate attention to environmental constraints as defined by hydroclimate, soils, topography, geology, etc. This process may be facilitated by twin arrangements between research institutes in industrialized and Third World countries.

Ways have finally to be found to create the necessary partnership on the national scene among the public, NGOs, and governments; and within the international community among intergovernmental organizations, NGOs, and scientific associations.

CONCLUSION

The current situation calls for strategies based on a new water awareness, founded on a basic understanding of the particular role played by water for life and civilization on Earth:

— water is central to practically all issues of environment and develop-

ment *in the tropics and subtropics: environmental protection is necessary to make development possible;*
— strategies (multi-sectoral in character) have to address the multicause environmental challenges emerging from water scarcity, water pollution, and water-related land fertility degradation;
— strategies have to acknowledge regional differences in terms of environmental vulnerability;
— strategies in water-scarce regions should strive towards maximum productivity per flow unit of water available;
— strategies should take an integrated approach to land productivity and water resources in order to strive at sustainable land productivity.

It is crucial that the present 'water blindness' of environmental and development experts, originally founded on a climatic bias in their original concepts and perceptions, be urgently mitigated so that water issues be given adequate attention. It is essential to focus not only on visible water but also on invisible water, and not merely on man-induced environmental problems but also on the problematic environmental preconditions for human activities that characterize the tropics and subtropics, and in particular their large environmental vulnerability.

III / Water Resources Management

16 / Groundwater Quality Management

A. DAS GUPTA

INTRODUCTION

Groundwater has always been considered to be a readily available source of water for domestic, agricultural, and industrial use. However, with increase in water demand, this resource is being overexploited in many areas. The quality of the underground water is also affected by changes in land-use and an increase in wastewater disposed into the environment. The extent to which the quality is affected by either natural processes or human activities varies with the hydrogeologic and climatic settings. In bygone years, the development of groundwater resource was normally limited to the long-term safe yield of the basin based on hydrologic budget, no account being taken of how the groundwater quality might change with time as a result of human interference. However, the present state of development should be limited to sustainable yield, taking into consideration both quantity and quality aspects of the resource. As such, efforts are being made for a complete understanding of the phenomenon of contaminant transport in subsurface environment and how the impacts of contamination can be mitigated by proper development and management practices.

Following a review of the existing condition of groundwater development in selected countries in the Asia and Pacifix region, the attempt here is to assess the state of development and how far this level of development is sustainable on a long-term basis when all probable environmental consequences—in particular, the water quality degradation—are considered. The need for a proper groundwater monitoring programme is emphasized to obtain background information on water quality, factors affecting it, and the trend in water quality change required for groundwater quality management.

GROUNDWATER USE

Groundwater has been contributing significantly to the socio-economic development of the majority of countries in the Asia and Pacific region. The groundwater utilization by various sectors in selected countries is shown in Table 1. In Kirabati, a Pacific island country, groundwater is the only source of water supply, apart from restricted practices in rain-water harvesting. Groundwater is an important source of water supply for irrigation in India and Pakistan. For instance, India obtains 40 per cent of its irrigation water from groundwater. In Malaysia, good quality surface water was readily available until about 25 years ago. However, a considerable increase in water demand has caused severe shortage in water supply, and groundwater resource has increasingly assumed a significant role in supplementing the surface water resource. In Thailand, with increased requirement of water due to population growth and the expansion of national economic development programmes over the last two to three decades, the water demand could no longer be satisfied by the surface water resource alone, and groundwater resource had to be utilized to meet the demand. In the Philippines, groundwater has been used primarily for domestic water supply. About 28 per cent of the total population were supplied with groundwater tapped from wells and springs. Another sector in which groundwater is utilized is industry.

Table 1. Groundwater utilization (million cu m/year) in selected countries in Asia and Pacific region (ESCAP, 1987)

Country	Domestic/ Municipal	Irrigation	Industry	Total	Percentage of Total Water Use
Australia	1424	1297	111	2832	NA
Bangladesh	1710	5997	24	7731	NA
Guam	NA	NA	N.A.	35	75
India	4600	1,43,500	1900	1,50,000	NA
Indonesia	3640	11	33	3684	NA
Iran	NA	NA	NA	NA	41
Japan	NA	NA	NA	NA	16
Kirabati	NA	NA	NA	NA	100
Malaysia*	60%	5	35	100	NA
Pakistan	NA	40,000	NA	40,000	NA
Philippines	2000	NA	1000	3000	35
Thailand	541	202	181	924	NA

* Absolute figures not available.
NA = data not available or not separately reported.

About 50 per cent of total industrial water requirement is satisfied by groundwater (ESCAP, 1987).

GROUNDWATER CONTAMINATION

The extensive use of and dependency upon groundwater dictate that this valuable resource be protected for both current and future uses. In most countries, groundwater development has taken place in an unsystematic and unplanned manner without much detailed scientific appraisal being made concurrently on the sustainability of the resource. As a result, this resource has been overexploited in many areas, producing long-term decline in water levels with associated adverse consequences such as land subsidence and deterioration of water into the aquifer. Chemical contamination—mainly from fertilizers, industrial wastes, and dumped solid wastes—as well as biological contamination, particularly that related to human waste contamination in dug wells, are common incidence of groundwater quality deterioration. Also, saltwater contamination problems exist in coastal areas (for example, in Thailand and Indonesia) as well as in inland areas (as in Pakistan).

Saltwater intrusion is the major water quality problem in the coastal region of the Jakarta basin. Electrical conductivity measurements indicate that an area highly contaminated by saline water (conductivity exceeding 2500 micromhos/cm) extends widely along the coastal plain. There are also instances of contaminated water supply wells occurring for more than 11 km inland from the sea of Java (Finney, Samsuhadi, and Willis, 1990). In Thailand, the groundwater quality problems are related to high concentration of chloride, sulphate, iron nitrate, and fluoride. High chloride and sulphate concentrations have been found in the northeastern region where rocksalts, gypsum, and anhydride exist. Saltwater encroachment due to depletion of water levels in aquifers in the Bangkok area is the main cause of inferior groundwater quality. High nitrate concentrations are found mostly in shallow aquifers in the northeastern region due to contamination from fertilizer (Vachi and Buapeng, 1984).

A number of studies have been conducted on groundwater quality aspect in some countries, but there is still need to assess the overall status of groundwater quality in this region. Shallow groundwater can easily be polluted. In some cases, even deeper groundwater aquifers are not completely protected against pollution as there are hydraulic contacts between shallow and deeper aquifers. Thus, protective measures are necessary where shallow groundwater is being use for domestic water supply. This is particularly important in developing countries—Indonesia, Malaysia, Myanmar, Philippines, and Thailand—where a large number of rural population depends upon shallow wells for water supply. The prevalence of communicable diseases (gastro-enteritis and diarrhoeal diseases) in these countries is associated with inadequate water quality—both surface water and groundwater (UNESCO, 1984).

There are four primary sources of groundwater pollution: the movement into groundwater of bacteria, nutrients, salt, toxics, and other pollutants from agricultural practices, and urban and industrial effluents; the percolation of bacteriological and chemical contaminants from human wastes into and between aquifers through shallow dug wells or by abandoned wells not properly plugged; saltwater intrusion associated with groundwater pumping; and the movement of contaminants between interconnected ground and surface water bodies (Hurd, 1979).

From land surface, contaminants infiltrate downward through the soil, unsaturated zone and finally reach the aquifer. As the contaminant travels through the system, attenuation of the contaminant may take place. Attenuation includes those mechanisms that reduce the rate of movement of the contaminant through processes such as dilution, dispersion, mechanical filtration, volatilization, biological assimilation and decomposition, precipitation, absorption, ion exchange, oxidation–reduction, and buffering and neutralization. The degree of attenuation that can occur is a function of (a) the time that the contaminant is in contact with the material through which it passes, (b) the grain size and physical and chemical characteristics of the material through which it passes, and (c) the distance that the contaminant has travelled. In general, for any given material, the longer the time and greater the distance, the greater the effects of attenuation. In a similar manner, the greater the surface area of the material through which the contaminant passes, the greater the potential for absorption of the contaminant and, hence, for attenuation.

GROUNDWATER PROTECTION

Most contaminants are detected sometime after entering the subsurface. Weeks, months, or years may pass before a problem is noticed. The contaminant may have travelled a considerable distance and affected a large portion of an aquifer before pollution is recognized. Even if the source is identified and removed, and no further contaminants enter the groundwater flow system, the 'damage' to the groundwater may persist for a long time: a time span stretching across tens, hundreds, or thousands of years may be necessary to flush the contaminants out of the groundwater flow system. Existing groundwater contamination problems will become more troublesome in the future because of the long time factors involved in the decay of the pollutants; the slow movement of the affected groundwater body; the exhaustion of the soil's ability to reduce the concentrations of, or to remove, specific pollutants; and the ever-increasing volume and complexity of contamination fluids. Because of the extremely slow movement of groundwater within an aquifer and the subsurface geological discontinuities, pollutants introduced into an aquifer at one location will usually constitute a localized or, perhaps, a regional problem. Since groundwaters lack any significant assimilative capacity, such pollutants will likely remain in the aquifer. Six factors, all local or regional in nature, determine the extent of groundwater pollution. Four of them—soil, geology, climate, and hydrology—exist in nature and are beyond man's capacity to control, although they may be modified. The other two factors, land use and growth patterns, are subject to control by man through planning and management.

The complex society in which we live generates all types of waste: chemical, liquid, and solid, sanitary, industrial, hazardous, toxic, and a host of others. It is necessary that these wastes are properly treated before they are disposed of in any natural environment. How can we dispose of these wastes safely? The usual practice is to use the ground surface as a disposal medium for liquid and solid wastes. It is obvious that materials leak from these disposal sites and end up in the groundwater. Therefore, disposal sites should be properly designed, constructed, operated, and monitored to protect the groundwater from the leachate. To ensure that aquifers are not contaminated, or that they will not be contaminated in the future, a hydrogeological study is necessary and groundwater monitoring requirements must be established.

It is acknowledged that the water table aquifers face the most immediate threat because of their general lack of natural protection. The situation is particularly acute in karstic or fractured rock aquifers, which have only thin soil covers and shallow sand, and gravel aquifers. Should the latter contain bank-filtered (i.e. induced-recharge) wells, pollution may occur both from vertical infiltration from the surface and laterally from polluted surface-water courses. In all cases where the quality of groundwater in unconfined aquifers is of concern, full recognition must be given to its relationship with surface-water quality. Similarly, the position of water supply wells with respect to the natural recharge areas of the groundwater flow system in which they are installed should be established, so that precautionary measures may be taken in the siting of potential contamination sources on the recharge area. The direct contamination of deep confined aquifers is usually limited by the presence of low permeability confining layers; but it must always be borne in mind that these aquifers may become contaminated by indirect recharge via their outcrop and/or recharge areas, and that such areas require protective measures if the future uses of such aquifers are not to be compromised. Contamination of deep confined aquifers may also occur by the leakage of polluting liquids from above or below, along the line of ineffectively-grouted casing, or through faults in confining layers.

There are two basic problems in dealing with groundwater contamination: (a) handling existing cases and (b) preventing new occurrences. The goals under the former situation will be to protect groundwater users and to prevent further degradation of water quality. The control measures to achieve these goals then call for inventory of sources of contamination; defining and monitoring contaminated groundwater bodies that are considered hazardous; controlling the use of groundwater already affected or threatened by contamination and providing alternate sources of supplies when needed; and containing or clearing up of pollution when economically and technically feasible. For the second problem situation, the goal will be to protect groundwater resources. This needs preparation of realistic guidelines and enforcement of regulations that are truly protective. Also, new technology and how it is being utilized is to be publicized. Considerable research efforts are needed to develop appropriate procedures to minimize environmental effects of the various potential sources of contamination and to make a complete documentation of conditions at existing key sites of groundwater contamination as a guide for future research.

Groundwater contamination is a socio-economic problem that has its roots in technological development. Its solution requires a scientifically sound and well-formulated public policy grounded in broad-based public participation which includes the private sector as well as the government. The lack of any one of these elements is likely to impede viable progress toward the prevention, or reduction, of groundwater contamination. No simple solution can address the problem adequately and comprehensively. To effectively prevent groundwater contamination, one must be aware of the sources of contamination, understand the movement of contaminants through porous media, and ascertain the technical socio-economic reasons that permit, encourage, and, indeed, make groundwater contamination the widespread phenomenon that it is today in many countries.

MONITORING AND LEGISLATION

Monitoring is an essential element of the maintenance and management of groundwater resources. The rate of migration of contamination may lead to extensive damage to the aquifer which could persist for a considerable period of time. Meyer (1973) defined monitoring of groundwater quality as a scientifically-designed programme of continuing surveillance, including direct sampling and remote quality measurements, inventory of existing and potential causes of change, and analysis and predicting of the nature of future quality changes. The groundwater quality monitoring process comprises the following action steps: monitoring strategy; monitoring objectives; monitoring programme; and monitoring system and methodology (Vrba, 1987).

The long-term planning, strategy, and policy for national and regional groundwater resources is based on the analysis and implementation of data obtained from the relevant monitoring programme. Unfortunately, groundwater quality monitoring has not been a regular programme but rather considered on an *ad hoc* basis as part of environmental monitoring programmes. In most cases, only scattered data, both in the spatial and temporal context, are available and this is inadequate for an assessment of the trend on a national or regional basis. Different methods for the design of monitoring networks and for data acquisition are used, depending on the objectives of monitoring. Steps and methodology of groundwater quality monitoring were described by Tinlin and Everett (1978). Ward (1979). Everett (1983), EPA (1985), and others which could be used as a guideline for launching similar activities, particularly in many developing countries of the Asia and Pacific region.

Through monitoring, an attempt is made to gain knowledge about the groundwater quality by taking samples from the total population. However, all too often authorities are concerned with ensuring that samples are collected properly, and they do not conduct any further assessment on the state of the system from the analysis of sample data. For sample data to yield information on the quality of water, monitoring programmes must be statistically designed and the data analyzed, using statistical concepts, and correlated with water use and hydrologic changes.

The principal reasons for the lack of effectiveness of the existing monitoring programmes in dealing with groundwater contamination problems are deficiencies in the technology currently available to satisfy economic, social, and political restraints; inadequate budgeting and staffing, together with the diverse interest of regulatory agencies; and a general lack of understanding as to how various human activities degrade groundwater quality.

Water legislation in general, and groundwater legislation in particular, are the means to effective implementation and enforcement of any desired water policy: but legislation by itself does not constitute the panacea for solving problems. Any legislation, to be effective, must be the result of water policy decisions which should precede its enactment and be based on the political, technical, economic, social, legal, and institutional factors prevailing in any one country. What is more, water legislation is strongly influenced by the legal system followed and it must take into consideration the sociological, religious, and philosophical character of the people of any particular country or region. The purpose of water legislation is to ensure, on the basis of water availability, the optimum use of such resource and its conservation, in order to satisfy present and future water demands for every type of utilization. This may be achieved by bringing the existing and future uses of water under unified, coordinated, or centralized administrative control. A basic Water Act should contain also a statement of national policy on water pollution control so that there is a clear-cut legal basis on which to promulgate subsequent detailed regulations.

SOME ISSUES AND PROSPECTS

In order to provide adequate groundwater protection, the first step is to gain a thorough understanding of all the issues involved. It should be noted in this connection that the groundwater problem, aggravated by increasing pollution, is a complicated as well as a critical one. The basic issues involved in developing an effective protective/management system are:

1. *The fragmentation of authority in and among various agencies*: conflicting goals of water agencies and users should be reconciled through interaction in the development of a groundwater management plan by all interested parties or their elected representatives.

Improved and continued cooperation among them is an integral part of the solution.

2. *The matter of authority itself*: how much uniformity or variety is needed in the matter of jurisdiction over groundwater management? In other words, what are the roles of different water agencies in respect of groundwater management?

3. *Interrelations*: quality and quantity of groundwater: groundwater vis-a-vis surface water. A pertinent question requires resolution: is there enough water of the right quality for the use of citizens? Groundwater and surface water are closely related in the hydrologic cycle and must be considered together in any comprehensive water quality management programme.

4. *Non-degradation*: here the focus is on the question, how good does groundwater quality need to be? Those in the water industry generally accept a three-level categorization of water: finished drinking water; water that can be drunk if purified; and groundwater adequate for uses other than drinking (industrial processes, irrigation, etc.). In this context, a question presents itself: what are the factors determining which level should receive priority protection and who is the decision-maker? The sorting of aquifer in terms of their quality serves as a starting point.

5. *Measures being tried or considered by different authorities responsible for groundwater protection*: these fall into four broad groupings:

(a) Standards—which mean a set of numerical limits on the allowable concentrations of particular contaminants that relate to the use of an aquifer. Standards themselves do not prevent pollution. The main use of standards is in setting an objective legal basis for further, more active pollution control measures or for determining the permissible changes in groundwater quality. It is difficult to draw the cause-and-effect relationship between control measures and attainment of the standards, leaving the controls open to challenge.

(b) Recharge zone protection for critical zones. Non-degradation, according to certain observers, is the goal to aim for in these zones. This is an objective they support because isolation of aquifer segments is more feasible for groundwater than for surface water.

(c) Land-use controls serve to prohibit pollution of groundwater resources. However, carrying out such controls across what could be a large number of political boundaries in a recharge zone is not always easy.

(d) Effluent limits restrict discharges. In the case of lower-priority areas, many geologists and hydrologists regard effluent limits as an effective means of restricting discharges into the groundwater.

CONCLUSION

Groundwater serves as the main source of water supply for drinking and other domestic needs, as well as for agricultural needs plus meeting the need of commercial and industrial developments in many parts of the Asia and Pacific region. As such it is essential that every effort be made to protect this resource as a valuable natural resource. One possible solution for groundwater protection is the establishment of groundwater quality standards. The purpose of such standards is to protect public health and welfare and maintain the quality of groundwater in all usable aquifers for domestic, industrial, and agricultural water supplies. A legal basis must exist and the prescribed steps must be followed as dictated by the rule-making process. The backbone of such a standard rests on the completion of a hydrogeological study which is necessary to determine background water quality information, to set up the monitoring programme, and to outline the sampling strategy for determining when the water quality changes are taking place and what is the significant change. One must understand the behaviour of contaminant in the subsurface so that environmental impact can be predicted.

Groundwater contamination may be reduced by thoroughly evaluating and monitoring contaminating sources such as disposal facilities and by responding quickly and effectively when a contamination problem is detected. Several steps can be taken to minimize the incidence of groundwater contamination and to limit the extent of contamination once this is clear:

1. An inventory, and subsequent evaluation, in a particular area of existing and potential sources of contamination would determine the relative significance of contamination potential of the various sources. Such an inventory might include human waste disposal facilities, municipal and industrial wastes disposal system, landfills, mining areas, salt stockpiles, and perhaps others. Some potential sources may be poorly regulated. Such information would provide a basis for developing guidelines or regulations to evaluate potential sources.

2. It is also important to delineate those areas geologically most sensitive to environmental degradation. This would include areas in which

geological materials are naturally unsuitable for waste disposal and those in which existing or potential aquifer use might be jeopardized if contaminants reach groundwater.

3. In addition to groundwater protection, plans or strategies must be developed to limit contamination once this is detected. Cooperative efforts among agencies are needed to develop a plan for an early evaluation of each incident and an appropriate response based on the hydrogeologic setting, the nature of the contaminant, and the extent of contamination.

4. The role of hydrogeologists in regulatory agencies should be strengthened to provide proper evaluation of potential sources of contamination and to aid in remedial actions when groundwater is contaminated.

5. The public should be educated on a long-term basis about groundwater and pollution. In many cases, private entities disposing wastewater are unaware of the impact of their operation on groundwater quality. Protection of groundwater quality requires a long-range perspective by water users and potential polluters, often difficult in today's economic climate.

6. Academic training of groundwater professionals and hydrogeologists should have equal emphasis on groundwater quantity and quality aspects. In the current academic programme, prime consideration is usually given to groundwater development and aquifer testing, and water quality may receive only minor consideration. All important aspects of groundwater pollution evaluations such as soil chemistry, water chemistry, geochemistry, pollution sources, and flow and transport processes in the unsaturated zone should be an integral part of the academic training so that professionals can address the problem effectively. Also, an exposure to other fields such as engineering, mining, and agriculture would be an added necessity.

7. Several lines of needed research are suggested by the evaluation of case histories in this region:
   (a) the movement of contaminants in the unsaturated zone;
   (b) groundwater monitoring and sampling techniques;
   (c) techniques for removal of contaminants from the subsurface;
   (d) documentation of groundwater contamination cases for possible application to future problems.

REFERENCES

Economic and Social Commission for Asia and the Pacific (ESCAP). 1987. 'Water Resources Development in Asia and the Pacific: Some Issues and Concerns', *Water Resources* Series no. 62, United Nations, New York.

Environmental Protection Agency (EPA). 1985. *Groundwater Monitoring Strategy*, United States Environmental Protection Agency, Washington, D.C.

Everett, L. G. 1983. *Groundwater Monitoring*, General Electric Company, New York.

Finney, B. A., Samsuhadi, M. S., and Willis, R. 1990. Groundwater Management in the Jakarta Basin. *Groundwater and the Environment*. Second International Groundwater Conference, Kota Bahru, Malaysia.

Hurd, M. 1979. The 208 Planning Approach to Groundwater Protection: A Program Review, *Groundwater*, vol. 17, no. 2, pp. 136–41.

Meyer, C. F. 1973. *Polluted Groundwater*, United States Environmental Protection Agency, Report EPA-600/4-73-0016, Washington, D.C.

Tinlin, R. M. and Everett, L. G. 1978. *Establishment of Groundwater Quality Monitoring Programmes*, Proceedings, Symposium of American Water Resources Association, Minneapolis.

United Nations Educational, Scientific and Cultural Organization (UNESCO). 1984. *Workshop on Groundwater in Rural Water Supply*. Report, Lahustein, Federal Republic of Germany.

Vachi, R. and Buapeng, S. 1984. *Groundwater Quality Problems in Thailand*, International Symposium on Hydrochemical Balances of Freshwater Systems, Uppsala, Sweden.

Vrba, J. 1987. 'Groundwater Quality Monitoring—Strategy, Objectives, Programmes and Methods', *Vulnerability of Soil and Groundwater to Pollutants*, Proceedings and Information No. 38, Netherlands Organization for Applied Scientific Research TNO. The Hague, The Netherlands.

Ward, R. C. 1979. 'Regulatory Water Quality Monitoring', *Water Resources Bulletin*, vol. 15, no. 2, pp. 369–80

17 / Water Management in Japan after World War II

Y. TAKAHASI

INTRODUCTION

The history of Japan after the Second World War is an extraordinary story of a country transcending economic poverty to become a world economic giant. A radical transformation has accompanied this development not only in the socio-economic but also in the water-related fields.

First, drastic changes mark this era: increases in population, Gross National Product, water demand, flood damage after the Second World War (Figs. 1, 2, 3, and 4 respectively) and the change in industrial sructure (Fig. 5). To cope with these rapid changes, several measures have been introduced. For example, multipurpose reservoirs, hydroelectric dams, saline barriers, and river improvement works have been constructed. (Figure 6 shows the increase in hydroelectric capacity.)

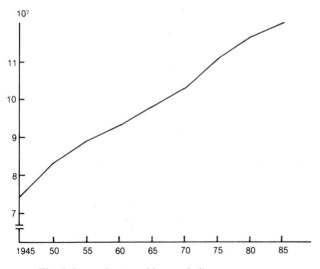

Fig. 1. Increasing trend in population

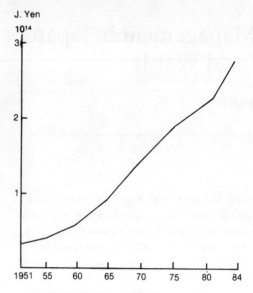

Fig. 2. Increasing trend in Gross National Product

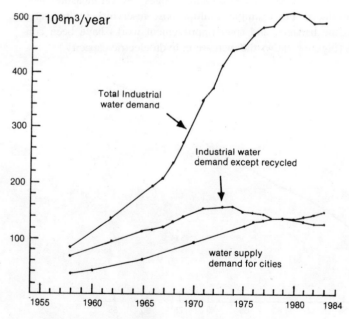

Fig. 3. Increasing trend in water demand

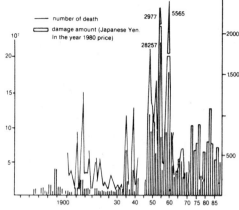

Fig. 4. Trend in flood damage

Though Japan always progressed rapidly on the economic and industrial fronts in this period of nearly half a century, the actual conditions have changed gradually. The period of 45 years after the War may be divided into three categories based on socio-economic and related hydrological considerations: (a) the severe flood damage period from 1945 to 1959; (b) the so-called water shortage period from 1960 to 1973; and (c) the period after 1974 emphasizing the environment and amenity.

SEVERE FLOOD DAMAGE PERIOD: 1945 to 1959

Unfortunately, severe and frequent storm-rainfalls were caused by extraordinarily strong typhoons at the end of the rainy season from June to July, further damaging the devastated land almost every year. Especially in 1953 and 1959, the flood damage was extremely tragic. The Ise-Bay Typhoon in 1959, which is often compared with the 1953 storm-surge in the Netherlands, lashed mainly the coast of the Ise-Bay, including South-Nagoyn, killing more than 5100 inhabitants.

Almost all of the important rivers in Japan have experienced breaking of levee, victimizing more than 1000 people annually. The river works focused on flood damage repair and flood control. In addition to river enlargement and improvement works, multipurpose reservoirs were built for flood control, irrigation, and hydroelectricity purposes after the enactment of the Integrated National Land Development Act in 1950 which activated comprehensive river development.

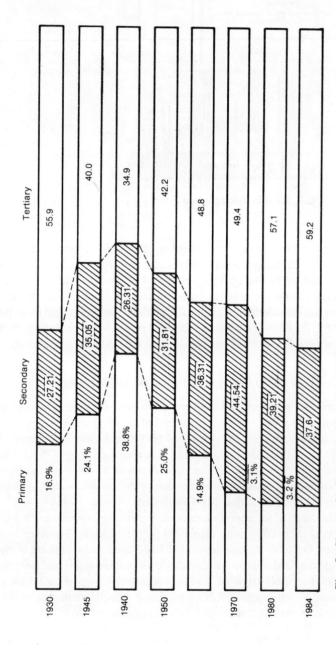

Fig. 5. Change of industrial structure since 1930

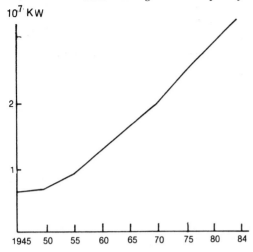

Fig. 6. Increase in hydroelectric capacity

Further, the Electric Development Promotion Act in 1953 emphasized the construction of large-scale dams for hydroelectric power development in order to recover and activate the industrial sector which had declined owing to the war.

It should be noted that the remarkable rate of modernization and economic growth since the end of the last century was influenced largely by the massive scale of flood control works. In fact, the rapid land development in this century necessitated large-scale improvement works with continuous levee systems, because the agricultural development and urbanization was concentrated in alluvial plains which are prone to inundation. Industrialization too has advanced in the same plains and the seaside regions where it is difficult to avoid natural disasters. In general, continuous levee systems have been consistently built in the middle and downstream reaches of important rivers where they flow through large alluvial plains with floodways and cutoffs in several cases, in order to protect rice fields and urbanized areas. As a result of these works, the productivity of farmland has rapidly increased, and the extent of regularly-flooded areas has markedly diminished. On the other hand, flood flows have become concentrated within the river channels between continuous levees on almost all rivers in the country, thereby intensifying peak discharges, raising the level of river stages, and increasing the velocity of flood waves. This implies that flood regime is decisively influenced by human activities, including the flood control works themselves and economic development in the basins. That is why the increase in flood discharge for the same amount of storm-rainfall has become one of the most important reasons for the successive severe flood damages.

Rapid changes in the factors affecting the condition of river basins are clearly visible in Japan, a country that achieved industrialization in a relatively short time.

WATER SHORTAGE: 1960 TO 1972

A high economic growth period marked the latter half of 1950 when a large section of the Japanese population migrated to urban areas. Though this spurt in Japan's economy was made possible because the labour population from farm and forest areas was attracted to urban and industrial areas, this led to a rapid increase in water demand in the urbanized and industrialized areas, especially in big cities such as Tokyo, Nagoya, and Osaka and the industrial zones along the Pacific coast. Heavy-chemical industries, which were the driving force of the high growth rate of the Japanese economy, needed plenty of water. Figure 3 shows the sharp increase in water demand for industries during this period.

A representative case of water shortages in important cities was the severe water deficiency experienced in Tokyo in 1964, just before the Tokyo Olympic Games. The reasons for this shortage are: low precipitation in the rainy season, rapid increase in water demand beyond the predictions, and delayed development for water resources.

Though the Water Resources Development Acceleration Act was formulated at the same time that the Water Resources Development Co-operation was established in 1961, it was not in time to tackle Tokyo's water shortage in 1964. However, since the latter half of 1960, with the acceleration in water resources development, it became possible to curtail the wide disparity between the supply of and the demand for water, except in a few cities where the population continued to expand. A number of dams were constructed from 1950 to 1970 to meet the increasing demands for municipal and industrial water supply and also for hydroelectric power. For example, the number of dams higher than 15 m, constructed between 1951 and 1978, is 304 for irrigation purposes, 222 for hydroelectric power, and 226 for multiple purposes emphasizing flood control. As a result, there are now few major rivers without dams, and their appearance at upper river reaches have changed strikingly since the 1950s.

It is also important to note the emergence of an unusual type of flood disaster in newly-urbanized areas during this period. The soaring population in large cities and their suburbs was an impetus to urban development, claiming lowland areas along the river course, marshes, and paddy fields which served as natural reservoirs during heavy storm-rainfalls. The first of this new type of flood disaster occurred during the Kanogawa Typhoon in 1958 in a newly-urbanized area in Tokyo. In the 1950s and 1960s when Tokyo's population spiralled, housing became an urgent problem and residential areas could not control extension of their boundaries to low land or near river courses, where the land was vulnerable to inundation.

It must be noted that almost all urbanization emerged from vast paddy fields which acted as natural reservoirs in Asian monsoon regions, including Japan. That is, urbanization in these regions led to more reduction of the flood-retention capacity than anywhere else in the world. During the high economic growth period, which corresponded with the time of rapid urbanization, this type of flood disaster spread from large cities to the surrounding areas and local central cities where population growth lagged behind that of large cities.

Keeping pace with the recovery from devastated land and the active development on land and water resources through the high economic growth, the Gross National Product and the standard of living have risen remarkably (Fig. 2). On the other hand, people's awareness and appreciation of living standards and changing lifestyles, and their expectations from and evaluation of public works, including dam construction, river improvement works, and other related facilities have changed. In the case of dam construction, in addition to compensation cost for submerged houses, the affected people began to demand aftercare services in their new jobs and altered life. Further, the towns too demanded measures for revitalization of the region around the submerged village, because the village often showed signs of decline after the dam's completion. During the next period, a new policy for these problems was introduced.

ENVIRONMENT AND AMENITY PERIOD: 1973 TO DATE

The period commencing 1973 faced many new and hitherto unexperienced conditions, and may be labelled the period for environment and amenity. The oil crises of 1973 deeply influenced not only the Japanese economy but also the water problem.

First of all, the trend towards increasing water demands by the municipal and industrial sectors slowed down or stopped altogether after the oil crises, because the governmental policy had no option but to enforce economy of resources, not only oil but also even water. Before the oil crises, the cost of dam construction had already escalated due to the paucity of suitable dam sites and the increase in compensation costs, including the so-called 'social cost'. In other words, water became a 'precious' and 'irreplacable' resource.

The Special Measures Law concerning Upstream Area Development was enacted in 1973 to stimulate the economy of dam-site areas which are generally less attractive to settlers as compared to urban areas further downstream. The law means that the social value of water developed in the upperstream is recognized, and also tries to find a solution to the conflicting interests between the upstream and the downstream, arising from the dam construction. Several months before the oil crises in 1973, the water supply bureau of Tokyo Metropolitan Government had presented to the public a new proposal on economizing water use, as the water resources development for Tokyo had been delayed owing to the anti-dam movement, lack of funding, etc.

Stoppage or weakening of the water demand increase in large cities and industrial sectors was caused by a combination of the above-mentioned factors. To economize on water resources, several kinds of engineering methods were applied. For instance, recycled water had already been used broadly in modern industry, especially cooling water in steel and iron companies (by construction of a cooling tower). Since the 1970s recycling systems were gradually adopted by municipal authorities. For example, Shinjuku Sub-Center of Tokyo, a group of skyscraper buildings, used recycled water for toilets, etc. by introducing the combined-unit treating station. Use of treated wastewater is also adopted by a group of buildings for recovery of dried-up channel and moat, and for water in parks, etc. In some buildings with broad roofs, rainwater is collected in a reservoir constructed in an underground room.

Water pollution in urban rivers, channels, and lakes awakened public awareness to the importance of environmental issues associated with increased urbanization, especially as water pollution in large cities has intensified since the latter half of the 1950s. In Tokyo, water pollution on the River Sumida began in 1950 with the outbreak of the Korean War.

At the central government level, after the Diet for pollution control in

1970, several kinds of anti-pollution measures were adopted, such as the enactment of new laws, and financial increase in sewerage works. To counter the new type of flood disaster in urbanized areas which has been continuing since the high economic growth period, several kinds of river works are now in the planning and construction stage or have been completed in many cities, using new types of structural and non-structural measures. New structural measures, such as underground by-pass channels and underground reservoirs for flood diversion, are being introduced in many cities. Another new measure is the multipurpose reservoirs along the river course. In view of the paucity of land in cities, the reservoirs are usually used for parks, training courses for cars, residential apartments, schools, etc. These buildings in the reservoir are equipped with pilotis preparing them for flood time.

Since the latter half of 1970, citizens began to make new demands for recovering amenity and accessibility to the river. The high levees which had been constructed against floods and high tide had reduced easy access to the river and destroyed aesthetics. Now, the Sumida River in Tokyo and several other rivers have begun a new urban redevelopment project on the riverside land, called 'super embankment', to ward off disastrous floods. That is, the ground level along the river is being raised to the top level of the embankment, stretching over 50 m, where new urban development is now underway. At the same time, the environment of the river-front has been improving by the construction of revetment with a gentle slope or by planting trees and promenades on the super embankment or high river bed along the river. In other words, 'super embankment' projects are based on the needs of both flood control and amenity.

CONCLUSION

During the last 45 years, the main topics of interest in water-related sciences and technologies such as hydrology, water resources planning and management, and the like have changed with the socio-economic requirements and the engineering capabilities mentioned above. During the years 1945–59, research emphasis was on flood forecasting, levee protection, evaluation of flood damage, etc. From 1960–73, the focus was on the prediction of water demand, planning of water resources development, sedimentation in reservoirs, and strategies for preventing water shortages. In the years following 1974, the environmental topics related to water pollution, aesthetic design of the river front, ecological balance between river works, water resources development, and natural environment gained prominence.

The active period of Japanese history after the Second World War is important in the water management field in areas such as severe flood control works, urgent water resources development, and emphasis on ecological topics. Japanese engineers had to rise to each new challenge brought about by rapid development. Looking back on the period of the last half-century, it may be said that the hydrologists and water resources engineers have contributed well to the establishment of a firm and safe infrastructure. This experience, with its advantages and disadvantages, can be taken as a lesson on world water management practice, especially for the developing countries where urbanization has just started.

ACKNOWLEDGEMENT

I would like to thank Dr S. Herath for language corrections in the manuscript.

REFERENCE

Takahasi. Yutaka, 'Integrated water management in urban areas in Japan', Proceedings of International Symposium-cum-Seminar by IHP, Nagoya, 1989, pp. 1–8.

18 / Agricultural Drainage Water Reuse in Egypt

M. ABU-ZEID AND S. ABDEL-DAYEM

INTRODUCTION

Agricultural drainage water in the area south of Cairo flows back to the Nile river. In the Nile delta, drainage water is collected by an intensive network of covered and open drains which ultimately discharge into the northern lakes and the Mediterranean Sea. Extensive monitoring programmes in force since 1984 have determined the spatial and temporal variations of the quantity and salinity of drainage water in the Delta area (El-Quosy, 1990).

During the past decade, Egypt launched an ambitious programme towards achieving higher water-use efficiency to cope with the increasing water demands. The future improvement of the irrigation system, the better allocation of available water resources, and the efficient utilization of irrigation water will affect the quantity and the quality of agricultural drainage water. The introduction of this programme effected a sharp decrease in the natural flow of the River Nile (Abu-Zeid and Abdel-Dayem, 1990). The water releases from the High Aswan Dam decreased and the irrigation and drainage discharges declined proportionately. Meanwhile, the salinity of drainage water increased (Abdel-Dayem and Abu-Zeid, 1991).

Our analysis of the historical discharge and salinity data on the drainage water in the Nile Delta is an attempt to determine the trends and tendencies of their changes. Our study, which focuses on the east, the middle, and the western parts of the Delta, includes a discussion of the effect of improved water management on drainage water quantities and qualities.

TEMPORAL VARIATIONS OF DRAINAGE WATER

Seasonal Variations

The water of the main drainage system is composed mainly of on-farm drainage (surface and/or subsurface) and canal tail-water losses. The latter portion varies according to the type, length, and area served by the canal. Maximum tail-water flow usually occurs in the fall when evapotranspiration is relatively low and crops are at their mature stage. Upward seepage of saline and brackish groundwater, sea water intrusion, and industrial and domestic wastewater also reach the drainage system. The available data on drainage water provide information only on the quantity and salinity at different strategic locations within the drainage network in the Delta. There is no definite information yet on the concentration of other agricultural and industrial chemicals and biological contaminants.

A remarkable variation in the monthly flow of drainage water to the sea is apparent, particularly during the period July–October (Fig. 1). At this time, about one million acres in the Nile Delta, which are cultivated with rice, remain ponded with water over the growing season. During the same season, the rest of the Nile Delta is cultivated mainly with maize and cotton. An enormous quantity of irrigation water is used during this period to mitigate the high summer evapotranspiration and the excessive deep percolation.

The quantity of drainage water decreases in November after the summer crops are harvested. Part of the agricultural area remains fallow during November before the farmers finish preparing their lands for the winter crops. The pre-irrigation of winter crops is mainly responsible for the drainage water flow increase in December. During the rest of the winter season and spring (from January till May), the drainage water flow is generally less than in summer. It drops too low during February (Fig. 1) when the irrigation system is not operated for three weeks for maintenance. The drainage flow during February is mainly due to the subsurface flow of groundwater to the drains. A strong correlation exists between the monthly quantities of irrigation and drainage water flowing to the sea at the same period (Fig. 2).

A correlation between the irrigation and the drainage water quantities, on the lines of the relationship shown in Fig. 2, was made on a regional basis. The pairs of data used in the correlation represent periods of well-identified flow characteristics such as the peak flow period (June–October), the winter period (November–January), the spring period (March–April), and the closure period. The relationships representing the three regions of the Delta are as follows:

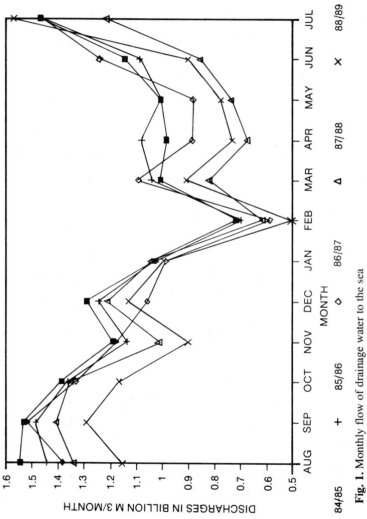

Fig. 1. Monthly flow of drainage water to the sea

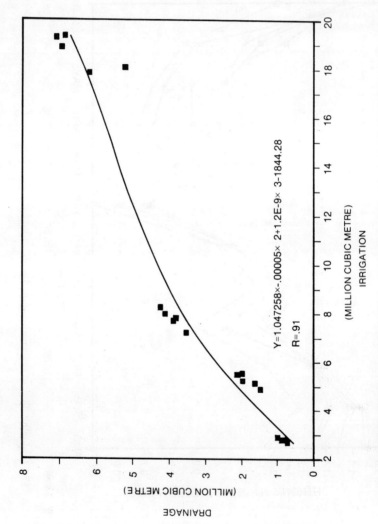

Fig. 2. Relationship between Nile inflow and drainage water outflow in the Delta

For the east: $D = 0.332\,I - 4.6 \times 10^{-6}\,I^2 - 124.6$ (1)
with $r^2 = 0.82$

For the middle: $D = 0.699\,I - 4.3 \times 10^{-5}\,I^2 - 322.9$ (2)
with $r^2 = 0.96$

For the west: $D = 0.933\,I - 8.4 \times 10^{-5}\,I^2 - 589.5$ (3)
with $r^2 = 0.95$

where D is the drainage water flow in a given season in million m^3, I the total water used in the same period in million m^3, and r^2 the correlation coefficient. Poor correlation was obtained when similar relationships were examined on a monthly basis, apparently due to time lag between the periods of drainage and the irrigation. The foregoing three equations may be used in predicting the drainage outflow during a period similar to those considered in their derivation. They are site-specific and represent the physical characteristics of each region.

The monthly variations in the quantity of drainage water reused in irrigation follow the same distribution pattern as the drainage water to the sea. More drainage water is reused during the summer season; however, its average salinity is rather uniform and often less than 1.5 mmhos/cm (975 ppm). Very limited quantities of drainage water of higher salinities (1.5–2.0 mmhos/cm) are used in February.

The high variability characterizing the salinity of drainage water over the area of the Nile Delta is generally related to the quantity (Fig. 3). The salinity of drainage water during the period July–October is the lowest over the year. It is influenced by the low salinity of the drainage water from the rice fields (Abdel-Dayem and Ritzema, 1987). The weighted average of the subsurface drainage water salinity during this period varies between 3 mmhos/cm and 4 mmhos/cm. The drainage water salinity generally increases in winter and becomes very high in February during the closure period of the irrigation system.

Annual Variation

The total drainage water flowing annually to the sea since 1984–85 is shown in Fig. 4. In general, the quantity of drainage water diminished with time: from a total of 14.3 billion m^3/year in 1984–85 it dropped to 12.0 billion m^3/year in 1988–89. A noticeable drop in the annual flow occurred in 1987–88 when the total flow out of the Delta to the sea decreased by about 1.3 billion cu m as compared with the preceding year. This decrease may be attributed to the tight control on water diver-

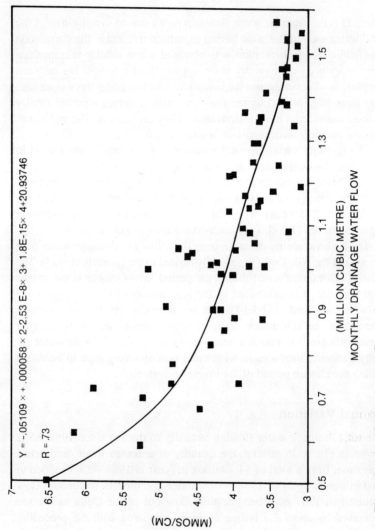

Fig. 3. Salinity of drainage water flow to the sea

sion and distribution imposed by the government to tackle the shortage in the Nile flow due to continuous drought conditions in the upper Nile basin. In the same year, the Nile water diverted to the Delta was less than the previous year's flow by about 1.6 billion cu m (Abdel-Dayem and Abu-Zeid, 1991).

Indications for improved irrigation water use are not limited to the decrease in irrigation water supply but realized at the same time by the increase in the area of agricultural lands. The cultivated area in Egypt has extended from 6.1 million acres in 1980 to 7.2 billion acres in 1990 (Biswas, 1991). This implies a more efficient water use per unit area. The effect of this improvement on drainage water was a decrease in the drain outflows and increase in their salinities. The overall weighted average of the salinity increased to 4.2 mmhos/cm in 1988–89 as against 3.71 mmhos/cm in 1984–85.

The drainage water reused annually in irrigation has diminished during the last two years by about 10 per cent. It is worthwhile to note that this decrease accompanied the decline of Nile water flow during the same period. This is strong evidence of the increase in water-use efficiency as the decrease in the Nile water has not been compensated for by a similar quantity of drainage water. The salinity of the reused drainage water has slightly increased but still remained within the 1.5 mmhos/cm limit.

SPATIAL VARIATION OF DRAINAGE WATER

Drainage Water to the Sea

The quantities of drainage water flowing to the sea from the three regions of the Nile Delta are approximately the same (Fig. 4). In 1988–89, the annual drainage discharge to the sea from the eastern, middle, and western regions were 4066, 4092, and 3868 million m^3 per year, respectively. The drainage water per unit cropped area for the three regions was 2129, 2930, and 2830 m^3 per year per acre, based on the agricultural land survey area of 1988 (EPSA, 1988). The corresponding total irrigation water used in the three regions during the same year (Nile water, reused drainage water, and groundwater) were 7016, 8240, and 8674 cu m/year/acre, respectively. Thus, the drainage water as fractions of the irrigation supplies were 0.30, 0.36, and 0.33, respectively.

The foregoing analysis implies that the unit area of land in the eastern region receives less irrigation water and produces less drainage water.

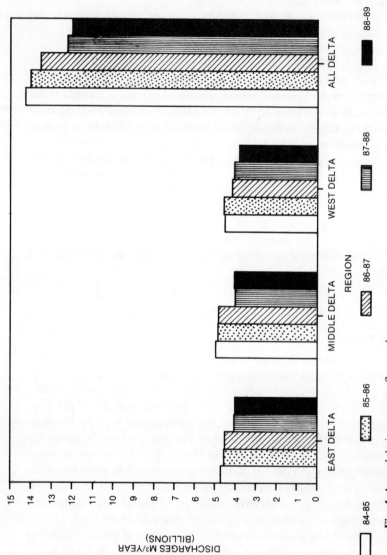

Fig. 4. Annual drainage water flow to the sea

Meanwhile, the drainage/irrigation ratio in this area is the lowest among the three regions. The central part of the Delta, on the other hand, produces the highest drainage rate per unit area and the highest drainage/irrigation ratio. The ratio being higher in the middle Delta (although the irrigation gift is not the highest) suggests that the high drainage rate in this area may be related to lower irrigation efficiency, higher drainable porosity, or excessive seepage water to the area. Of these three possibilities, the last sounds the most acceptable as the irrigation system in the middle region is as efficient as in the rest of the Delta. Meanwhile, the heavy soils of the middle region are not expected to have significantly higher drainable porosity than the soils in the east and the west. On the other hand, a significant part of the central area is subject to upward seepage from the deep aquifer (Farid *et al.*, 1979).

The average salinity of drainage water flowing to the sea is low in the east and highest in the west. In 1988–89, the average salinities of drainage water in the eastern, middle, and western parts of the Delta were 2.85, 3.95, and 6.09 mmhos/cm. This implies a higher potential for drainage water reuse in the east, from a salinity point of view. The variability of drainage water salinity is higher in the west. A correlation between the quantity and salinity of drainage water in each region produced a third degree parabolic relationship with correlation coefficients of 0.59, 0.72, and 0.4, respectively. The high variability in drainage water salinity in the east and the west of the Nile Delta can be attributed to the kind of soils, crops, topography, and land development, and the extent of pollution. These factors are more uniform in the middle region than in the east and the west.

Reused Drainage Water

The quantity of drainage water annually reused for irrigation in the east is always more than in the middle and the west (Fig. 5). In 1988–89, 1424 million m³ were reused in the east, 674 million m³ in the middle, and 536 million m³ in the west. Their salinities were 1.52, 1.44, and 1.63 mmhos/cm, respectively. The more water reused in the east is justified by the lower salinity of the drainage water available in this region. This also may explain the increase in water reused in the east while the middle and western parts of the Delta registered a decrease.

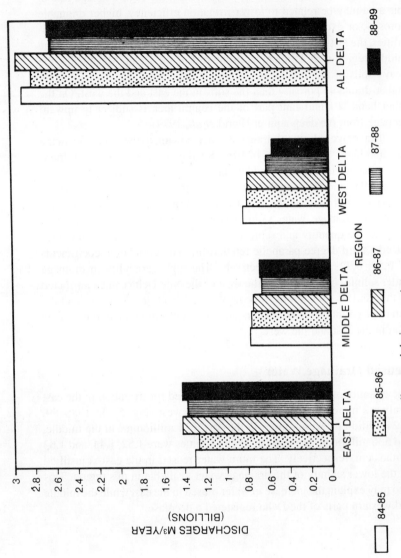

Fig. 5. Quantity of annually reused drainage water

FUTURE TRENDS AND IMPLICATIONS

The objectives of the current water policies in Egypt are to improve irrigation efficiency and maximize the use of the available water resources. The improvement in the irrigation system efficiency and on-farm water management is expected to yield less drainage water. The decrease in drainage water quantity will eventually increase its salinity (Fig. 2). The improvement will, however, take place over a relatively long time during which drainage water will continue to be an important water resource. Furthermore, under heavily increasing demand for irrigation water, it may be necessary in the future to consider using drainage water of higher salinities under controlled management conditions.

The pollution of drainage water by agricultural chemicals, industrial wastes, and sewage water would seriously limit the availability of drainage water for reuse. The extent of pollution and the levels of contamination from each source, with their temporal and spatial variations, should be determined. The existing monitoring network should be extended to measure the chemical and biological pollutants in the drainage water. Effective action plans should be implemented to control the disposal of waste materials and minimize the pollution of drainage water.

The prediction of future changes in drainage water quantity and quality is quite a complicated process. A regional water distribution and management simulation model (Amer and de Ridder, 1990), which is still at the calibration and verification stage, will be used for this purpose. For quick and approximate estimate, the relationships outlined above may be used.

CONCLUSION

The variations in drainage water outflow is strongly related to the changes in the water inflow to the Delta. Drainage water flow is therefore too high during the summer season when rice is grown. Less drainage flow occurs during the winter. The salinity of the drainage water is inversely proportional to the quantity of flow. Influenced by the tight control on irrigation supply and distribution, the annual drainage flow to the sea decreased since 1984, registering a sharp drop in 1987–88. The total annual flow measured in 1988–89 was 12.0 billion m³ year.

Although drainage water per unit area in the eastern region is less than in the middle and the west, it is of better quality from the salinity point of view. Thus, more drainage water is reused in the east. However, the total quantity reused in the Delta has decreased slightly during the last two years. The total quantity of drainage water reused in 1988–89 was 2.6 billion cu m/year.

With further improvement in irrigation and water management, the drainage water quantity will continue to decrease while its salinity increases. Pollution of the drainage water by agricultural, industrial, and domestic wastes is a serious threat to its quality and potential use. A prediction of changes in drainage water quantity and salinity is not easy due to the complexity of the system; however, rough estimates can be made on the basis of the drainage/irrigation relationships determined in this chapter.

REFERENCES

Abdel-Dayem, S. and Abu-Zeid, M. 1991. *Salt Load in Irrigation and Drainage Water in the Nile Delta.* African Regional Symposium on Techniques for Environmentally Sound Water Resources Development, Alexandria.

Abdel-Dayem, S. and Ritzema. 1987. *Subsurface Drainage Rates and Salt Leaching in Irrigated Fields.* Proceedings of the 3rd International Workshop on Land Drainage, Columbus, Ohio.

Abu-Zeid,. M. and Abdel-Dayem, S. 1990. *The Nile, the Aswan High Dam and the 1979–88 Drought.* Transaction of the 14th ICID Congress, vol. I-C, Q43, R26, Rio de Janeiro.

Amer, M. H. and de Ridder, N. A. (eds). 1990. *Land Drainage in Egypt.* Drainage Research Institute/International Institute for Land Reclamation and Improvement, Cairo.

Biswas, A. 1991. *Land and Water Management for Sustainable Agricultural Development in Egypt: Opportunities and Constraints.* Report submitted to FAO, Project TCP/EGY/0052, Rome.

El Quosy, D. 1990. *Spatial and Temporal Variability of Drainage Rates in the Nile Delta.* Symposium on Land Drainage for Salinity Control in Arid and Semi-Arid Regions, vol. 3, Cairo.

EPSA. 1988. *National Project for Agricultural Land Survey.* Egyptain Public Authority for Survey (EPSA), Ministry of Public Works and Water Resources, Egypt.

Farid, M. S., Hefny, K., and Amer, A. 1979. *Hydrological Aspects of the Nile Delta Aquifer.* Water Resources Planning in Egypt, Proceedings of International Conference, Cairo.

19 / Potential Effect of Global Warming on Evapotranspiration in Egypt

M. R. SEMAIKA AND M. A. RADY

INTRODUCTION

Water, which is an essential ingredient of life, offers many conveniences. So much so that fresh water, not oil, is becoming the most dominant resource issue worldwide. Of the many factors contributing to the consumption of water, a major influence is environmental temperature.

Since the Villach Conference in Austria in 1985, atmospheric models suggest that our planet faces unprecedented changes in its climatic regimes (M. K. Tolba, 1989). Global warming is expected to increase the intensity of the global hydrological cycle (Mitchell, 1989). Precipitation and temperature patterns, soil moisture requirements, and the physical structure of the vegetative canopy play important roles in the hydrologic system. Changes in these phenomena, because of CO_2, have the potential to affect the quantity, quality, timing, and spatial distribution of water demand and water supply, and thereby to threaten an upheaval not over several millennia, but in the time span of the next two generations.

In Egypt, the Water Distribution and Irrigation Systems Research Institute, Water Research Center, is responsible for the different activities related to the distribution and effective use of irrigation water. The Institute planned an in-depth study of expected potential effects of the global climate change, particularly the increase in crop evapotranspiration. The current investigation attempts to predict the expected increase in the evapotranspiration of some of the major crops cultivated in Egypt in different areas, using reference crop evapotranspiration estimated by the Hargreaves and Samani climatic equation, and to suggest alternative solutions to this problem.

METHODOLOGY

Two locations were selected to represent the significant differences in climatic changes for middle and lower Egypt, namely, the areas encompassing Giza and Kom Ombo. Reference crop evapotranspiration was estimated for both areas, using the Hargreaves-Samani equation (Hargreaves and Samani, 1985) and an average of ten years climatic data as an input for each area. The equation may be stated as follows:

$$ET_0 = 0.0023 \text{ Ra TD}^{0.5} (T + 17.8)$$

where
ET_o is the reference crop evapotranspiration;
RA, the extraterrestrial solar radiation, $cal/cm^2/day$;
TD, the mean maximum minus mean minimum temperature (in °C);
T, the mean air temperature over the month considered (in °C); and
0.0023, the Hargreaves–Samani coefficient.

This equation was calibrated under Egyptian conditions for the Giza and Kom Ombo areas (Semaika and Molden, 1988). The coefficients of the calibrated equations were

0.00350, the Semaika–Molden coefficient for the Giza location
0.00346, the Semaika–Molden coefficient for the Kom Ombo location

In the study reported by Semaika and Molden (1988), the calibrated equations were found to be the most consistent of 20 well-known equations for estimating the reference crop evapotranspiration in both the Giza and Kom Ombo areas. The assumed increase in air temperature was used as an expected effect due to global warming, T+2, T+5, and T+7 °C, where T is the average of ten-year climatic data for each area.

The crop coefficient of the different crops—wheat, field beans, cotton, and corn—for the Giza and Kom Ombo areas and for the Hargreaves–Samani equation (Semaika and Rady, 1987 and Semaika and Armanious, 1989) were calculated, using actual field-measured evapotranspiration. The actual evapotranspiration ET_c of the different crops was calculated for the two locations; the differences between the actual evapotranspiration at (T + 0) and (T + the assumed air temperature increase) was calculated as a percentage of the actual ET_c at T + 0 °C.

RESULTS AND DISCUSSIONS

Values of estimated reference crop evapotranspiration ET_o for Giza and Kom ombo areas, representing middle and upper Egypt, are given in Table 1. The data shows that the ET_o values increased as a result of rising temperature, reaching its maximum values for (T+7) °C. The ET_o values for Kom Ombo were higher than those for Giza due to the high T values at Kom Ombo. These results are to be expected since the Hargreaves–Samani equation uses the temperature values as the main input besides the extraterrestrial solar radiation. The highest values of ET_o were registered in June in both areas.

Actual crop evapotranspiration, ET_c, was calculated for Giza (Figs. 1–4) and for Kom Ombo (Figs. 7–10), for wheat, field beans, cotton, and corn, using the crop coefficients, K_c, for each crop and each area (Semaika and Armanious, 1989) and the ET_o for each air temperature in each area ($ET_c = K_c * ET_o$). Monthly ET_c values for each crop increased due to the increase in air temperature, reaching a maximum in March for wheat and field beans and in July for cotton and corn in both areas. In the same time, it could also be noticed that the area of increase in ET_c for these months was the greatest although the assumed average increase in air temperature was the same among the different months overall the growing season. This indicates that the most significant effect of global warming will be in the months with the maximum water requirements. Therefore planners of the irrigation water resources in Egypt should give this point serious consideration.

Figures 5 and 11 illustrate the seasonal ET_c and the seasonal ET_c increase for the different crops in both areas due to the assumed average

Table 1. Reference crop evapotranspiration (mm/day) for Giza and Kom Ombo areas estimated by calibrated Hargreaves–Samani equation for T+ the assumed average air temperature increase

Location	Jan	Feb	Mar	Apr	May	Jun	Jul	Aug	Sep	Oct	Nov	Dec
Giza												
T + 0	2.77	3.62	4.94	6.78	8.23	9.05	8.51	7.92	6.76	5.31	3.64	2.74
T + 2	2.99	3.89	5.27	7.20	8.68	9.51	8.94	8.32	7.12	5.61	3.87	2.94
T + 5	3.31	4.30	5.77	7.82	9.37	10.19	9.58	8.92	7.65	6.06	4.22	3.24
T + 7	3.53	4.58	6.10	8.24	9.82	10.65	10.00	9.31	8.00	6.36	4.45	3.44
Kom Ombo												
T + 0	3.66	4.63	6.23	8.16	9.51	10.16	9.74	9.49	8.16	6.73	4.84	3.68
T + 2	3.94	4.96	6.63	8.61	9.99	10.64	10.20	9.94	8.57	7.08	5.13	3.94
T + 5	4.36	5.46	7.22	9.28	10.70	11.36	10.89	10.61	9.17	7.62	5.58	4.33
T + 7	4.64	5.80	7.62	9.73	11.17	11.84	11.35	11.05	9.57	7.97	5.88	4.60

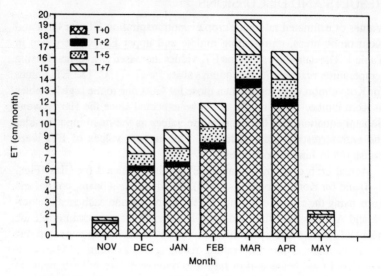

Fig. 1. Expected evapotranspiration of wheat due to temperature increase in Giza area

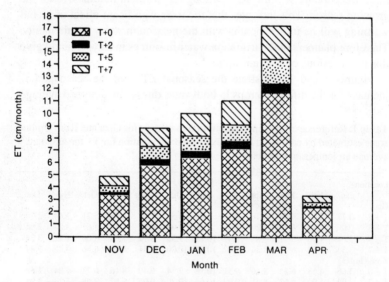

Fig. 2. Expected evapotranspiration of field beans due to temperature increase in Giza area

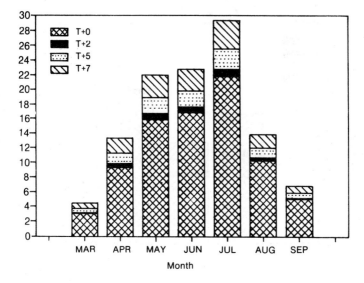

Fig. 3. Expected evapotranspiration of cotton due to temperature increase in Giza area

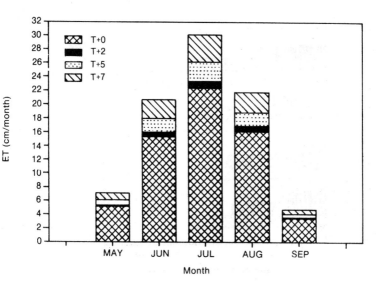

Fig. 4. Expected evapotranspiration of corn due to temperature increase in Giza area

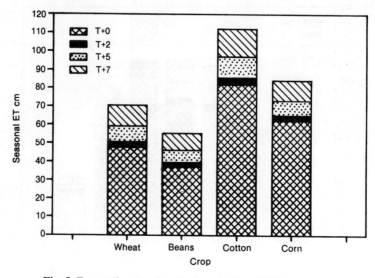

Fig. 5. Expected seasonal evapotranspiration of different crops due to temperature increase in Giza area

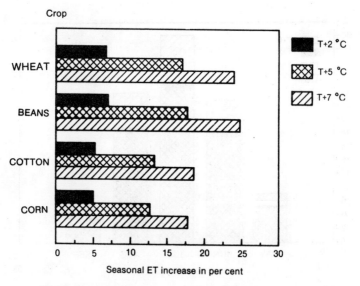

Fig. 6. Expected increase in seasonal ET of some crops for Giza area due to global warming

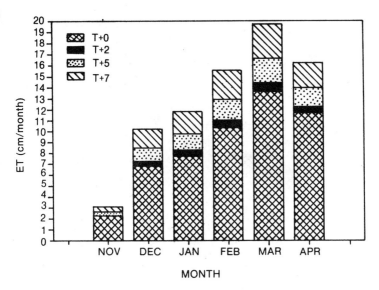

Fig. 7. Expected evapotranspiration of wheat due to temperature increase for Kom Ombo area

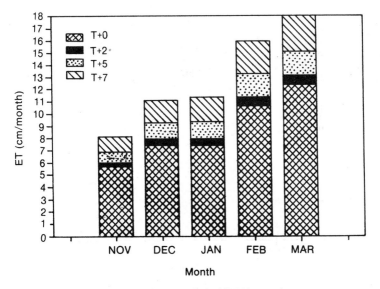

Fig. 8. Expected evapotranspiration of field beans due to temperature increase for Kom Ombo area

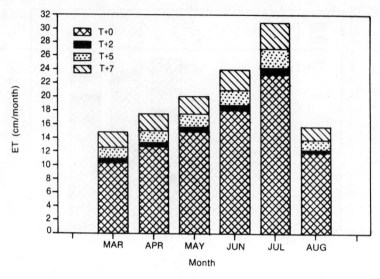

Fig. 9. Expected evapotranspiration of cotton due to temperature increase for Kom Ombo area

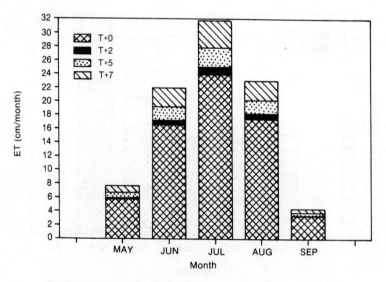

Fig. 10. Expected evapotranspiration of corn due to temperature increase for Kom Ombo area

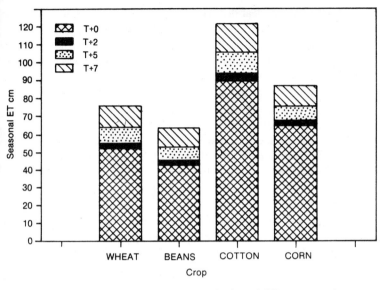

Fig. 11. Expected seasonal evapotranspiration of different crops due to temperature increase in Kom Ombo area

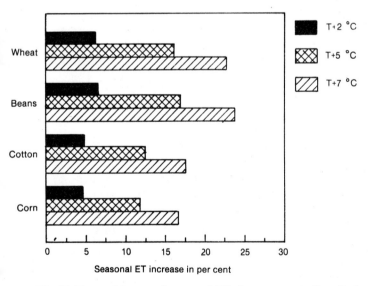

Fig. 12. Expected increase in seasonal ET of some crops in Kom Ombo area (due to global warming)

air temperature. It is clear that the greatest increase in seasonal ET_c is for cotton since it has the longest summer growth season, whereas field beans register the smallest increase in ET_c as they have the shortest winter growth season. The increase in ET_c for field beans was the highest in both areas, whereas corn showed the lowest increase, indicating that the warming effect has the most significant influence on winter crops. Further, the impact is greater in Giza than in Kom Ombo where the temperature is higher.

The increase in the ET_c values ranged from 4.8 per cent to 24.9 per cent. These values indicate the effect of global warming on the demand for irrigation water resources which may create planning problems with the limited irrigation water resources of Egypt.

Figures 6 and 12 summarize these effects for the different air temperature increases on the seasonal ET_c for the different crops. The data illustrate the greater effect on the cooler short growth seasons, especially in the area of low air temperature (Giza). At least about 0.7 milliard m³ of irrigation water would be needed to overcome the increase in ET_c for

Table 2. Predicted increase in ET_c expressed as percentage of differences between the seasonal actual crop evapotranspiration for (T + O) and (T + the assumed air temperature) for Giza and Kom Ombo areas

Temperature	Seasonal evapotranspiration (cm)			
	wheat	field beans	cotton	corn
Giza				
T + 0 °C	47.78	37.26	81.88	62.34
Increase %	00.00	00.00	00.00	00.00
T + 2 °C	51.07	39.91	86.25	65.51
Increase %	6.88	7.11	5.33	5.09
T + 5 °C	56.00	43.88	92.80	70.27
Increase %	17.20	17.77	13.33	12.72
T + 7 °C	59.29	46.53	97.16	73.44
Increase %	24.08	24.87	18.67	17.81
Kom Ombo				
T + 0 °C	52.47	43.62	90.74	66.67
Increase %	00.00	00.00	00.00	00.00
T + 2 °C	55.94	46.62	95.33	69.84
Increase %	6.62	6.88	5.06	4.75
T + 5 °C	61.15	51.13	102.22	74.59
Increase %	16.55	17.21	12.66	11.88
T + 7 °C	64.63	54.13	106.82	77.76
Increase %	23.17	24.09	17.72	16.63

the current cultivated areas of wheat, field beans, cotton, and corn crops in Egypt if the temperature increases by 2 °C; and as much as 2.64 milliard m³ of irrigation water would be required if the temperature increases by 7 °C due to any global warming. These values will be greater if we consider that the overall irrigation efficiency may be decreased under these conditions.

Unless irrigation and crop management planning take these results into consideration Egypt will face a serious problem of insufficient crop production in the event of global warming.

HOW TO OVERCOME THE PROBLEM

We propose the following guidelines for possible implementation by planners under the Egyptian conditions:

— Agronomists should work towards raising different crop varieties of shorter growing season. They should also work towards producing short varieties of different crops.
— The use of anti-evaporation and anti-transpirant chemicals to reduce water losses from plant surfaces and/or from the soil surface, especially during the late growth season, should be considered. Researchers working in this field obtained different results (Bowers and Hanks, 1961; Slatyer and Bierhuizen, 1964; Gerad and Chambers, 1967; Davenport *et al.*, 1972; Fuehring, 1973; Guhathakurta, 1973; De Boodt, 1974; Hillel and Berliner, 1974; Davis and Kosolowiski, 1975; Kreith *et al.*, 1975; Anter and De Boodt, 1976; Semaika and Metwally, 1983). Some people objected to the application of these materials either because of their toxicity or their retardant effect on plant growth. But one cannot discount their efficacy under conditions of global warming.
— The possibility of harvesting some crops before complete maturity for air drying should be considered.
— Consideration should be given to the possibility of shifting the time of planting of different crops in certain areas to the cooler months to reduce evapotranspiration in order to match, as much as possible, with the original ones at (T+0), where $ET_{c(t)}$ = constant × $T_{(t)'}$, since $ET_{c(t)} = K_{c(t)} ET_{o(t)} = K_{c(t)} 0.0023 \, Ra \, TD^{0.5} (T + 17.8)_{(t)}$, as (t) is a specific air temperature and Ra is dependent on the latitude and the time of the year only.

In this regard, we tried different scenarios (Tables 3 and 4), shifting the

Table 3. Different scenarios proposed to overcome the increase in evapotranspiration of wheat, field beans, cotton, and corn due to global warming

Wheat crop

Temperature	Oct	Nov	Dec	Jan	Feb	Mar	Apr	May	days	ET cm before	ET cm after
T + 0	-	7	31	31	28	31	30	5	163	47.78	47.78
T + 2	-	22	31	31	28	31	20	-	163	51.07	47.69
T + 5	12	30	31	31	28	31	-	-	163	56.00	47.93
T + 7	24	30	31	31	28	19	-	-	163	59.29	47.89

Field beans crop

Temperature	Oct	Nov	Dec	Jan	Feb	Mar	Apr	days	ET cm before	ET cm after
T + 0	-	20	31	31	28	31	10	151	37.26	37.26
T + 2	13	30	31	31	28	18	-	151	39.91	37.31
T + 5	31	30	31	31	28	-	-	151	43.88	38.10
T + 7	31	30	31	31	28	-	-	151	46.53	40.35

Cotton crop

Temperature	Jan	Feb	Mar	Apr	May	Jun	Jul	Aug	Sep	Oct	Nov	days	ET cm before	ET cm after
T + 0	-	-	16	30	31	30	31	31	20	-	-	189	81.88	81.88
T + 2	-	20	31	30	31	30	31	16	-	-	-	189	86.25	81.82
	-	-	-	-	25	30	31	31	30	31	11	189	86.25	80.54
T + 5	12	28	31	30	31	30	27	-	-	-	-	189	92.80	81.97
	-	-	-	-	14	30	31	31	30	31	22	189	92.80	81.86
T + 7	15	28	31	30	31	30	24	-	-	-	-	189	97.16	81.91
	-	-	-	-	6	30	31	31	30	31	30	189	97.16	82.02

Corn crop

Temperature	Mar	Apr	May	Jun	Jul	Aug	Sep	Oct	days	ET cm before	ET cm after
T + 0	-	-	16	30	31	31	12	-	120	62.34	62.34
T + 2	-	9	31	30	31	19	-	-	120	65.51	62.88
	-	-	-	22	31	31	30	6	120	65.51	62.76
T + 5	-	26	31	30	31	2	-	-	120	70.27	62.74
	-	-	-	8	31	31	30	20	120	70.27	62.90
T + 7	3	30	31	30	26	-	-	-	120	73.44	62.20
	-	-	-	-	30	31	30	29	120	73.44	62.55

Table 4. Different scenarios proposed to overcome the increase in evapotranspiration of wheat, field beans, cotton, and corn as an effect to increase in air temperature due to global warming by shifting time of planting in Kom Ombo area

Wheat crop

Temperature	Month								Season		
	Sep	Oct	Nov	Dec	Jan	Feb	Mar	Apr	days	ET cm before	ET cm after
T + 0	-	-	10	31	31	28	31	30	161	52.47	52.47
T + 2	-	-	30	31	31	28	31	10	161	55.94	52.38
T + 5	-	31	30	31	31	28	10	-	161	61.15	52.94
T + 7	18	31	30	31	31	20	-	-	161	64.63	54.69

Field beans crop

Temperature	Month							Season		
	Sep	Oct	Nov	Dec	Jan	Feb	Mar	days	ET cm before	ET cm after
T + 0	-	-	30	31	31	28	31	151	43.62	43.62
T + 2	-	20	30	31	31	28	11	151	46.62	43.68
T + 5	24	31	30	31	31	4	-	151	51.13	43.91
T + 7	28	31	30	31	31	-	-	151	54.13	45.87

Cotton crop

Temperature	Month											Season		
	Jan	Feb	Mar	Apr	May	Jun	Jul	Aug	Sep	Oct	Nov	days	ET cm before	ET cm after
T + 0	-	-	31	30	31	30	31	31	-	-	-	184	90.74	90.74
T + 2	3	28	31	30	31	30	31	-	-	-	-	184	95.33	90.99
	-	-	-	4	31	30	31	31	30	27	-	184	95.33	90.87
T + 5	15	28	31	30	31	30	19	-	-	-	-	184	102.22	90.57
	-	-	-	-	13	30	31	31	30	31	18	184	102.22	90.79
T + 7	22	28	31	30	31	30	12	-	-	-	-	184	106.82	90.50
	-	-	-	-	1	30	31	31	30	31	30	184	106.82	90.81

Corn crop

Temperature	Month								Season		
	Mar	Apr	May	Jun	Jul	Aug	Sep	Oct	days	ET cm before	ET cm after
T + 0	-	-	15	30	31	31	12	-	119	66.67	66.67
T + 2	-	15	31	30	31	12	-	-	119	69.84	66.84
	-	-	-	26	31	31	30	1	119	69.84	66.89
T + 5	-	30	31	30	28	-	-	-	119	74.59	66.93
	-	-	-	13	31	31	30	14	119	74.59	66.71
T + 7	5	30	31	30	23	-	-	-	119	77.76	66.89
	-	-	-	6	31	31	30	21	119	77.76	66.91

time of planting wheat, field beans, cotton, and corn in both Giza and Kom Ombo areas to the cooler months and calculating the evapotranspiration of these crops to offset the expected evapotranspiration increase. These scenarios showed a large potential for overcoming the global warming problem; but there is concern about the feasibility from the standpoint of the different environmental requirements for each plant.

CONCLUSION

In order to study the effect of any expected global warming on the evapotranspiration of some crops in two different locations in Egypt, we used:

1. Calibrated Hargreaves-Samani equation to estimate ET_0 for two important locations in Egypt which have the most significant differences in climate; and
2. Average of ten-year climatic data, assuming an average increase in air temperature by 2 °C, 5 °C, and 7 °C.

The actual evapotranspiration, ET_c, for wheat, field beans, cotton, and corn was calculated, using the crop coefficient K_c for each crop under each area and the values of ET_0 for each air temperature.

Data showed a significant increase in ET_c for the different crops and the different locations due to any expected global warming. The maximum increase occurred at the months registering the maximum water consumption although the assumed increase in the average air temperature was constant all through the months of the growth seasons. The maximum increase in the seasonal ET_c was for the cotton crop since it has the longest summer growth season while the beans have the minimum as it has the shortest winter crop. The minimum ET_c increase per cent was for the shortest summer corn crop, while the maximum was for the shortest winter field beans crop, which indicates that the warming will have its most significant increase effect on the shortest winter crops. The percentage increase in ET_c of the different crops in the Giza area was greater than that for Kom Ombo where the temperature is higher. The values of ET_c increase ranged between 4.75 per cent for corn at Kom Ombo by increasing the temperature by 2 °C, and 24.87 per cent for field beans in the Giza area by increasing the temperature by 7 °C. This will no doubt affect the plans for distribution of the limited water resources in Egypt.

Different solutions are suggested for overcoming the problem; for instance, producing short growth season and short varieties, using anti-evapotranspiration chemicals and harvesting the crops before complete maturity. Another proposal envisages different scenarios for shifting the time of planting of the different crops to offset the increase in ET_c.

Water resources planners and agronomists should work diligently to select the most suitable solutions to this critical problem threatening Egypt's water resources. Conducting different experiments under controlled climatic conditions in greenhouses may produce positive results. Also, studies should take into consideration climatic factors other than temperature that significantly affect the evapotranspiration processes of the different crops, for instance, relative humidity and wind velocity as well as the interaction between these climatic factors.

REFERENCES

Anter, F. and de Boodt, M. 1976. 'Preliminary Results on the Direct Effect of Conditioners on Plant Growth and Nutrient Uptake', Med. Fac. Landbouw, Rijks Univ. Gent. 41–1. 287–291.

de Boodt, M. 1974. 'Soil Conditioning, Its Effect on Water Use and Some Physical Properties of Soils', Lecture at the Soil Lab. NRC. Cairo, Egypt, March.

Bowers, S. and Hanks, R. J. 1961. 'Effect of DDAC on Evaporation and Infiltration of Soil Moisture', *Soil Sci*, 93, 344–46.

Davenport, D. C., Fisher, M. A., and Hagan, R. M. 1972. 'Some Counteractive Effect of Antitranspirants', *Plant Physiol.* 49, 722–24.

Davis, W. J. and Kozolowiski, T. T. 1975. 'Effect of Applied Abscisic Acid and Plant Water Stresses on Transpiration of Woody Angiosperm', *Fores. Science*, 21, 2 191–95.

Fuehring, H. D. 1973. 'Effect of Antitranspirants on Yield of Grain Sorghum under Limited Irrigation', *Agro. Jou.* 65, 348–51.

Gerad, C. and Chambers, G. 1967. 'Effects of Relative Coatings on Soil Temperatures, Soil Moisture and Establishment of Fall Bell Peppers', *Agro. Jou.* 59, 4 293–96.

Guhathakurta, P. 1973. 'Effect of Antitranspirant Phenyl Mercuric Acetate on Some Conifer Seedlings'. A preliminary study, *Indian Forester*, 99, 8, 499–504.

Hargreaves, G. H. and Z. A. Samani. 1985. 'Reference Crop Evapotranspiration from Temperature'. Applied Engineering in Agriculture, Am. Soc. of Agr. Engr. vol. 2, November.

Hillel, D. and Berliner, P. 1974. 'Water Proofing Surface Zone Soil Aggregates for Water Conservation', *Soil Sci.*, 118, 2, 131–35.

Kreith, F., Taori, A., and Anderson, J. E. 1975. 'Persistence of selected antitranspirants', *Water Resources Research*, 11, 2, 281–86.

Mitchell, A. 1989. 'Greenhouse and Climate change', *Review of Geophysics*, vol. 27 (1).

Mostafa, K. T. 1989. 'Climate Change and Water Management', special invited lecture, International Seminar on Climatic Fluctuations and Water Management, Meridian Hotel, Cairo, Egypt, September.

Semaika, M. R. and Molden, D. J. 1988. 'Reliable Methods for Estimating ET_0 with Minimum Climatic Data under Egyptian Conditions', Western Society of Crop Science, Colorado State University, Colorado, USA, June 13–16.

Semaika, M. R. and Shanahan, J. F. 1988a. 'A Comparison of Methods for Estimating Potential Crop Evapotranspiration in Egypt', Inter. Summer Meeting of the A.S.A.E., Rushmore Plaza Civic Center Rapid City. SD June 26–29.

Semaika, M. R. and Shanahan, J. F. 1988b. 'The Reliability of Several Methods of Estimating Reference Crop Evapotranspiration as Affected by Crop and Growing Season in Egypt', Western Society of Crop Science, Colorado State University, Colorado, USA, June 13–16.

Semaika, M. R. and Armanious, S. D. 1989. 'On the Management of Crop Coefficient when Estimating Crop Evapotranspiration', ICID, Tokyo, Japan, October 15–25.

Semaika, M. R. and Metwally, S. Y. 1983. 'Effect of some Chemicals on Evaporation and Transpiration', PhD Thesis, Soil Science Department, Faculty of Agriculture, Ain Shams University.

Slatyer, R. O. and Bierhuizen, J. E. 1964. 'The Influence of Several Transpiration Suppressants on Transpiration, Photosynthesis and Water Use Efficiency of Cotton Leaves', *Australian Jou. Bio. Sci.*, 17, 131–46.

20 / Tubewell Drainage and Regional Groundwater Planning in Egypt

K. HEFNY, FATMA ATTIA, AND ALBERT TUINHOF

INTRODUCTION

More than 2500 years ago, groundwater in Egypt was used to irrigate about one million acres of fertile land. Water was generally conducted to the lands by gravity through nearly-horizontal tunnels. In the Western desert, there are still ample signs of ancient irrigation by deep wells.

In many parts of Egypt, the use of groundwater for irrigation continued over time. In the Nile Valley and Delta (Fig. 1), groundwater was used for supplementary irrigation during the low-flow season of the Nile, whereas in the desert it has always been the only source of water. After construction of the High Aswan Dam (HAD), most farmers in the old lands abandoned their tubewells and relied on surface water alone. Recently, farmers started to dig new wells to alleviate seasonal and spatial shortages of surface water supplies.

GROUNDWATER DEVELOPMENT

Needs for Groundwater Development

Agricultural production in the Nile Valley and Delta faces two major constraints: a shortage of irrigation water, either seasonally or spatially; and waterlogging. The limited available surface water supplies are completely utilized at present. Any further expansion of lands for cultivation has therefore to depend on other water resources. Groundwater development has the potential to alleviate the present constraints in agricultural water management and to cope with the increasing water demands for domestic purposes.

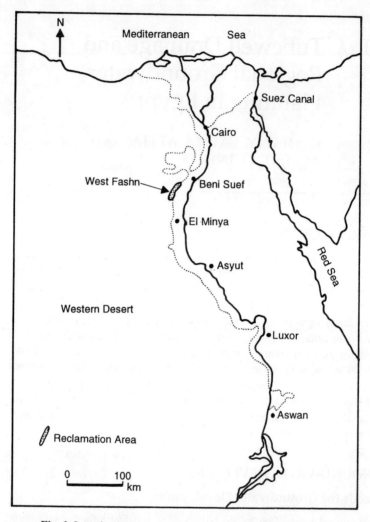

Fig. 1. Location map

Main Aquifers

The main aquifers in Egypt can be distinguished in granular rocks and fissured and karstified rocks (RIGW/IWACO, 1988).

The alluvial aquifer, which is the main water-bearing formation in the

Nile Valley and Delta, consists of Quaternary and Later Tertiary sand and gravel beds, intercalated with clay lenses. The aquifer thickness decreases from 300 m at Suhag to a few metres at Cairo, then increases northwards to about 1000 m near the Mediterranean coast. The aquifer is overlain, in about 70 per cent of the area, with clay-silt layers of thickness ranging, on an average, from 10 m (Valley) to 25 m (Delta). The main source of replenishment is the seepage from the surface water systems. The alluvial aquifer is underlaid with a thick bed of Pliocene clays which is generally regarded as the impervious base of the aquifer. Laterally, the aquifer system is bounded with carbonate rocks.

The Nubian Sandstone aquifer system is part of a regional hydrogeological system extending into Libya, Sudan, and Saudi Arabia. It constitutes the main aquifer in the Western Desert of Egypt, and extends below the alluvium in the Nile Valley and North Sinai.

The Moghra aquifer, dominating the north-western portion of the Delta, is another granular aquifer system with a regional spread. The salinity is brackish to saline in the major part of the aquifer.

Local and low productive aquifers are found along the coastal zones and in the fissured carbonate and crystalline rocks. These aquifers have hardly been explored yet.

Groundwater Potential for Development

Recent studies carried out by the Research Institute for Groundwater (RIGW) made the following observations:

1. Groundwater in the Nile Alluvium is not a resource in itself. The thick aquifer underlying the Valley and Delta may be considered a large storage reservoir, which is replenished by seepage from the surface water system. The total amount of fresh groundwater stored in the Nile Valley and south Delta amounts to 500 billion m^3 (the storage capacity of Lake Nasser is about 162 billion m^3). Of the annual replenishment of about 8 billion m^3, about 3 billion m^3/year flows back to the Nile. The groundwater quality in the Valley and south Delta is generally suitable for irrigation.

2. Groundwater in the Tertiary sediments on the fringes of the Valley and Delta is of medium potential. The sources of replenishment are either from the adjacent alluvium, or from occasional runoff from *wadis*, or from the adjacent carbonate rocks. Its quality depends on the source and amount of replenishment; the continuity of the re-

source, in terms of quantity and quality, depends on the type of irrigation. Irrigation with both groundwater and surface water (conjunctive use) is the most promising.

3. Groundwater in the Nubian Sandstone aquifer receives very little replenishment, which generally occurs outside Egypt. Its quality—fresh in the south, and becoming brackish to saline towards the north—depends on the existing hydrogeological conditions.

Groundwater Development Plans

The basic information used in the development of groundwater plans is:

1. rate and distribution of present extractions;
2. present quality of groundwater;
3. land-use and sources of irrigation;
4. aquifer characteristics and boundary conditions;
5. type and rate of recharge;
6. depth to groundwater and aquifer productivity; and
7. drainage conditions.

This data makes it possible to determine the additional amount of water that can be pumped, the total pumping head, and the expected change in groundwater quality. Priorities are decided according to econ-

Table 1. Groundwater development plan

Location		Purpose	Extractions (billion m^3/yr)		
			present	additional (planned)	total
Nile alluvium and adjacent desert fringes	Nile Valley	Tubewell drainage		65	65
		Land reclamation	50	49	99
		Conjunctive use	386		
				1210	2126
		Domestic supply	530		
	Nile Delta	Land reclamation	690	510	1200
		Conjunctive use	590		
				495	1480
		Domestic supply	395		
Remaining desert area		Land reclamation			
			675	2625	3300
		Domestic Supply			
	Total		3316	4954	8270

omic returns. Taking into account these priorities, the RIGW identified the regional geographic distribution and magnitude of future pumpage (RIGW/IWACO, 1989c). Table 1 summarizes the groundwater development plan.

TUBEWELL DRAINAGE

Previous Experience

Groundwater extraction schemes for land drainage purposes (tubewell drainage) started at the beginning of this century. In Arizona (USA), where large areas in the Salt River Valley were waterlogged 40 years ago, pump irrigation helped in eliminating most of the problem. The same situation holds in other parts of the USA, for instance, in the San Joaqin Valley (California) where hundreds of drainage wells are used for water table control and irrigation water supply.

In West Pakistan, in the Indian basin, tubewell drainage was applied to solve extensive waterlogging problems resulting from modern irrigation development. Similar experiences are reported from the USSR.

Feasibility of Tubewell Drainage

Tubewell drainage cannot be regarded merely as a substitute for tile drainage. Feasibility of tubewell drainage, which depends on the hydrogeological conditions of the area, is limited to aquifers having relatively high transmissivity (more than 5000 m²/day) and a relatively low hydraulic resistance of the top semi-confining layer (less than 1000 days).

Groundwater quality is also an important factor affecting the feasibility of tubewell drainage. Brackish or saline groundwater which cannot be used for irrigation should be disposed of from the well field area. Fresh groundwater can be used for irrigation, either alone or after being mixed with surface water, thus increasing the benefits of tubewell drainage.

The hydrogeological conditions in the major part of the Nile floodplain are conducive to tubewell drainage. A pilot area study in Minya (RIGW Iwaco, 1986; Attia and Tuinhof, 1989) showed that tubewell drainage is indeed a technically feasible option for land drainage in the Nile Valley and economically attractive to the country, especially when large capacity wells are installed.

Application of Tubewell Drainage

The major part of the Nile floodplain is already under tile drains or is planned to become so in the future. Tile drain systems are easier to operate and require less energy and skilled labour than tubewell systems. Technical constraints for tile drainage are a feature of the waterlogged area of the floodplain adjacent to reclaimed desert lands where high upward seepage is customary (Fig. 2).

In some of the waterlogged areas, open interceptor drains were constructed, intercepting 10-20 per cent of the seepage as they penetrate only the top of the aquifer. Deeper drains are difficult to construct due to the type of subsurface soil (fine sands). Hence, application of tubewell drainage has top priority in these waterlogged areas. The MPWWR re-

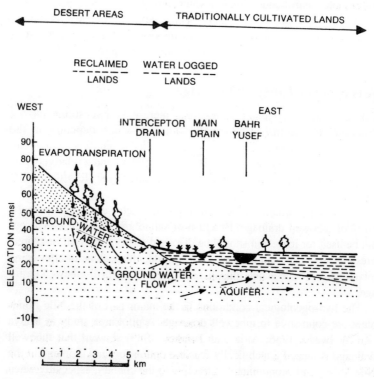

Fig. 2. Groundwater flow from reclaimed desert areas

quested the RIGW to conduct the necessary studies and designs for drainage well fields. Table 2 gives some characteristic data of three reclamation projects and adjacent waterlogged areas.

Drainage Well Fields in Nile Valley

The RIGW has designed tubewell drainage well fields in the three first areas (Table 2). The West El Fashn (RIGW/IWACO, 1989b) and West

Table 2. Characteristic data of reclaimed desert areas

Name	Reclaimed Area		Badly-drained and Waterlogged Area	
	Cultivated area (feddan)	Surface water supplied (million m^3/y)	Area (feddan)	Seepage rates (mm/day)
West of Tahta	5000	46	2000	1.3
West El Fashn	12,100	216	14,000	1.5
West Samalut	7500	176	20,000	1.5
Edfu/Kom Ombo	12,000		9500	
Esna	17,000		9500	

Note: 1 feddan=0.42 ha

Table 3. Simplified overall water balance of reclaimed desert areas

Water Balance Component	West of Tahta		West El Fashn	
	million m^3/yr	mm/day	million m^3/yr	mm/day
Inflow of surface water	46	9.0	216	8.1
Applied water for irrigation	32	6.3	156	5.8
- evapotranspiration	23	4.5	68	2.5
- sub-surface drainage	9	1.8	88	3.3
Percolation from canals	14	2.7	60	2.3
Total groundwater outflow	9+14=23		88+60=148	
Inflow to main canals/ drains	2		37	
Seepage to floodplain	21		111	
Required well field capacity	35		160	

Samalut well fields are complete and were put into operation in 1990. Studies and designs for other areas were carried out in 1990-1991.

The studies included extensive field surveys, water balance computations (Table 3), and simulation runs with a numerical groundwater flow model in order to test different alternative options and designs.

In the three studies it was found that:

1. Seepage from (unlined) canals in reclaimed sandy desert areas amounts to 30 per cent of the delivered surface water.
2. In order to maintain a groundwater depth of 1 metre in the existing waterlogged area, the well field capacity should be at least 40-50 per cent higher than the total seepage rate from the reclaimed area to the old land.
3. Tubewell drainage in waterlogged areas due to desert reclamation is economically more feasible than the lining of conveyance canals.

CONCLUSION

For groundwater development, the RIGW distinguishes three main planning regions, viz. the Nile floodplain, the desert fringes adjacent to the Nile floodplain, and the remaining desert area. In each of these regions, priorities on the type and design of groundwater systems for agriculture differ. The quota of groundwater required for domestic use is much smaller and should be incorporated with priority, particularly in areas where groundwater is the only freshwater resource.

Nile floodplain

Within the Nile floodplain the first priority is given to tubewell drainage in the existing waterlogged areas. The second priority is given to groundwater pumpage for irrigation water supply in areas with spatial or seasonal shortages.

Drainage well fields have been designed in three areas and constructed in two of them. No experience has been gained yet with the operation and maintenance of well fields. Field experiences are also needed to verify the design of well fields with respect to the applied drainage criterion (water depth of 1 metre).

Desert fringes

Groundwater development in the desert fringes should be based on the conjunctive use of groundwater and surface water in order to minimize the constraints of groundwater pumpage (increase of salinity and falling groundwater tables).

In the absence of sufficient surface water from the Nile, it is worthwhile to consider the conjunctive use of groundwater and treated sewage water from the urban areas in the Nile floodplain.

Remaining desert areas

Exploitation of the fossil groundwater reserves in the remaining desert areas should be based mainly on economic considerations and take into account the steady increase in pumping cost and deterioration in water quality with time.

REFERENCES

Attia, Fatma and Hefny, K. 1984. *Effect of Pumping Groundwater on Land Drainage*, Proc. of the Second National Conference on the Problems on Land Degradation in Egypt, Minya, Egypt. 10 pp.

Attia, Fatma and Tuinhof, A. 1989. 'Feasibility of tubewell drainage in the Nile Valley', *Land Drainage in Egypt*, Egyptian-Dutch Advisory Panel on Land Drainage in Egypt, Cairo.

RIGW/IWACO. 1986. 'Feasibility of Vertical Drainage in the Nile Valley-Minya Pilot Area', Final Report, RIGW (MPWWR), Cairo.

RIGW/IWACO. 1988. 'Hydrogeological Map of Egypt, scale 1:2,000,000, Explanatory note to the map', RIGW (MPWWR). Cairo.

RIGW/IWACO. 1989a. 'Development of Groundwater for Irrigation and Drainage in the Nile Valley—Groundwater Development in the area west of Tahta', Final Report, RIGW (MPWWR), Cairo.

RIGW/IWACO. 1989b. 'Development of Groundwater for Irrigation and Drainage in the Nile Valley—Groundwater Development in the area west of El Fashn', Final Report, RIGW (MPWWR), Cairo.

RIGW/IWACO. 1989c. 'Groundwater potential in the Nile Valley and Delta', RIGW (MPWWR), Cairo.

21 / Socio–economic Impacts of Water Development: Case Study of Mula Project

S. Y. KULKARNI

INTRODUCTION

In ancient mythology, water is equated with life. Human beings need it for sustenance, cultivators need it for agricultural production, and industries need it for running of the plants. The sustainability of agricultural production is dependent mainly on irrigation as a crucial input.

The history of irrigation in Manarashtra, the third largest state in India, goes back to the sixteenth century. This history is replete with descriptions of various irrigation and water works carried out from time to time by various emperors to meet agricultural needs. The Phad system of irrigation, which has farmers' involvement, was in use 350 years back.

India's economy has been predominantly agriculture-based and, as of today, about 65 per cent of the population is dependent on agriculture. Water resources projects have played a dominant role in the development of this agriculture and in stabilizing and making the country self-reliant in foodgrain production.

MAHARASHTRA'S WATER RESOURCES

Prior to independence, the irrigation potential of Maharashtra was about 0.27 million ha.Construction of irrigation projects—major, medium, and minor—have contributed immensely to the water needs and primarily to the agricultural needs. During various plan periods, 18 major dams, 140 medium dams, and 1365 minor irrigation schemes have been constructed, and by June 1988 an irrigation potential of 2.27 million ha had been created.

In comparison with many other states in the country, Maharashtra is poorly endowed in respect of water resources. Nearly one-third of the state is drought-prone and even the remaining part of the state has to cope with a large variation in rainfall. What is worse, some areas are plagued by drought in alternate years or even over a continuous period of two to three years.

NEED FOR AUGMENTING WATER RESOURCES

As per the Maharashtra Irrigation Commission Report, 1962, the total water resources of the state are 11.1 million km^3, of which only 5.7 million km^3 of water can be augmented by storage and used for agriculture and drinking. It was estimated that even after full development of the available potential, only 26 per cent of the culturable area can be brought under irrigation, making it imperative that the water resources in Maharashtra be augmented.

The need for water resources development through irrigation projects is not only for agriculture but also for generating hydropower. Hence the need for the optimum development of water resources.

A CASE STUDY: THE MULA PROJECT

The river Mula rises in the Sahyadri range and flows eastwards before meeting the river Pravara, near Newasa in Maharashtra. The Mula project comprises a dam near Rahuri with canals on the left bank and right bank to provide irrigation to the drought-prone areas in the Ahmednagar district of Maharashtra. The Mula dam, completed in 1970–71, forms a reservoir with a live storage capacity of 609 hm. The canals were progressively completed a few years later. More than half the command area lies in Newasa taluka and the rest in Rahuri, Shevgaon, and Pathardi talukas. The principal isohyet in the command area is of 600 mm. The Mula Project Report, 1956, lists the average rainfall at Rahuri and Newasa as 538 mm and 574 mm, respectively, with an average of 32 and 37 rainy days, respectively. Nearly half the command area has deep soils (more than 2.5 m deep) and a quarter each medium (0.5 m–2.5 m deep) and shallow soils (less than 0.5 m deep). About 62 per cent of the land, which is flat, has less than 1 per cent slope, about 26 per cent has 1–2 per cent slope, and only 12 per cent of land has slope steeper than 2 per cent.

With an average rainfall of less than 600 mm, the command area was drought-prone until irrigation commenced. About 150 villages now benefit from the irrigation.

ECONOMIC RETURNS FROM WATER RESOURCES

At the project formulation stage, the concept of benefit-cost ratio is applied to work out the feasibility of the project. Different approaches have been presented for the benefits that have accrued from the irrigation project. In the present study, the economic rate of return (ERR) approach has been applied, and the computer model developed by Mr S. R. Daines of USA has been modified to meet the Indian conditions and has been used in carrying out a study of three irrigation projects in the state of Maharashtra: a major project, the Mula; a medium irrigation project, the Chulbund; and a minor irrigation project, the Siddhanath.

For project evaluation, agricultural data was collected by designing formats in coordination with the Agriculture University and Irrigation Department. For compiling irrigation data, the random method of sampling was used and samples extended to cover the command, influence, and control areas. Field samples included interviews with the farmers to obtain data related to the in inputs applied and the output obtained.

The status of areawise samples collected during the rapid appraisal survey of the Mula Irrigation Project is noted in Table 1. (Figures within parentheses indicate the number of samples.) The results from the survey were tabulated and the differences in arithmetic means for the sampled groups were utilized in the income, employment, health, and benefit-cost computer models.

The model was developed with 'Plan-Perfect' software. Irrigation data such as expenditure during and after execution of the project, and

Table 1 Area-wise Samples of Mula Irrigation Project

Command Farms		Influence Area Farms		Control Farms and Landless Families	
Head	(40)	Groundwater	(40)	Control farms	(40)
With well	(20)	With well	(20)	With well	(20)
W/O well	(20)	W/O well	(20)	W/O well	(20)
Mid	(40)	Lift area	(40)	Landless families	(80)
With well	(20)	With well	(20)	Command	(20)
W/O well	(20)	W/O well	(20)	Groundwater influence	(20)
Tail	(40)	Economic influence area	(40)	Economic influence area	(20)
With well	(20)	With well	(20)	Control area	(20)
W/O well	(20)	W/O well	(20)		

year-wise areas of irrigation, was compiled and overall coordination was rendered in preparation of this model. The model gives the ERR for irrigation projects after analysis of

(a) foodgrain yield and crop area increase;
(b) influence area indirect benefits;
(c) crop diversification;
(d) indirect income; and
(f) health benefits.

Considering these factors, the ERR for the Mula project worked out to 19.15 per cent which (discounting the year 1986) is about 7 per cent above the frequently-used international minimum value of 12 per cent. The contribution in ERR by benefit type, as identified, is:

		%
Health	...	0.39
Indirect/Landless	...	2.05
Influence Area	...	1.11
New Crops (Wells)	...	2.71
New Crops (Canals)	...	10.56
Foodgrains	...	2.33
Total ERR		19.15

BENEFITS

Benefits flow for the Mula command in the above analysis are divided into five groups (as defined earlier). The relative contribution of each of these benefit types to Mula's total ERR is 19.15 per cent.

Income-Irrigation Crop Diversification

The dominant benefit type is the income to command farmers resulting from the cultivation of new crops which would not be possible without irrigation. This single factor accounted for more than three-fourths of the total benefit, and for 10.56 per cent of the total 19.15 per cent ERR. The crop diversification included a variety of crops such as sugarcane, groundnut, fruits, vegetables, and fodder crops.

Protection Offered during Drought

The study of the Mula project for economic evaluation covered conditions prevailing during a good year (1988–89) and a drought year (1987–

88). The bar chart (Fig. 1) represents the difference in income per hectare planted between the command control area and the influence control area.

Command Farm Income per Hectare

Direct farm income was substantial in both bad and good years, but the difference between the two groups was much greater in a bad year. This is mainly because controlled groups farms have to make planting decisions before the rainfall year is known to be good or bad, which cannot be avoided. Irrigation farms may offer to wait for their investments in planting.

New crops grown with all irrigation confined to the command area is the second largest benefit contribution to Mula's ERR with 2.71 per cent.

Foodgrain Yield and Crop Area Influence

Improvement in foodgrain yields and increase in crop area contributed 2.33 per cent to Mula's overall ERR. This shows that with availability of assured water from irrigation projects, crop diversification takes place, resulting in a good contribution to ERR.

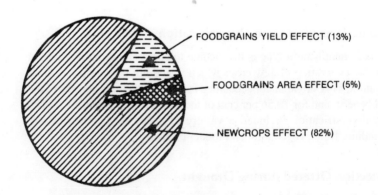

Fig. 1 Mula: Percentage of income impact by source

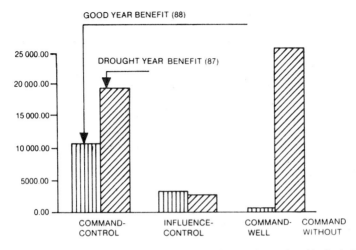

Fig. 2. Mula: Comparison of income impact in good and bad rainfall years

Influence Area Indirect Benefits

The 'Influence Areas' referred to income benefits associated with irrigation occurring to farms and families outside the command in those close areas 'influenced' by the irrigation project. The present study defined and sampled farms and families in three types of influence area:

(a) those located in the groundwater influence area where system recharge benefits well-water supply;
(b) those located in lift areas where water from canals or tanks is pumped for irrigation;
(c) those farms or landless families located in communities close to the command where irrigation facilities have created family employment opportunities in sugar factories, etc.

Thus, income benefits from the influence area contributed 1.11 per cent to Mula's overall ERR of 19.15 per cent.

Indirect Employment and Landless Family Benefits

The indirect and landless family benefits refer to income benefits from irrigation which flow from indirect (non-crop) employment of farm and landless families living inside the command. All these impacts have not

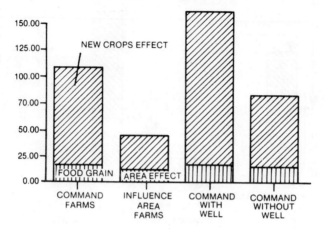

Fig. 3. Employment impact by source effect

made large contribution to the ERR of the Mula project. Their importance in an equity sense is larger, since most of the benefits flow to the unemployed and most disadvantaged groups, namely, the landless poor.

The important impact as farms in the commands is over 100 per cent days of increased labour per hectare planted. Influence area farms increased employment by roughly 40 per cent days per hectare.

Health Impact

Health impact is estimated in terms of number of workdays lost due to illness. The analysis exhibited a consistent pattern of sharply reduced illness rate after the introduction of irrigation. The reduction is by more than half, from roughly 20 days to less than 8 days, indicating a gross saving of 12 days. During the same period, the control group made a slight improvement of about 1.5 days saving. Therefore, the net saving of 10.5 days is the impact of irrigation.

Wetland Effect

The study also indicated a negative impact of proximity to water which however existed both before and after the introduction of irrigation.

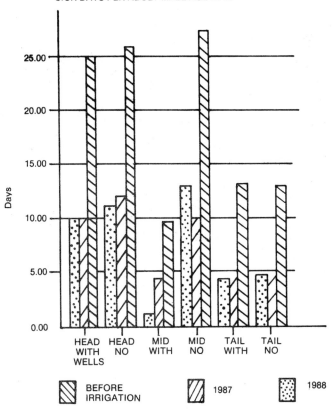

Fig. 4. Mula: Health impact on adult males

Health impact evaluation of the Mula project indicates that irrigation substantially reduced the illness and subsequently narrowed the gap between those living in the vicinity of standing water and those far away from this essential facility.

CONCLUSION

It is apparent from the case study that the Mula Project has resulted in a good Economic Rate of Return (19.15 per cent) and has also shown benefits by way of:

(a) economic impact on areas outside the command;
(b) groundwater influence impact; and
(c) improvement in health.

Thus, major dams have their place in society, serving to improve the economic status of the agricultural community. Water resources development therefore has priority in India's Five-Year Plans. No development project, whether in irrigation or industry, can be beneficial without creating some impact on the environment. Development and environment are two sides of the same coin.

ACKNOWLEDGEMENT

The author is grateful for the encouragement and guidance given by Shri S. T. Deokule, Secretary (I), Irrigation Department, G O M during the conduct of this study. The assistance rendered by Mr. S. R. Daines in the use of the computer model developed by him and its application to the irrigation project impact evaluation study in Maharashtra is also gratefully acknowledged.

REFERENCES

Daines, S. R. 1989. *Irrigation Impact Evaluation System.*
Kulkarni, S. Y. 1990. *Economic Evaluation of Irrigation Project for Environmental Impact Assessment.*

22 / State and Perspectives of Aral Sea Problem

GENADY N. GOLUBEV

BEFORE THE CATASTROPHE

The Aral Sea, the fourth largest lake in the world, surface-wise, and the second in the Soviet Union (after the Caspian Sea), is a closed lake with only two rivers. Amudarya and Syrdarya, flowing into it. A few more rivers, for instance, Zerafshan, Tedzhen, and Murgab, no longer reach Amudarya as they once did long ago. Canals branch out from the two main rivers, the largest being the huge Karakum Canal. The Aral Sea serves as the main (but not the only) collector of waters in this widespread region with a surface measure of about 2 million sq km. Approximately 70 per cent of the territory belongs to the USSR, the rest forming part of Iran and Afghanistan. The Soviet section is shared by five republics, recently the constituent parts of the USSR. As of the beginning of December 1991, four republics have proclaimed themselves as independent states.

While the population around and near the lake shores exceeds 3 million, the basin provides shelter to no less than 32 million inhabitants. Most of the population lives nearabout where the middle reaches of the rivers emerge from the mountains. It is an area of ancient civilizations with millenia of irrigation, the oldest one dating back to 6000 BC. By the middle of this century, the irrigated area in the Aral Sea basin approximated 5 million ha.

The Aral Sea is situated in an arid region with annual precipitation of about 100 mm. At the border between the plains and the mountains precipitation is between 400 mm and 500 mm and, in the mountains which form the zone of the river runoff formation it is higher—at some points exceeding 2000 mm. The total amount of precipitation in the Aral Sea region is about 500 km^3 a year. The river runoff is about 120 km^3. Of this amount, Syrdarya and Amudarya carry from the mountains approximately 110 km^3. The groundwater resources of acceptable quality which are not connected with the river runoff are assessed at 45 km^3 a year (Glazovsky, 1990).

In the historic past, oscillations of the meteorologic and hydrologic conditions in the basin were quite large and, as a result, there were pronounced changes in the state of the Aral Sea. The water level varied within 20 m, being sometimes much higher and sometimes lower than at present. The rise and the fall of the civilizations in the basin were related to the development and the decline of irrigation in the basin and, hence, also influenced the state of the lake.

A century before 1960, about half of the Amudarya and Syrdarya runoff was used for irrigation and lost for natural evapotranspiration in the middle and lower reaches of the rivers; the other half flowed into the Aral Sea, which measured 66,000 km^2 (excluding the islands). The water level was oscillating within 2–3 m. The volume of water was 1066 km^3 (Nikolaeva, 1969). The maximum depth was 69 m and the average depth, 16 m. The salinity of water was about 10 g/l. These morphometric data are commonly used now as a reference point when discussing the state of the lake.

STRATEGY FOR DEVELOPMENT

At the end of the 1950s and the beginning of the 1960s, the leadership of the USSR made a decision on an extensive development of irrigation in the Aral Sea basin. From the 1950s through the 1970s, it was believed that irrigation would resolve many of the problems besetting the country's agriculture and its social and economic spheres. The irrigated Central Asia had a prominent place in this technological fix. It was expected that the expansion of the irrigated lands would bring a drastic increase in cotton production with an upswing in the textile trend and its products; that a part of the cotton produce would be exported, bringing hard currency into the country; that the region would be the main source of fruits and vegetables for the whole country; that the production of rice and meat would go up, satisfying the demand of the region. And last, but not the least, it was expected that all those developments would provide enough jobs for the rapidly-growing population of the region.

In short, the expansion of irrigation in Central Asia should have brought a prosperity both to the region and to the country as a whole. It was clear to the water resources experts and, through them, to the rulers that one of the main side-effects would be a deterioration of the Aral Sea. But this was deemed a small sacrifice on the altar of dazzling development. Any water expert in the country knew the saying of the famous Russian climatologist A. I. Voevkov (published in 1908) that the Aral Sea is a mistake of Nature because waters collected from the mighty mountain systems go finally to a sparsely populated depression and evaporate. And the common thought was that Nature's folly could and should be corrected. Thus the technological fix has been combined with a narrow, sectoral support from science. Even if a comprehensive impact assessment of the development plans for the region had ever been made, it has never been divulged to the government or the public. Besides, the role of the latter at that time was to applaud the rulers and not to participate in the decision-making.

Since the decision on the massive development of irrigation has been made, the investments in agriculture, including irrigation, have increased drastically. For instance, in Uzbekistan, the most populated of the five republics, during the period of 1961 through 1985 the investments in agriculture were 45 billion roubles. Of this amount, at least 24 billion roubles were reserved for irrigation and related activities. With the official exchange rates prevailing at the beginning of the 1980s, these figures correspond to US $64 billion and US $34 billion. It would not be gross exaggeration to say that the investments in agriculture in the basin of the Aral Sea over the last 30 years were close to 100 billion roubles. A half of this went into irrigation, the area of irrigated lands in the Aral Sea basin increasing from 5 million ha to about 8 million ha.

HYDROLOGICAL IMPLICATIONS

The consumption of water was, and still is, excessive, basically because of the lack of interest in economizing on it. Irrigation canals are mostly unlined. The largest one is the Karakum Canal which takes about 10–12 km^3 of water a year from Amudarya River westward, running in many places through a desert. But even where the lining was planned it usually has not been made because the builders, after having dug a part of the conduit, filled it with water without putting in the lining and reported on the work as accomplished in accordance with the design. Additional pay for the advanced accomplishment of the construction quotas and diversion of the illegally-saved materials to the black market were the premiums for such corruption. More lining has, however, been put in the canals built more recently.

Efficiency of the irrigation systems is between 0.55 and 0.65 only (Glazovsky, 1990) due to the seepage from the unlined distributing canals and a predominantly furrow method of watering. Water consumption by crops exceeds the necessary one by 150–200 per cent. On an average, about 17,000–18,000 m³ of water is utilized per hectare of cotton (Oreshkin, 1990) and between 25,000–55,000 m³ per hectare of rice (Glaxovsky, 1990).

In the Amudarya and Syrdarya River basins, some water once used for irrigation returns to the river and can be reused. Even keeping this in mind, it is obvious that the development of new irrigated lands covering an area of 3 million ha would utilize all the water resources available in the Aral Sea basin by 1960. With the 17,000 m³ per hectare the water consumption by the plants would be at least 51 km³ a year. Taking an average efficiency of the irrigation systems as 0.6, we can obtain the amount of water used by new irrigated areas as 85 km³ per year. If we add some unknown, but considerable, volume lost from the main irrigation canals, we could arrive at the figure of water consumed by the new irrigation developments. Apparently, this figure is close to 100 km³ a year. For comparison, before 1960 the average amount of water flowing annually into the Aral Sea was about 56 km³.

Thus, even accounting for the repetitive use of the agricultural returned waters, no considerable inflow to the Aral Sea could be expected under the circumstances. In fact, the inflow dropped to 11 km³ by 1975 and 0 by 1980. In the 1980s, the rivers did not reach the Aral Sea every year and when they did the inflow did not exceed a few km³. As a result, the Sea has been shrinking since the beginning of the 1960s while the concentration of dissolved salts has been increasing (Oreshkin, 1990) (Table 1).

The former lake bottom is a salty desert (*solonchaks*) and serves as a source of salts dispersed by the wind. The rest of the Aral Sea is at the

Table 1. Details of the Aral Sea, 1960–90

Year	Water Level (m a.s.l.)	Area (thou. km²)	Volume (km³)	Salts Content (g/l)
1960	53.3	67.9	1090	10
1965	52.5	63.9	1030	10.5
1970	51.6	60.4	970	11.1
1975	49.4	57.2	840	13.7
1980	46.2	52.5	670	16.5
1985	42.0	44.4	470	23.5
1990	39.0	38.0	300	29.0

brink of a division into a deeper western part and a more spacious shallow eastern part. The northeastern part, called the Little Sea, is also practically separated.

Drastic changes have occurred in the hydrographic networks in the basin of the Aral Sea. A good part of the water infiltrated into the soil in the irrigation systems, and conduits appear in many newly-formed lakes and marshes situated in the desert. Sarykamysh Lake, the largest, collects the water northwest of the lower reach of Amudarya river. It has an area of 3000 km^2 and a volume of 26 km^3. The dissolved salts content of its water is at present 12–13 g/l. Another lake, Arnasai, has an expanse of 1800–2400 km^2, a volume of 12–20 km^3, and the salt content of its water is 4–13 g/l (Glazovsky, 1990). The Arnasai Lake collects water from the middle reach of the left bank of the Syrdarya river. In the irrigated areas, a new, sample network of the irrigation and drainage canals has been formed. The level of groundwater has increased drastically in many places due to the seepage. There, the salinization of soils is a nagging problem. Along the riverbeds, the groundwater level has diminished due to the drop in the river water levels. The deltas of the two principal rivers have completely changed their regime and mostly dried up. Consequently, the unique ecosystems have disappeared and many endemic species face the danger of extinction.

ENVIRONMENTAL IMPLICATIONS

Because of the agricultural returned waters, the salinity in the Syrdarya and Amudarya progressively increases downstream. In the lower reaches of Syrdarya the average salts content has increased from 0.8 g/l in 1960 to 2.8 g/l in 1985, and in Amudarya it has gone up to 1.7 g/l (Glazovsky, 1990). Hence, though the rivers are currently the main source of water supply, its quality does not meet required standards. In addition, the level of fertilizers application on the irrigated lands exceeds 10–15 times the average for the whole of the USSR, and a part of the fertilizers leaches down into the rivers. Even more, the level of pesticides application seems to be the highest in the world to the detriment of the water quality both in the rivers and the Aral Sea. In the Autonomous Republic of Karakalpakya situated along the lower reaches of Amudarya, 118,000 tonnes of pesticides, i.e. about 10 kg per person per year, have been used over the last 20 years (Oreshkin, 1990).

The hydrological consequences (hydrographic features, water resources and their quality) of the development strategy adopted 30 years ago could have been predicted. Many other effects, mostly environmental, were more difficult to foresee. An aboriginous, to a large extent endemic, fish fauna was adapted to the brackish water of the Sea because it has evolved from the freshwater species. It could survive 13 g/l but the higher salinity has killed all the fish. The fishery which provided the main occupation of the population around the lake has gone, along with the annual catch of 44 thousand tonnes of rare and valuable fish. People there have lost their main source of income.

Large changes have occurred in the environment. The direction, intensity, and composition of the salts transport have modified considerably. The expansion of irrigation has led to the increase of the salts movement, mostly with the drainage runoff. N. Glazovsky (1990) has calculated that the salts transport in the Aral Sea basin has increased about two times and is now 118 million tonnes a year. It constitutes a huge amount of three billion tonnes of salts removed within the basin during the time in question. Of this volume, 60 per cent is accumulated in the nearby ecosystems, in small new lakes and marshes, 27 per cent go to the two large new lakes, Sarykamysh and Arnasai, and 13 per cent to the Aral Sea. Moreover, the transport of sodium, chlorine, sulphate, and magnesium has increased much more than that of the other main ions such as calcium and carbonate.

Wind erosion of the former bottom of the Aral Sea has increased greatly, from 50–360 per cent in different points around the lake. The salts transport goes along with it, taking away between 1000 and 10,000 t/km^2 per annum. For the whole former lake bottom it comes to 40–150 million tonnes a year (Glazovsky, 1990).

Transport of salts with the drainage water, the wind, and the groundwater, together with the raise of the groundwater level, leads to the progressive salinization of soils. Soils with a medium or high degree of salinization occupy 35–80 per cent of the irrigated areas in Central Asia. The land losses due to water management activities there have reached 1 million ha (Rosanov, 1984).

HEALTH IMPLICATIONS OF ENVIRONMENTAL DETERIORATION

The environmental degradation, namely, unacceptable drinking water quality, high salt content of the air, and, apparently high level of the pesticides residue in the agricultural produce endanger human health in the Aral Sea basin. The worst situation arises where these hazardous factors merge into the most unfavourable combination, that is, in the lower reaches of the two rivers and around the lake.

In the lower reaches of the Syrdarya river, the morbidity has increased 20 times over the last 20 years. Infant mortality in a number of districts exceeds 110 per 1000, that is, three times more than the average for the USSR and comparable with the figures for the least developed countries. The number of cancer cases in the Autonomous Republic of Karakalpakya is seven times the all-Union level. Over 90 per cent of the population are prone to anaemia, the number being 60 times more than the average for the USSR. In the same Autonomous Republic, 46 per cent of the women have genetic disorders of different kinds, and in its capital, Nukus, the breast milk of all the 35 mothers in a sample study was found unsuitable for feeding. Clearly, the area in the environs of the lake is in a state of catastrophe, and the environment of the whole Aral Sea basin is not much better. The water level of the Aral Sea is, therefore, an indicator of the difficult socio-economic situation in the entire basin.

RESULTS OF THE IRRIGATION DEVELOPMENT STRATEGY

Nor can it be said that the pitiful state of human health and the environment is compensated for by remarkable achievements in the economy of the region. The plans to convert the whole of Central Asia into a blossoming garden have failed miserably. The region has been converted into an area for cotton monoculture. The production quotas of cotton increased steadily over the years, though the export expectations were not fulfilled, and even some cotton of good quality had to be imported to produce textiles. Though it has not yet been published, there are indications that the important user of local cotton was the military-industrial complex, producing fuel for missiles, gunpowder, and the like. As in many other regions and cases, the decades-long military orientation of the country has brought disaster to that potentially-prosperous area.

The yields and the total harvest of cotton were on the rise through the 1960s and 1970s, having increased almost twice, but from 1980 they began to decline due to the salinization of soils and the monoculture. The quality of the cotton produced is generally low.

Pesticides indiscriminately used and sprayed from the air over both the fields and the villages have adversely affected the health of the inhabitants. Revenue from the cotton plantations was not used wisely enough in the development of such social amenities as education and medical services. In addition, students were obliged to spend about two months collecting cotton at the expense of their education. Even the reforms have not changed much during the last six years.

Though the region has the highest rate of population growth in the country, no fertile lands supplied with enough water are available any more. The developing irrigation could not absorb the growing population, and unemployment is high. Tensions between the neighbouring nations intensified. In a number of places, the national boundaries drawn in the 1920s do not adequately reflect current realities, and any border change may lead to ethnic confrontation. The management of a large, multinational lake basin under these conditions would not be a simple task.

It is obvious now that the development strategy of the Aral Sea basin, which is the centre and the main part of Soviet Central Asia, adopted 30 years ago was faulty. It has led to environmental catastrophe, maybe the worst in the world. The strategy has proved to be unsustainable. The damage to the environment and the economy of the region, assessed in terms of the costs of the necessary corrective measures, is at least 37 billion roubles (Glazovsky, 1990). A new development strategy for the Aral Sea basin therefore requires immediate attention.

POSSIBLE DEVELOPMENT ALTERNATIVES

A priority activity is the expeditious improvement of the environment for the population of the Aral Sea basin, particularly in the vicinity of the lake. During the last three years, major pipelines stretching to a total length of 1900 km have been built to transport water of acceptable quality. About 300 desalinating installations have been put into operation. These measures have provided water supply for 58,000 people. Improvements were also made in the health service for the population. The use of aircraft in spraying toxic pesticides and defoliants has been forbidden, and the application of pesticides is more restrained than before. Provision of food of good quality is also on the agenda, but a meaningful impact in this sphere is nowhere near in the current difficult times of food shortage. The suggested corrective measures can alleviate the distress of the people but would be insufficient for solving the crisis.

The crisis may be solved only if the strategy of development is changed. A comprehensive, long-term programme of land-and-water resources management should be a cornerstone of the new strategy. It should be geared to clear-cut goals: dropping low productivity lands from irrigation; increasing efficiency of the irrigation systems; drastic reduction of water applied for a unit of cropland; diversification of crops and liquidation of the monoculture of cotton; optimal use of fertilizers and pesticides; and transition to the integrated pest-management systems.

The new strategy must transcend the modern land-and-water management programme. It should tackle the roots of the catastrophe, addressing principal social and economic problems such as population control; a balanced ratio between the demand and the supply of cotton; an appropriate structure of the crop and livestock production; development of the agricultural extension services; conversion of industry from military production; considerable improvement of the social amenities, including education at all levels and medical services. Much care should be devoted to cooperation among the nations of the region in whatever political forms they may evolve as the only basis for lasting, sustainable development of the rich territory which used to be called Soviet Central Asia and where the Aral Sea basin has the central position.

It has already been mentioned that the deterioration of the Aral Sea is an indicator of the troubles haunting its basin. A special programme to save the Sea would not reach a desirable objective whereas a long-term sustainable development strategy, if successful, would bring about a stabilization and even raise the level of the lake water.

Currently, however, a sustainable development programme for Central Asia is nowhere in sight and it is doubtful whether, even under the most favourable circumstances, it would appear within a few years. In the meantime, the social situation continues to deteriorate and the water level of the Aral Sea keeps dropping. To stabilize it at the present level, an inflow of about 35 km^3 a year is necessary. It is possible, and even economically feasible, to save this amount of water by implementing a part of the land-and-water management programme mentioned above. To stop irrigating 15 per cent of the lowest productivity lands would save about 20 km^3 of water. Control of the water seepage from the canals and more efficient watering of the crops would contribute at least another 20 km^3. One has to emphasize, however, that technological remedies must harmonize with a careful analysis of the socio-economic implications of such measures.

The complex environmental catastrophe that enshrouds the Aral Sea and its basin is a warning to be remembered worldwide.

254 / Genady N. Golubev

REFERENCES

Glazovsky, N. F. 1990. *Aral Crisis: the Reasons of Emergence and the Ways for Solution* (In Russian). Nauka, Moscow.

Nikolaeva, R. V. 1969. Principal Morphometric Parameters of Aral Sea (In Russian). In: *Problems of the Aral Sea*. Nauka, Moscow.

Oreshkin, D. B. 1990. *Aral Catastroph*e. Znanye, Moscow.

Rozanov, B. G. 1984. *Fundamentals of the Environmental Science* (In Russian). MGU, Moscow.

23 / A World Water Resources Bank

MICHAEL CURLEY

INTRODUCTION

Throughout the world small water systems suffer from a lack of independent capital. New projects and reconstruction of older projects are most often dependent upon and funded directly by government appropriations. Relying on a national or regional unit of government for funding puts freshwater needs into direct competition with other critical human needs such as public health and education. For certain projects, there may be no alternative. In areas of great poverty and deprivation, clean drinking water may have to be provided free, by government, to all users, simply as a matter of public health or basic humanity. But for water systems in areas where even modest user charges are possible, there should be working alternatives. Wherever there are funds, no matter how modest, which can meet annual payments, such systems should be able to finance earmarked projects without government funds, or at least without considerable government funding.

HANDICAPS OF SMALL WATER SYSTEMS

Small water systems are unable to reach the international credit markets, both because of their limitations and because the market is unfamiliar with the borrower and the quality of the required credit. They tend to be at the mercy of the prevailing local banking community. This is truly an infelicitious position. Because of the trend to massive disintermediation which began in the 1970s, banks are under global pressure to shorten maturities and to lend only at floating rates. Water system assets are, on the other hand, long term by nature and should be paid for over their service life. Also, floating interest rates play havoc with systems that are generally unable to adjust user charges with the speed and frequency required to match loan payments. Furthermore, bankers are loath to lend against assets that cannot readily be repossessed and sold at a high percentage of their original cost. Water mains, storage tanks, and treatment facilities hardly fit this bill.

Notwithstanding the negatives, there are two major positive aspects of water economics which can best be expressed by the simple tautology: water is a necessity; everyone uses it. These simple facts constitute the inherent strengths of water economics. What is needed is a new financial regime which will maximize the economic strengths of water systems and minimize their weaknesses. To accomplish this goal, we must understand the economic implications of these strengths. Let us first consider the concept of water as a necessity.

A VIABLE LOAN PROGRAMME

Although using experiences in one country always has serious drawbacks in terms of valid analogies to other countries, there is a programme in the United States which may offer some valuable insights which might be applicable on a broader scale.

Since 1940, the Farmers Home Administration (FmHA) of the U.S Department of Agriculture has had a programme of grants and loans for the capital improvement projects of water and wastewater systems which serve rural communities. FmHA defines a rural community as one having a population of 10,000 or less. In the United States, there are about 60,000 water systems, about 20,000 of which are privately owned and the balance of which are constituted as units of local government. Since 1940, FmHA has made over 30,600 loans, totalling over $30 billion to water systems which are units of local government or, if privately owned, not-for-profit cooperatives.

The astonishing aspect of the FmHA programme is that in its entire 50-year history there have been less than 20 defaults! By defaults, FmHA means a permanent cessation of payment on a loan. In contrast, delinquencies, which FmHA defines as more than 30-days late on a payment of over $100, have run over time at a fairly consistent rate of about 1 per cent. At the close of the last fiscal year, for example, 0.87 per cent of FmHA water and wastewater loans were delinquent.

FmHA offers loans to water and wastewater systems for capital improvement projects, which can mean anything from the installation or replacement of new mains to the construction of a treatment facility. FmHA provides no funds for operations. Loans may be repaid over 40 years. Interest rates charged, at present, are between 5 per cent and 7 per cent. In addition, FmHA also has grant funds available. These grants are used to reduce project costs for poorer communities. For example, a water system with only 100 users might need a capital improvement project totalling $1 million. With a 40-year loan at 5 per cent, the water system would have an annual loan payment of about $50,300. The annual payment for each of the system's 100 users (assuming equal charges) would be $583 a year, or over $48 per month. This would be an onerous burden, especially on a community of poorer families. In such cases, once FmHA had assessed both the vital need for the project and the limited ability of the system users to pay, it might well provide $ 750,000 of the $1,000,000 project cost in the form of an outright grant to the system, with the balance, i.e. $250,000, in the form of a loan. This would reduce the system's payment to about $14,600 per year, which would, in turn, reduce the users' annual payment to $146, i.e. a little over $12 a month.

The first question that arises is whether the FmHA loan programme itself could be financed through the international credit market instead of by the United States government. The answer to this question is 'yes'. Several years ago, as part of the Reagan administration's effort to reduce the federal debt, FmHA actually sold about $1.8 billion of its loans to the public. The vast majority of the loans, from its water and wastewater programme, were sold without any guarantee whatsoever of the federal government. Other than the fact that in the United States the interest on such loans is exempt from federal income taxation, and hence such loans pay a lower rate which is attractive only to U.S. taxpayers, there is no reason at all why such loans could not have been sold in the international credit market.

A NEW FINANCIAL REGIME

The next question is: what insights can be gained from the FmHA programme which might be useful in structuring a new financial regime for small water systems.

The most obvious fact about water, itself, is that it is a physical necessity. One can survive only a few days without water, even under the best climatic circumstances. Because water is an essential ingredient of life, this necessity can be used as a lever to enforce payment of water charges. In other words, the penalty for the non-payment of a water bill in the United States is a cutoff of water service! This is not nearly as draconian as it seems. The cutoff is not implemented immediately, but generally only when about 90 days or more after payment due-date have elapsed. But the threat of penalty is always there and it is always real.

At this point, it is well to note that there are financial assistance programmes available in the U.S. for the payment of water bills of poorer citizens. No one is denied water because he is poor. Cutoff penalties are aimed at lax or indifferent users, not at poor ones. In any given service area, the water charges will amount to only a very small percentage of the income of the average household. So, the system's water charges will likely be affordable to the vast majority of the system's users.

There are two principles at work here. The first is that the payment of one's water bill must be absolutely compulsory. To the extent that a water service district embraces an area where there are poor persons, some extrinsic mechanism must be used to provide for them. This could take many forms. Their bills could be paid by government subsidy. Or the poorer consumers could simply be exempted from water charges by the system itself, where the system is financially strong enough for wealthier consumers to absorb the dues from the non-payers. But regardless of who pays, the principle must be established that at least *some* people *must* pay. A corollary to this principle, of course, is that the more people who do pay, i.e. the broader the system's economic base, the more reliable will be the system's ability to pay its debt in a full and timely manner.

This brings us to the second principle: affordability. Regardless of how many of a system's users may be exempted or subsidized, it is critical that the payments levied against the balance of the system users who do pay be reasonable in three ways. First, they must be reasonable in terms of the average income of the system's users. They cannot be expected to pay a significant share of their total income just for water. Second, the charges must be reasonable in terms of the quality of the service they receive. Users cannot be expected to pay full cost for turbid or contaminated water or low pressure or intermittent service. Third, water charges must be reasonable in relation to those charged for the same quality of service in adjacent areas.

Thus, for any geographic or service area to become a part of a successful private financial regime, the user charges in that area must be both reasonable and obligatory.

A final insight which might be drawn from the FmHA programme has to do with the supervision of the water system by higher authority. In the U.S., local water systems are supervised by a country or state health department. They are also supervised by environmental regulatory authorities. Finally, in some areas, they are also regulated as to rates and quality of service by a state utility regulation commission on behalf of the system's users or rate-payers. The point here is that the Department of Agriculture has absolutely no jurisdiction whatsoever over water. They simply provide the funds for rural systems to build or improve their systems. But, in conducting its programme, FmHA makes use of 50 state offices and 264 district offices, each of which is staffed with knowledgeable experts in various aspects of realizing water projects. They are also able to advise on administrative and financial matters. They are even able to assist a district in convincing its users that the benefit inherent in a planned project will outweigh its costs. While it is clearly impossible to gather empirical data on why water and wastewater loans do not default, it is reasonable to believe, after studying and discussing FmHA procedures with those on both sides, that one of the principal reasons for the outstanding credit history of the programme is the superlative administrative and technical support offered by FmHA to its borrowers.

Therefore, the third insight which may be relevant is that, for small systems to be able to fund their own capital needs through a private credit mechanism, there must be in place an adequate administrative support network to advise and assist such systems on all aspects of their capital projects.

Thus far we have addressed the basic structure of a possible, new financial regime in that we have determined that, for such a concept to be successful, user payments must be affordable but obligatory. We have also observed that a strong supervisory mechanism should also be present to support small system management. Now, let us turn to what the institutional structure of a new financial regime might look like.

INSTITUTIONAL STRUCTURE

There are two major principles involved in the creation of an institutional structure for a new financial regime for small water systems. The first of these might be called *payment intermediation.*

The second part of our water tautology was: everyone uses it. To this, we may now add: since everyone uses it, everyone must pay for it. It is absolutely critical that there be as many individual sources of payment as possible. In addition to having a large number of payment sources, it is also critical that these payments be made not to the system but to an intermediary acting on behalf of the system's creditors. This procedure is called payment intermediation. It has two closely-related purposes. First, it eliminates the credit risk of having the funds under the control of the system's management. This is not to impugn any managers. It is simply a principle of credit that the fewer hands that touch funds, the better. The second purpose relates to the law of large numbers and the probability of non-payment. The probability that any given water system will default is vastly higher than the probability that all 1000 of its individual customers will default simultaneously for unrelated causes. In short, by having the 1000 individual customers, rather than the one system, pay, we have dramatically increased the odds that payment will actually be made. The role of the payment intermediary is, thus, crucial to the structure of a new financial regime.

A COST-EFFECTIVE NETWORK

Such a new financial regime would necessarily begin at the local level. Here, it is proposed that local water systems band together to form what might be termed credit cooperatives. The strength at the local level is the complete comprehension of system operators of the requisite needs, reasonable water charges, operating costs, and environmental factors. Participating systems would borrow through the cooperative, and knowledgeable local operators would constitute its credit committee.

This leads us to the second major principle involved in the creation of an institutional structure for a new financial regime: *security intermediation*. This means the creation of an independent layer of collateral as a buffer between the borrower and the lender. This critical element is achieved by allowing each participating system to borrow a small percentage more than the actual project cost and by placing such funds in the hands of the cooperative's payment intermediary. These 'overborrowed' funds would then be held as common collateral for all of the funds borrowed by the cooperative. The key to the value of this collateral is that it is pledged for all the members of the credit cooperative, not just the one borrower. The financial basis of the cooperative would, thus, be that each participating system would borrow a fixed percentage more than it needed for its project. The surplus would be retained by the cooperative as pledged security for all of the loans of all of the participating systems. In addition, the cooperative would require that the water charges of the participating systems be paid directly by the users to a payment intermediary, which would be a bank or other fiduciary, and which would also serve as the cooperative's loan administration.

The local cooperative would fund members' loans by borrowing from a regional or national cooperative of which the local cooperative would be a participating member. The structure of the regional or national cooperative would be identical to that of the local cooperative. It would, in fact, be 'a cooperative of cooperatives'.

The regional or national cooperative would, in turn, obtain its funds from an international credit cooperative which would also be of identical structure and which might be called a *World Water Resources Bank*. This institution would obtain its funding directly from the international credit markets, where it would borrow at long terms and at fixed rates. Such funds would be passed through the network of regional and local cooperatives, and thence to the individual system borrowers. The fixed rates would assure stability of local user charges and ease the system's financial planning. The long term on the debt would have the doubly beneficial effect of minimizing user charges while spreading payments over the long service life of system assets.

Is such a process cost-effective for the local water system? Even if the local system loses (through the defaults of other systems in its cooperative) its entire overborrowing, such a process would still be cost-effective. A reasonable overborrowing amount would be 10 per cent. Through the international credit market, the system should be able to reduce its rates by more than 10 per cent, thereby more than offsetting the loss. Furthermore, by just being able to borrow for a 20-year term, instead of a five-year term, the system would be able to reduce its annual burden by up to 56 per cent.

A World Water Resources Bank would have its greatest impact in areas where the population growth is relatively steady and the income level is stable, if modest. In such areas, if water charges were affordable and water payments were obligatory, several water systems could easily join in creating a credit cooperative and designate a payment intermediary. As and when systems needed to fund capital projects they would borrow through the cooperative, where they would also overborrow a small percentage of the project amount. These funds would be held by the payment intermediary as common collateral for all of the cooperative's borrowings.

Affordable water rates. Mandatory payments. Local credit cooperatives. Overborrowed funds as common collateral. Payment intermediation. Security intermediation. These are the critical elements which combine to create a truly powerful credit device. These simple elements constitute the basal and institutional structure for a World Water Resources Bank. By effectively collecting larger and larger bases of water system users, through an expanded network of credit cooperatives, and by using overborrowed funds as common collateral, the powerful credit device embodied in the concept of a World Water Resources Bank can be put to work for the benefit of all.

To the extent that certain water systems become part of a World Water Resources Bank credit structure, they would no longer have to rely on their national government to provide funds for their capital projects. And, to the extent that governments no longer had to fund projects in financially-viable areas, they could redirect those financial resources to poorer areas of greater need.

CONCLUSION

The creation of a World Water Resources Bank will not be a panacea for the world's water problems. Providing safe drinking water to the poorest and most remote areas will always be the direct burden of government. However, a World Water Resources Bank could ease some of the pressure on national budgets by creating a private mechanism to fund at least some of the world's water needs. If the need for clean drinking water is ever to escape the lengthening queue for scarce government resources, there must be an alternative source of funding, at least for financially viable systems. On the other hand, the long-term, fixed-rate financial needs of small water systems are anathema to the modern banking industry. And, the international credit markets which specialize in such funding are, in today's world, unreachable. A World Water Resources Bank, however, sitting atop a series of concentric circles of security intermediation mechanisms, such as regional and local credit cooperatives, could have access to the international credit markets. This would then create a private structure for obtaining the long-term, fixed-rate capital which local water sytems need to reach their goal of providing safe drinking water to the peoples of the world.

24 / Role of Nationalized Banks in Financing Water Resources Development in India

R. L. DEWAN

INTRODUCTION

Increase in irrigation facilities has been one of the main strategies for acceleration of agricultural production in India. Accordingly, it was proposed to use major, medium, and minor irrigation schemes to increase the irrigation potential from 67.5 million ha at the end of the Sixth Plan (1984–85) to 80.4 million ha by the end of the Seventh Plan (1989–90). Of the additional potential of 12.9 million ha, the contribution of minor irrigation schemes alone was 8.6 million ha (67.6 per cent) and the balance of 4.3 million ha was envisaged through major and medium projects. For utilization of the potential, the target was 10.9 million ha, 7 million ha from minor irrigation and 3.9 million ha from major and medium irrigation. The actual achievements are listed in Table 1.

The tabulated data shows that in the first four years of the Seventh Plan (up to 1988–89), 8.63 million ha were added against a projected target of 10.97 million ha. The shortfall of 2.34 million ha has been reported to be due mainly to a lesser achievement of 1.49 million ha in the field of minor irrigation alone, the balance registering the deficiency of major and medium projects where the major constraint was the increase in cost of most of the projects resulting from delay in their execution due to problems of land acquisition and clearance of forests. In the case of minor irrigation projects, inadequate funding has been the main reason behind the comparatively higher shortfall, a factor that our financing institutions would do well to scrutinize.

Table 1. Development of irrigation potential and its utilization

					(Million ha)	
	7th Plan	85–86	86–87	87–88	88–89	89–90
Project	85–90 Targets		Achievement			Target
Major and Medium Irrigation						
Potential	4.30	0.51	0.46	0.68	0.69	0.82
Utilization	3.90	0.49	0.66	0.53	0.53	0.63
Minor Irrigation						
Potential	8.60	1.52	1.63	1.62	1.72	1.95
Utilization	7.00	1.32	1.36	1.41	1.55	1.74
Total						
Potential	12.90	2.03	2.09	2.30	2.41	2.77
Utilization	10.90	1.81	2.02	1.94	2.08	2.37

FUNDING FROM BANKS

While the bulk of funds for execution of major and medium irrigation projects is provided by the government, minor irrigation schemes, which include not only the exploitation of groundwater such as dug wells and tubewells but also small surface water diversion schemes, storage tanks, and lift irrigation projects, are financed by banks. It is in this context that the role of banks in fortifying the irrigation infrastructure, particularly in the area of minor irrigation, emerges as an important factor.

The banking industry in India has a wide network of 58,568 branches, 57 per cent of which operate in rural areas and contribute substantially towards the growth of agriculture. The banks are providing liberal credit assistance to almost all sections of society for a variety of purposes. In agriculture, clientele ranges from small and marginal farmers to corporate entrepreneurs such as state-owned corporations engaged in minor irrigation schemes, land development, electricity boards, and rural electrification.

Banks in India are under obligation to ensure that 40 per cent of their credit is allocated to the priority sector and 18 per cent to direct agriculture, irrigation being a part of both. Credit for water resources development, therefore, gets high priority from the banking industry for consolidation of infrastructural support necessary for increased production in the agricultural sector.

TERMS OF LENDING

Banks generally provide medium-term loans for minor irrigation schemes at 10 per cent interest, which is repayable in five to seven years, depending upon the repayment capacity of the borrowers against hypothecation of assets created through bank loans and mortgage of agricultural lands as security. In the case of small and marginal farmers, however, the mortgage of lands is not necessary.

Project appraisal, which determines eligibility for bank financing, covers six different aspects: economic, technical, managerial, organizational, commercial, and financial. The main consideration in deciding to grant a loan is, however, the *benefit and cost factor*. Any irrigation project with a benefit–cost ratio (B/C Ratio) of more than 1.5 is acceptable from the economic point of view. A lesser ratio may also be acceptable in the case of drought-affected areas. The benefit is estimated as a difference in the net values of the agricultural produce before and after irrigation, and the cost comprises the stipulated rate of interest on the capital cost of the project.

The priority sector advances of public sector banks constituted 42.3 per cent of net bank credit at the end of June 1990 as against the 40 per cent target. Bank advances to weaker sections at the end of June 1990 were 11 per cent over the target of 10 per cent. Although public sector banks as a group are yet to achieve the target of direct finance to agriculture of 18 per cent of net bank credit which was required to be reached by March 1990, their progress towards this goal is noteworthy.

DIVERSE PROBLEMS

Judging from the standpoint of beneficiary farmers, handicaps may be in the nature of lack of credit, complicated procedure of securing bank loans, unavailability of power supply when needed, and shortage of water. The problems being faced by the government and the financial institutions are mainly the delay in the execution of projects and defaults by beneficiary farmers in timely repayment of government dues and bank loans. The position of recovery of agricultural dues of the banks and irrigation loans is not quite satisfactory. The percentage of total recovery is around 50 per cent. It varies from area to area and state to state. The recovery performance in developed states such as Haryana, Punjab, and western UP is better than that in other states—Bihar, Orissa, and the northeast regions, for example.

Several factors are responsible for the unsatisfactory recovery in some areas, namely, natural calamities which are beyond human control, lack of intensive follow-up by field-level functionaries of credit institutions, and inadequate support by the state governments with regard to recovery of dues. Moreover, the grant of small credits sanctioned to numerous accounts under the priority sector with a view to reaching the target as prescribed in the national policy of the country, and the supervision required for proper utilization of such loans by the borrowers entails work that requires additional man-power. However, commercial banks may not welcome additional staff, and this personnel shortage may also lead to poor recovery in small rural areas.

AGENDA FOR IMPROVEMENT

A large share of agricultural development earmarked for water resources is indicative of the high dependence of agriculture upon irrigation. This trend is likely to continue. Hence the greater need for laying stress on economic efficiency in planning, implementation, and management of irrigation projects. The most important aspect, which has not received adequate attention so far, relates to proper techno-economic appraisal of irrigation projects. Water being a scarce commodity, its exploitation, preservation, and utilization need skilful handling by the banks, government, and the ultimate consumers of water. The emphasis in bank operations should shift more towards effective exploitation of available resources through provision for training facilities, extensive education, etc.

Benefit–Cost Ratio

As already stated, an important consideration in determining the economic feasibility of irrigation projects is the benefit–cost ratio. This is obtained by discounting the estimated economic cost of benefits of the project. The use of 1.5 as the cutoff value for B/C ratio in the selection of a project has been an arbitrary decision. No distinction is made with regard to major, medium, and minor irrigation projects, though the life, gestation period, and dependability of each category of project would be quite different. Moreover, this criterion precludes incentive for detailed analysis of the financial merits of the project if the B/C ratio is equal to or greater than 1.5. For instance, this would not discriminate between two projects, one having a B/C ratio of 1.5 and the other 4.5. Again, the objectives of economic development in the country in general and of irrigation in particular are not adequately reflected in the B/C ratio. For instance, the employment generation and income redistribution for renewal of regional disparities do not find any place in the B/C ratio. In a vast country like India where there are glaring economic disparitites it is necessary to provide such criteria in the ambit of primary disparities benefits.

Recovery of Loan

As the volume of future bank lending for water resources development is likely to be determined more by the capacity of the borrowers to repay rather than the actual requirements of the funds to be utilized by them, recovery procedures should be more effective. In view of the increasing overdues, some authority may be especially designated exclusively to effect the recovery of bank loans. Groups, associations, and cooperatives of farmers are also expected to reduce the risk of default, but there have been mixed experiences in different countries in this regard. In India, these arrangements have not proved very successful despite their apparent advantages.

The other popular alternatives would be to educate borrowers for timely repayment of bank dues and to encourage good paymasters through financial rebates. Financial institutions should also amend the terms of sanction by rephasing the recovery schedule during national calamities. The follow-up system should be strengthened by banks to ensure regular contact with borrowers.

ACKNOWLEDGEMENTS

I am grateful to members of Oriental Bank of Commerce, New Delhi—Mr S. K. Soni, Chairman and Managing Director, Mr R. C. Kapoor, Executive Director, and Mr J. S. Tomar, Dy. General Manager—for their wholehearted cooperation and valuable suggestions. Their assistance in researching data greatly facilitated my study.

Index